taste of home
A+RECIPES
FROM SCHOOLS ACROSS AMERICA

taste of home
BOOKS

REIMAN MEDIA GROUP, LLC • GREENDALE, WI

taste of home Reader's Digest

A TASTE OF HOME/READER'S DIGEST BOOK
©2013 Reiman Media Group, Inc.
5400 S. 6oth St., Greendale WI 53129

EDITORIAL

Editor-in-Chief: Catherine Cassidy
Creative Director: Howard Greenberg
Editorial Services Manager: Kerri Balliet

Managing Editor, Print and Digital Books: Mark Hagen
Associate Creative Director: Edwin Robles Jr.

Editors: Janet Briggs, Sara Rae Lancaster, Christine Rukavena
Layout Designers: Nancy Novak, Catherine Fletcher
Contributing Layout Designer: Matt Fukuda
Production Coordinator: Dena Ahlers
Copy Chief: Deb Warlaumont Mulvey
Contributing Copy Editor: Valerie Phillips
Copy Editors: Mary C. Hanson, Alysse Gear
Content Operations Manager: Colleen King
Executive Assistant: Marie Brannon

Chief Food Editor: Karen Berner
Food Editor: Peggy Woodward, RD
Associate Food Editor: Krista Lanphier
Associate Editor/Food Content: Annie Rundle
Recipe Editors: Mary King; Jenni Sharp, RD; Irene Yeh

Test Kitchen and Food Styling Manager: Sarah Thompson
Test Kitchen Cooks: Alicia Rooker, RD (lead); Holly Johnson;
Jimmy Cababa
Prep Cooks: Matthew Hass (lead), Nicole Spohrleder,
Lauren Knoelke
Food Stylists: Kathryn Conrad (senior), Shannon Roum,
Leah Rekau
Grocery Coordinator: Molly McCowan

Photo Director: Dan Bishop
Photographers: Dan Roberts, Grace Natoli Sheldon, Jim Wieland
Set Styling Manager: Stephanie Marchese
Set Stylists: Melissa Haberman, Dee Dee Jacq

BUSINESS

Vice President, Publisher: Jan Studin, jan_studin@rd.com

General Manager, Taste of Home Cooking Schools: Erin Puariea

General Manager, tasteofhome.com: Jennifer Smith

Vice President, Magazine Marketing: Dave Fiegel

READER'S DIGEST NORTH AMERICA

Vice President, Business Development: Jonathan Bigham
President, Books and Home Entertaining: Harold Clarke
Chief Financial Officer: Howard Halligan
VP, General Manager, Reader's Digest Media: Marilynn Jacobs
Chief Marketing Officer: Renee Jordan
Vice President, Chief Sales Officer: Mark Josephson
General Manager, Milwaukee: Frank Quigley
Vice President, Chief Content Officer: Liz Vaccariello

The Reader's Digest Association, Inc.

President and Chief Executive Officer: Robert E. Guth

For other Taste of Home books and products, visit us at **tasteofhome.com.**

For more Reader's Digest products and information,
visit **rd.com** (in the United States) or see **rd.ca** (in Canada).

International Standard Book Number: **978-1-61765-178-6**
Library of Congress Control Number: **2012949663**

Pictured on front cover (clockwise from top right): Pork Chops with
Honey-Mustard Sauce, pg. 120; Chocolate Raspberry Cupcakes, pg. 225;
White Chicken Chili, pg. 113.

Pictured on back cover (from left to right): Flank Steak with Cilantro & Blue
Cheese Butter, pg. 153; Pasta with Eggplant Sauce, pg. 184; Chocolate Ganache
Peanut Butter Cupcakes, pg. 196.

Pictured on spine: Spanakopita Pinwheels, pg. 6.

Printed in China
3 5 7 9 10 8 6 4 2

contents

Introduction 4

Appetizers & Snacks 5

Soups, Sides & Salads 51

Entrees 109

Healthy Entrees 165

Desserts 187

Bake Sale Treats 223

Indexes 250

66As a parent volunteer, I contribute in various ways in both the library and my daughter's kindergarten class. As part of the WAY (We Appreciate You) committee, I contribute food to a monthly teachers' lunch called First Fridays. The teachers love it.99

—JAMIE MILLER MAPLE GROVE, MINNESOTA
*Volunteer, Heritage Christian Academy, Maple Grove, Minnesota
about her recipe, Pepperoni Lasagna Roll-ups, on page 111.*

VISIT
TASTEOFHOME.COM
FOR MORE

Do you have a dish you're ALWAYS asked to bring? We can't wait to hear about it! Enter one of our many national recipe contests online at **TASTEOFHOME.COM/CONTESTS** and you may win BIG!

Top-of-the-Class Recipes!

School is not only a great place to learn your ABCs, but to learn about delectable recipes. Teachers, administrators, support staff, coaches and parents **cook up an abundance of goodies** during the school year for class parties, bake sales, potlucks, special events and teachers' lounge snacks. That's why this book is **devoted to recipes shared in school hallways and classrooms across the nation.**

We received **more than 14,000 recipes** from schools around the country—from Kirkland, Washington, to Apopka, Florida. After sorting, testing and tasting contest recipes, the judges declared the **following the top three winners.**

The Grand-Prize Winner is **Chocolate Ganache Peanut Butter Cupcakes (page 196)**. Ronda Schabes won over our judges with her rich chocolate cupcakes with a surprise peanut butter center. She covers the cupcakes with a silky chocolate ganache, then tops that with a smooth peanut butter frosting that melts in you mouth. The seasoned baker said, "As soon as I took my first bite, I knew I had created **something divine!**" Our taste panel certainly agreed with her.

Chicken Marsala Lasagna (page 157) took second place. Bring your appetite when you sample Debbie Shannon's delectable, hearty entree. She layers lasagna noodles with a fantastic portobello mushroom-wine sauce that has bits of ham and chicken and a three-cheese spinach mixture—**absolutely delizioso.** Debbie's love of this classic dish inspired her to create her own version and make it sizeable enough to feed a crowd. At 12 servings, her lasagna is a **big success!**

Third place went to **Quinoa and Black Bean Salad (page 59)**, a healthy recipe developed by Yvonne Compton. She crowns quick-cooking quinoa with a festive mixture of orange peppers, red onion, black beans, corn, cherry tomatoes and avocado. A lime vinaigrette gives the **colorful dish wonderful flavor.** Yvonne likes to serve it as a side dish, but by increasing the serving size, it works just as well as an entree. Either way, our judges think you'll agree **this salad is fabulous.**

As you page through the book, you'll find recipes for appetizers, bake sales, potlucks, lunchtime, weeknight dinners, special occasions and much more. You can be assured these dishes will work in your kitchen, since the cooking professionals at *Taste of Home* tested them all. Each and every recipe has a beautiful full-color photo so you know what you're making. And the ingredients are available in most supermarkets.

> "Imagine the smiles on the faces of your family members when they taste a scrumptious dish from this cookbook. Don't delay. Cook up a winning recipe tonight. You'll be happy you did."

Creamy Basil-Feta Spread

PREP/TOTAL TIME: 15 MINUTES **MAKES:** 4 CUPS

- 2 packages (8 ounces each) cream cheese, softened
- 2 cups (8 ounces) crumbled feta cheese
- 1 jar (7 ounces) oil-packed sun-dried tomatoes, drained and chopped
- 1 cup minced fresh basil
  Wheat crackers

1. In a large bowl, beat cream cheese until smooth. Add feta cheese, tomatoes and basil; beat until combined. Transfer to a serving dish; refrigerate until serving. Serve with crackers.

Appetizers & Snacks

66 Every summer I just get a craving for this great cracker spread! It's even better with homegrown basil, and great to share at school for those beginning of the year meetings. 99

JENNY RODRIQUEZ PASCO, WASHINGTON
Teacher, Delta High School, Richland, Washington

Spanakopita Pinwheels

I'm obsessed with spanakopita. This is a quick and easy version, which I have used for teacher get-togethers and family events. I think it's simply wonderful with a glass of white wine.

—RYAN PALMER WINDHAM, MAINE
Teacher, Lake Region Middle School, Naples, Maine

PREP: 30 MINUTES + COOLING **BAKE:** 20 MINUTES
MAKES: 2 DOZEN

- 1 **medium onion, finely chopped**
- 2 **tablespoons olive oil**
- 1 **teaspoon dried oregano**
- 1 **garlic clove, minced**
- 2 **packages (10 ounces each) frozen chopped spinach, thawed and squeezed dry**
- 2 **cups (8 ounces) crumbled feta cheese**
- 2 **eggs, lightly beaten**
- 1 **package (17.3 ounces) frozen puff pastry, thawed**

1. In a small skillet, saute onion in oil until tender. Add oregano and garlic; cook 1 minute longer. Add spinach; cook 3 minutes longer or until liquid is evaporated. Transfer to a large bowl; cool.

2. Add feta cheese and eggs to spinach mixture; mix well. Unfold puff pastry. Spread each sheet with half the spinach mixture to within 1/2 in. of edges. Roll up jelly-roll style. Cut each into twelve 3/4-in. slices. Place cut side down on greased baking sheets.

3. Bake at 400° for 18-22 minutes or until golden brown. Serve warm.

"My love for teaching extends beyond the walls of East Alton-Wood River High School. When I'm not teaching my students the ins and outs of the English language or great American literature, I teach cooking classes on the weekends, maintain a food blog (barbaricgulp.com) and write for a monthly food magazine."

—KELLY GARDNER ALTON, ILLINOIS

Teacher, East Alton-Wood River High School, Wood River, Illinois

Caramelized Onion Dip

Once you taste this fabulous dip, you'll discover how much better it is than store-bought French onion dip. While it takes a little longer to make, I promise you'll never go back to packaged dip.

—KELLY GARDNER ALTON, ILLINOIS

PREP: 50 MINUTES + COOLING **MAKES:** 2 CUPS

- 2 **large onions, finely chopped**
- 2 **tablespoons olive oil**
- ¾ **cup sour cream**
- ¾ **cup plain Greek yogurt**
- 3 **teaspoons onion powder**
- ½ **teaspoon salt**
   Potato chips, corn chips and/or assorted fresh vegetables

1. In a large skillet, saute onions in oil until softened. Reduce the heat to medium-low; cook, stirring occasionally, for 30 minutes or until deep golden brown. Cool completely.

2. In a small bowl, combine the sour cream, yogurt, onion powder and salt; stir in two-thirds cooked onions. Transfer to a serving bowl; top with remaining onions. Serve with chips and vegetables.

BBQ Chicken Pizza Roll-Up

These slices make a fab, filling snack with loads of sweet and tangy flavor.

—TRACEY BIRCH QUEEN CREEK, ARIZONA

PREP: 15 MINUTES **BAKE:** 15 MINUTES + COOLING
MAKES: 2 DOZEN

- 1 tube (13.8 ounces) refrigerated pizza crust
- ¼ cup honey barbecue sauce
- 1½ cups (6 ounces) shredded part-skim mozzarella cheese
- 1½ cups shredded cooked chicken breast
- 1 small red onion, finely chopped
- ¼ cup minced fresh cilantro
- 1 teaspoon Italian seasoning, optional
- 1 egg white
- 1 tablespoon water
- ¼ teaspoon garlic powder

1. On a lightly floured surface, roll crust into a 12-in. x 9-in. rectangle; brush with barbecue sauce. Layer with cheese, chicken, onion, cilantro and Italian seasoning if desired.

2. Roll up jelly-roll style, starting with a long side; pinch seams to seal. Place seam side down on a baking sheet coated with cooking spray.

3. Beat the egg white and water; brush over the top. Sprinkle with the garlic powder. Bake at 400° for 15-20 minutes or until lightly browned. Cool for 10 minutes before slicing.

"I'm proud to be a staff member of Grand Bowler Elementary. The best part of my job is seeing students' progress throughout the school year. A close second would be the annual May Day dance, a school tradition that dates back 100 years!"

—NANCY LEAVITT LOGANDALE, NEVADA

Staff, Grant Bowler Elementary School, Logandale, Nevada

Fruit Salsa with Cinnamon Tortilla Chips

If you are serious about getting your fruit servings, this is a fun way to do it. The bright red fruit salsa is addictive. It is best eaten the day it is made.

—NANCY LEAVITT LOGANDALE, NEVADA

PREP: 20 MINUTES + CHILLING **COOK:** 5 MINUTES/BATCH
MAKES: 6 CUPS SALSA AND 16 DOZEN TORTILLA STRIPS

- 1 **pound fresh strawberries, finely chopped**
- 2 **medium apples, peeled and finely chopped**
- 1 **package (12 ounces) frozen unsweetened raspberries, thawed and well drained**
- 2 **medium kiwifruit, peeled and finely chopped**
- 3 **tablespoons peach or apricot preserves**
- 2 **tablespoons sugar**
- 1 **tablespoon brown sugar**

CINNAMON TORTILLA CHIPS

- **Oil for deep-fat frying**
- 10 **flour tortillas (10 inches)**
- ½ **cup sugar**
- 2 **teaspoons ground cinnamon**

1. In a large bowl, combine the first seven ingredients; cover and chill for 20 minutes or until serving.

2. In an electric skillet or deep-fat fryer, heat oil to 375°. Cut each tortilla in half; cut each half into 10 strips. Fry strips, a few at a time, until light golden brown on both sides. Drain on paper towels. Combine sugar and cinnamon; sprinkle over strips and toss to coat. Serve with salsa.

"During my career as an educator, I've taught both third and fourth grade as well as reading and language arts, math and science. A highlight of my career was receiving a Science and Math Improvement Grant from the Toshiba America Foundation in New York City to purchase a weather station for the school."

—**LISA ARMSTRONG** MURRAY, KENTUCKY
Teacher, East Calloway Elementary School, Murray, Kentucky

Jalapeno Hummus

Hummus is an easy, tasty and nutritious snack or appetizer. Friends are often surprised at the uncommonly good taste, and the jalapeno gives it a little kick. Serve with crackers, raw vegetables or tortilla chips.

—**LISA ARMSTRONG** MURRAY, KENTUCKY

PREP/TOTAL TIME: 15 MINUTES **MAKES:** 4 CUPS

- **2** cans (15 ounces each) garbanzo beans or chickpeas, rinsed and drained
- **⅔** cup roasted tahini
- **½** cup water
- **⅓** cup lemon juice
- **¼** cup olive oil
- **2** tablespoons minced garlic
- **2** tablespoons pickled jalapeno slices, chopped
- **1** tablespoon juice from pickled jalapeno slices
- **½** to 1 teaspoon crushed red pepper flakes
- **½** teaspoon salt
- **½** teaspoon pepper
- **⅛** teaspoon paprika
    Assorted fresh vegetables

1. Place first 11 ingredients in a food processor; cover and process until well blended. Garnish with paprika. Serve with assorted vegetables.

Hot Bacon Cheddar Spread

This is my go-to recipe when I'm having people over. The warm, luscious dip is always quite popular.

—CARA LANGER OVERLAND PARK, KANSAS

PREP: 30 MINUTES **BAKE:** 15 MINUTES **MAKES:** 3 CUPS

- 1 **package (8 ounces) cream cheese, softened**
- ½ **cup mayonnaise**
- ¼ **teaspoon dried thyme**
- ⅛ **teaspoon pepper**
- 1 **cup (4 ounces) shredded sharp cheddar cheese**
- 3 **green onions, chopped**
- 8 **bacon strips, cooked and crumbled, divided**
- ½ **cup crushed butter-flavored crackers**
   Assorted crackers

1. In a large bowl, combine the cream cheese, mayonnaise, thyme and pepper. Stir in the cheese, green onions and half the bacon. Transfer to a greased 3-cup baking dish.

2. Bake, uncovered, at 350° for 13-15 minutes or until bubbly. Top with crushed crackers and remaining bacon. Serve with assorted crackers.

❝I've been teaching first grade for 10 years. Working with children at such a young age is incredibly rewarding because I get to lay the groundwork for them to become lifelong learners.❞

—CARA LANGER OVERLAND PARK, KANSAS
Teacher, Chinn Elementary School, Kansas City, Missouri

Family-Favorite Turkey Egg Rolls

Finger foods give a party extra flair! This recipe is so easy, kids can help prepare it. Serve with sweet-and-sour or hot mustard dipping sauce.

—VIRGINIA REHM WAYNESVILLE, MISSOURI
Teacher, Waynesville Career Center, Waynesville, Missouri

PREP: 25 MINUTES **COOK:** 5 MINUTES/BATCH
MAKES: 1 DOZEN

- ½ **pound ground turkey**
- 4½ **cups coleslaw mix**
- 3 **tablespoons sesame seeds**
- 1 **tablespoon reduced-sodium soy sauce**
- 2 **teaspoons Worcestershire sauce**
- ¾ **teaspoon ground ginger**
- ½ **teaspoon seasoned salt**
- 12 **egg roll wrappers**
  Oil for deep-fat frying
  Sweet-and-sour sauce

1. In a large skillet, cook turkey over medium heat until no longer pink; drain. Stir in the coleslaw mix, sesame seeds, soy sauce, Worcestershire sauce, ginger and seasoned salt. Cook for 3-4 minutes or until cabbage is crisp-tender.

2. Place ¼ cup of turkey mixture in the center of one egg roll wrapper. (Keep remaining wrappers covered with a damp paper towel until ready to use.) Fold bottom corner over filling. Fold sides toward center over filling. Moisten remaining corner with water; roll up tightly to seal. Repeat.

3. In an electric skillet or deep-fat fryer, heat oil to 375°. Fry egg rolls, a few at a time, for 3-4 minutes or until golden brown, turning often. Drain on paper towels. Serve with sweet-and-sour sauce.

"I have volunteered in numerous capacities at Belpre Elementary School over the past few years. The best part of being a volunteer is seeing the smiles on the students' faces when they get to use the gym and playground equipment the school and PTO worked together to purchase."

—MARY JO SLATER BELPRE, OHIO
Volunteer, Belpre Elementary School, Belpre, Ohio

Pumpkin Mousse Dip

I originally received this recipe from my daughter's Girl Scout leader. The fluffy pumpkin dip is great served with gingersnaps or honey graham sticks, or with fruit such as apple or pear slices.

—MARY JO SLATER BELPRE, OHIO

PREP/TOTAL TIME: 10 MINUTES
MAKES: 16 SERVINGS (¼ CUP EACH)

- 1 **cup canned pumpkin**
- ½ **cup confectioners' sugar**
- 1 **package (3 ounces) cream cheese, softened**
- ½ **teaspoon ground cinnamon**
- 1 **carton (8 ounces) frozen whipped topping, thawed**
  Gingersnap cookies and/or pear slices

1. In a large bowl, beat the pumpkin, sugar, cream cheese and cinnamon until smooth. Fold in whipped topping. Refrigerate until serving. Serve with the gingersnaps and pear slices.

"I teach foods and nutrition and advise Northwood's Family, Career and Community Leaders of America organization. There's nothing like a student telling you that you've made a positive impact in their lives. To know I'm influencing students to make healthier choices and positive decisions makes my job exciting and rewarding."

—**JACKIE MILLIKEN** PITTSBORO, NORTH CAROLINA
Teacher, Northwood High School, Pittsboro, North Carolina

Bacon-Sausage Quiche Tarts

As a teacher, I attend many meetings and also have special celebrations with the rest of the staff. The other teachers are very fond of this treat and often request that I bring it to our functions.

—**JACKIE MILLIKEN** PITTSBORO, NORTH CAROLINA

PREP: 30 MINUTES **BAKE:** 10 MINUTES
MAKES: 40 APPETIZERS

- 2 **cans (12 ounces each) refrigerated buttermilk biscuits**
- 6 **uncooked breakfast sausage links, chopped**
- 2 **tablespoons chopped onion**
- 2 **tablespoons chopped fresh mushrooms**
- 2 **tablespoons chopped green pepper**
- 1 **package (8 ounces) cream cheese, softened**
- 2 **tablespoons heavy whipping cream**
- 3 **eggs**
- 1½ **cups (6 ounces) finely shredded cheddar cheese, divided**
- 5 **bacon strips, cooked and crumbled**

1. Split each biscuit into two layers; press each into an ungreased miniature muffin cup.

2. In a large skillet, cook sausage, onion, mushrooms and pepper over medium heat until meat is no longer pink and the vegetables are tender; drain.

3. In a large bowl, beat cream cheese and cream until smooth. Beat in eggs. Fold in ¾ cup cheddar cheese and the sausage mixture. Spoon 1 tablespoon into each cup. Sprinkle with bacon and remaining cheese. Bake at 375° for 10-15 minutes or until golden brown. Serve warm.

Turtle Chips

Salty-sweet, crunchy-chewy, so many sensations in one delectable bite. This is the absolute easiest recipe to make! Both kids and adults will be reaching for this goodie.

—LEIGH ANN STEWART HOPKINSVILLE, KENTUCKY
Teacher, Lacy Elementary School, Hopkinsville, Kentucky

PREP/TOTAL TIME: 25 MINUTES
MAKES: 16 SERVINGS (½ CUP EACH)

1 **package (11 ounces) ridged potato chips**
1 **package (14 ounces) caramels**
⅓ **cup heavy whipping cream**
1 **package (11½ ounces) milk chocolate chips**
2 **tablespoons shortening**
1 **cup finely chopped pecans**

1. Arrange whole potato chips in a single layer on a large platter. In a large saucepan, combine caramels and cream. Cook and stir over medium-low heat until caramels are melted. Drizzle over chips.

2. In a microwave, melt chocolate and shortening; stir until smooth. Drizzle over caramel mixture; sprinkle with pecans. Serve immediately.

Pork Canapes

People will relish these festive, pretty appetizers. They're relatively simple to prepare, but look impressive.

—RANEE BULLARD EVANS, GEORGIA
Teacher, Augusta Christian Schools, Martinez, Georgia

PREP: 35 MINUTES **BAKE:** 25 MINUTES
MAKES: 3 DOZEN

- 1½ teaspoons garlic powder
- 1 teaspoon dried rosemary, crushed
- 1 teaspoon dried thyme
- ¾ teaspoon pepper
- ½ teaspoon salt
- 2 pork tenderloins (¾ pound each)
- 36 slices French bread baguette (½ inch thick)
- ¼ cup olive oil
- ¾ cup garlic-herb spreadable cheese
- 3 tablespoons seedless raspberry or seedless strawberry jam
- 36 fresh thyme sprigs

1. In a small bowl, combine the first five ingredients; rub over meat. Place on a rack in a shallow roasting pan. Bake, uncovered, at 425° for 20-25 minutes or until a thermometer reads 160°. Let stand for 10 minutes. Cut each tenderloin into ¼-in. slices.

2. Brush bread slices with olive oil. Place on an ungreased baking sheet. Bake at 425° for 1-2 minutes or until lightly browned. Spread each with cheese; top with meat, ¼ teaspoon jam and a sprig of thyme.

Mozzarella Appetizer Tartlets

These little cups are so easy to make, but it looks like you spent a lot of time in the kitchen. I find that when I serve them I can't keep up with the demand. They are eaten up so fast and everyone wants more.

—CAROLYN BOROUGERDI IRVING, TEXAS

PREP: 25 MINUTES **BAKE:** 10 MINUTES
MAKES: 1 DOZEN

- ¼ cup olive oil
- 2 tablespoons Italian seasoning, divided
- 1 package (8 ounces) cream cheese, softened
- 1 teaspoon minced garlic
- 12 slices white bread, crusts removed
- 1 plum tomato, seeded and chopped
- 12 ounces fresh mozzarella cheese, cut into 12 slices

1. In a small bowl, combine oil and 1 tablespoon Italian seasoning; set aside. In another small bowl, combine the cream cheese, garlic and remaining Italian seasoning; set aside.

2. Flatten bread with a rolling pin. Brush one side with oil mixture; place oil side down in muffin cups. Spoon cream cheese mixture into each; top with chopped tomato and a cheese slice.

3. Bake at 350° for 10-15 minutes or until cheese is melted. Serve warm.

"I have been an instructional assistant for eight years at Northwestern Lehigh School District. Working in an elementary school is an adventure. The kids do and say things that make life interesting every day. But what I enjoy most is knowing that I'm helping students do better in subject areas in which they are struggling."

—**TAMMY REX** NEW TRIPOLI, PENNSYLVANIA
Staff, Northwestern Lehigh School District, New Tripoli, Pennsylvania

Bacon and Fontina Stuffed Mushrooms

What's better than lots of bacon and cheese in a mushroom cap? You'll be saying "yum"—and so will your guests.

—**TAMMY REX** NEW TRIPOLI, PENNSYLVANIA

PREP: 30 MINUTES **BAKE:** 10 MINUTES
MAKES: 2 DOZEN

- 24 **large fresh mushrooms**
- 4 **ounces cream cheese, softened**
- 1 **cup (4 ounces) shredded fontina cheese**
- 8 **bacon strips, cooked and crumbled**
- 4 **green onions, chopped**
- ¼ **cup chopped oil-packed sun-dried tomatoes**
- 3 **tablespoons minced fresh parsley**
- 1 **tablespoon olive oil**

1. Remove stems from mushrooms and set caps aside; discard stems or save for another use. In a small bowl, combine the cream cheese, fontina cheese, bacon, onions, sun-dried tomatoes and parsley. Fill each mushroom cap with about 1 tablespoon of filling.

2. Place on a greased baking sheet. Drizzle with oil. Bake, uncovered, at 425° for 8-10 minutes or until mushrooms are tender.

Shrimp Salad Cocktails

This appetizer looks elegant and beautiful in a stemmed glass...and it tastes even better. For a special touch, garnish each glass with an extra shrimp.

—SUE SONNENBERG NAPOLEON, OHIO
Staff, Hope School, McClure, Ohio

PREP TIME: 35 MINUTES **MAKES:** 8 SERVINGS

- 2 **cups mayonnaise**
- ¼ **cup ketchup**
- ¼ **cup lemon juice**
- 1 **tablespoon Worcestershire sauce**
- 2 **pounds peeled and deveined cooked large shrimp**
- 2 **celery ribs, finely chopped**
- 3 **tablespoons minced fresh tarragon or 3 teaspoons dried tarragon**
- ¼ **teaspoon salt**
- ¼ **teaspoon pepper**
- 2 **cups shredded romaine**
- 2 **cups seedless red and/or green grapes, halved**
- 6 **plum tomatoes, seeded and finely chopped**
- ½ **cup chopped peeled mango or papaya**
  Minced chives or parsley

1. In a small bowl, combine the mayonnaise, ketchup, lemon juice and Worcestershire sauce. In a large bowl, combine the shrimp, celery, tarragon, salt and pepper. Add 1 cup dressing; toss to coat.

2. Spoon 1 tablespoon dressing into eight cocktail glasses. Layer each with ¼ cup lettuce, ½ cup shrimp mixture, ¼ cup grapes, ⅓ cup tomatoes and 1 tablespoon mango. Top with remaining dressing; sprinkle with chives. Serve immediately.

Mango Salsa

Fresh mango adds eye-catching color and an interesting twist to this healthy and colorful fruit salsa.

—MALA UDAYAMURTHY SAN JOSE, CALIFORNIA
Teacher, Martin Murphy Middle School, San Jose, California

PREP/TOTAL TIME: 15 MINUTES **MAKES:** 2¼ CUPS

- 2 medium mangoes, peeled and finely chopped
- ¼ cup finely chopped red onion
- ¼ cup finely chopped green pepper
- ¼ cup finely chopped sweet red pepper
- 1 jalapeno pepper, chopped
- 3 tablespoons minced fresh cilantro
- 2 tablespoons cider vinegar
- 1 tablespoon sugar
- 1 tablespoon olive oil
- ½ teaspoon salt
- ½ teaspoon pepper
   Baked potato chips

1. In a large bowl, combine the first 11 ingredients. Chill until serving. Serve with chips.

Editor's Note: *Wear disposable gloves when cutting hot peppers; the oils can burn skin. Avoid touching your face.*

Layered Curried Cheese Spread

Pretty and tasty, this layered dip has become my signature appetizer. We make this for almost every party and family occasion we attend.

—**MELODY KIEFFER** KIRKLAND, WASHINGTON

PREP/TOTAL TIME: 20 MINUTES **MAKES:** 4 CUPS

- 1 **carton (8 ounces) whipped cream cheese**
- ¾ **cup shredded sharp cheddar cheese**
- 1 **teaspoon curry powder**
- 1 **bottle (9 ounces) mango chutney**
- ½ **cup flaked coconut**
- ⅓ **cup chopped pecans, toasted**
- 2 **green onions, chopped**
- ¼ **cup dried currants**
  Assorted crackers

1. Place the cream cheese, cheddar cheese and curry powder in a small food processor; cover and pulse until mixture is blended.

2. Spread onto a 10-in. round serving platter. Spoon chutney over top; sprinkle with coconut, pecans, green onions and dried currants. Chill until serving. Serve with crackers.

"I am a psychologist at Stow-Munroe Falls High School. The high school is home to several college and technical prep initiatives in business, aviation, pre-engineering and culinary arts. In this role, I enjoy helping students with disabilities map their life after high shool. It is exciting to see where their interests and skills will take them as they enter adulthood."

—HEIDI DER STOW, OHIO
Psychologist, Stow-Munroe Falls High School, Stow, Ohio

Pear-Blue Cheese Tartlets

Here, I've combined some of my favorite ingredients into a sensational bite-size package.

—HEIDI DER STOW, OHIO

PREP: 25 MINUTES **BAKE:** 10 MINUTES
MAKES: 2½ DOZEN

- 2 **large pears, peeled and finely chopped**
- 2 **tablespoons butter**
- 2 **tablespoons honey**
  Dash salt
- ¼ **cup mascarpone cheese**
- ¼ **cup crumbled blue cheese**
- 2 **packages (1.9 ounces each) frozen miniature phyllo tart shells**
- ¼ **cup finely chopped walnuts**

1. In a small skillet, saute pears in butter for 2-3 minutes or until tender. Stir in honey and salt; cook for 4-5 minutes or until pears are lightly browned. Remove from the heat; cool slightly. Stir in cheeses.

2. Fill each tart shell with 1½ teaspoons filling. Place on ungreased baking sheets. Sprinkle with walnuts. Bake at 350° for 6-8 minutes or until golden brown. Serve warm. Refrigerate leftovers.

Islander Nachos

Take a tasty trip to the tropics without leaving home with these Hawaiian-style snacks. This recipe was featured on a local cable TV cooking show that my students and I produce, called "Hannah Penn's Cook'n."

—JENNIFER HEASLEY YORK, PENNSYLVANIA
Teacher, Hannah Penn Middle School, York, Pennsylvania

PREP: 40 MINUTES **BAKE:** 10 MINUTES + COOLING
MAKES: 16 SERVINGS

- ⅓ cup plus 1 tablespoon sugar, divided
- 2 teaspoons ground cinnamon
- ⅓ cup honey
- ¼ cup butter, cubed
- 8 flour tortillas (8 inches)
- 4 ounces cream cheese, softened
- 1 teaspoon vanilla extract
- 1 container (8 ounces) frozen whipped topping, thawed
- ½ cup drained crushed pineapple
- 4 medium bananas, sliced
- 1 cup flaked coconut, toasted
- ½ cup chopped macadamia nuts, toasted

1. In a small bowl, combine ⅓ cup sugar and cinnamon; set aside. In a small saucepan, combine honey and butter. Cook and stir over medium heat until blended. Brush onto both sides of tortillas; sprinkle tops with sugar mixture.

2. Stack tortillas, top sides up; cut into sixths. Arrange the wedges, sugared sides up, in a single layer on ungreased baking sheets. Bake at 400° for 6-8 minutes or until crisp and golden brown. Cool completely on wire racks.

3. In a large bowl, beat cream cheese, vanilla and remaining sugar until creamy. Beat in whipped topping until blended. Fold in pineapple. Arrange tortilla wedges on a large serving platter. Spoon cream cheese mixture over wedges. Top with bananas, coconut and macadamias. Serve immediately.

Baked Reuben Dip

PREP: 10 MINUTES **BAKE:** 25 MINUTES **MAKES:** 8 CUPS

- 1 jar (32 ounces) sauerkraut, rinsed and well drained
- 10 ounces sliced deli corned beef, chopped
- 2 cups (8 ounces) shredded sharp cheddar cheese
- 2 cups (8 ounces) shredded Swiss cheese
- 1 cup mayonnaise
- ¼ cup Russian salad dressing
- 1 teaspoon caraway seeds, optional
  Rye crackers

1. In a large bowl, mix the first six ingredients; stir in caraway seeds, if desired. Transfer to a greased 13-in. x 9-in. baking dish. Bake at 350° for 25-30 minutes or until bubbly. Serve with crackers.

"Reubens are one of my all-time favorite sandwiches. My recipe combines all of the Reuben's flavors into a great party dip!"

—JEFFREY METZLER CHILLICOTHE, OHIO

Artichoke and Sun-Dried Tomato Bruschetta

My family expects me to bring this bruschetta to every function. The artichoke and sun-dried tomato combination is a tasty alternative to the traditional versions. I've even tossed the mixture with spaghetti for a fun change of pace.

—TERRY SKIBISKI BARRINGTON, ILLINOIS
Teacher, Hough Street Elementary School, Barrington, Illinois

PREP/TOTAL TIME: 30 MINUTES **MAKES:** 3 DOZEN

36 slices French bread baguette (½ inch thick)
2 tablespoons olive oil
2 cups marinated quartered artichoke hearts, drained
1 cup oil-packed sun-dried tomatoes, drained
1 garlic clove, minced
1 teaspoon dried oregano
1 teaspoon dried basil
1 cup (4 ounces) shredded Italian cheese blend, divided

1. Brush baguette slices with oil. Place bread on ungreased baking sheets. Bake at 400° for 6-8 minutes or until lightly browned. Place the artichoke hearts, tomatoes, garlic, oregano, basil and ½ cup cheese blend in a food processor; cover and process until coarsely chopped.

2. Spread 1 heaping tablespoon on each bread slice; sprinkle with remaining cheese. Bake at 400° for 5-10 minutes or until top is bubbly.

Phyllo-Wrapped Brie with Sun-Dried Tomatoes

My mom and I would always make this together. Using flaky phyllo dough is a different way to wrap up Brie.

—**KATIE KLEE** NOBLESVILLE, INDIANA

PREP: 10 MINUTES **BAKE:** 20 MINUTES + STANDING
MAKES: 8 SERVINGS

- 2 **tablespoons butter, melted**
- 1 **tablespoon oil from oil-packed sun-dried tomatoes**
- 4 **sheets phyllo dough**
- 1 **tablespoon chopped oil-packed sun-dried tomatoes**
- 1 **round (8 ounces) Brie cheese, rind removed**
  Assorted crackers

1. In a small bowl, combine butter and oil. Lightly brush one sheet of phyllo dough with some of the butter mixture; place another sheet of phyllo on top and brush with butter mixture. Repeat twice.

2. Cut layered phyllo into a 9-in. square; discard trimmings. Spread chopped tomatoes in the center of the square. Place Brie over tomatoes.

3. Brush corners of phyllo with 1 teaspoon butter mixture. Fold pastry over the cheese and pinch edges to seal. Place seam side down on a greased baking sheet. Brush with remaining butter mixture.

4. Bake at 350° for 18-22 minutes or until golden brown. Let stand for 10 minutes before serving with crackers.

Chesapeake Crab Dip

Our school is a Maryland Green School. As such, many of our students work to improve the health of our local treasure, Chesapeake Bay. Crab stars in this rich, creamy dip that reminds me of the importance of a healthy Bay.

—CAROL BRZEZINSKI MARRIOTTSVILLE, MARYLAND
Teacher, Triadelphia Ridge Elementary School, Ellicott City, Maryland

PREP: 20 MINUTES **BAKE:** 20 MINUTES **MAKES:** 2¼ CUPS

- 1 **package (8 ounces) cream cheese, softened**
- 1 **cup (8 ounces) sour cream**
- 1 **tablespoon lemon juice**
- 1 **teaspoon ground mustard**
- 1 **teaspoon seafood seasoning**
- ⅛ **teaspoon garlic salt**
- 3 **cans (6 ounces each) lump crabmeat, drained**
- ½ **cup shredded cheddar cheese**
- ⅛ **teaspoon paprika**
  Assorted crackers

1. In a large bowl, combine the cream cheese, sour cream, lemon juice, mustard, seafood seasoning and garlic salt. Fold in crab. Transfer to a greased 9-in. pie plate. Sprinkle with cheese and paprika.

2. Bake at 325° for 20-25 minutes or until bubbly. Serve warm with crackers. Refrigerate leftovers.

Shrimp Spring Rolls

I began making these egg rolls in my college food science course, and I have made them countless times since with my own students. For best results, make sure the filling is cool before placing it into wrappers and the oil is hot—the egg rolls should sizzle when put into oil.

—LAURA BAKKER OMAHA, NEBRASKA

PREP: 45 MINUTES **COOK:** 5 MINUTES/BATCH
MAKES: 1 DOZEN (1 CUP SAUCE)

- ½ **cup packed brown sugar**
- 1 **tablespoon cornstarch**
- ¼ **teaspoon chicken bouillon granules**
- ½ **cup cold water**
- ½ **cup red wine vinegar**
- ½ **cup finely chopped green pepper**
- 1 **jar (2 ounces) diced pimientos, drained**
- 1 **tablespoon reduced-sodium soy sauce**
- 2 **garlic cloves, minced**
- ½ **teaspoon minced fresh gingerroot**

SPRING ROLLS
- 2 **teaspoons cornstarch**
- ½ **teaspoon sugar**
- ¼ **teaspoon salt**
- 2 **tablespoons reduced-sodium soy sauce**
- ¾ **pound uncooked medium shrimp, peeled, deveined and chopped**
- 2 **garlic cloves, minced**
- 4 **teaspoons canola oil, divided**
- 2 **cups finely shredded cabbage**
- 1 **cup finely chopped fresh mushrooms**
- ½ **cup finely chopped water chestnuts**
- ½ **cup shredded carrot**
- 4 **green onions, thinly sliced**
- 12 **egg roll or Chinese spring roll wrappers (6-8 inches)**
  Oil for deep-fat frying

1. In a small saucepan, combine the brown sugar, cornstarch and bouillon granules. Whisk in water and vinegar until smooth. Add green pepper, pimientos, soy sauce, garlic and ginger. Bring to a boil. Cook and stir for 2 minutes or until thickened; set aside.

2. In a small bowl, combine the cornstarch, sugar and salt. Stir in soy sauce until smooth; set aside.

3. In a large skillet or wok, stir-fry shrimp and garlic in 1 teaspoon oil until shrimp turns pink. Remove and keep warm.

4. Stir-fry the cabbage, mushrooms, water chestnuts and carrot in remaining oil for 2-3 minutes or until carrot is crisp-tender.

5. Stir the cornstarch mixture and add to the pan. Bring to a boil; cook and stir for 1-2 minutes or until thickened. Add the shrimp and green onions; set aside to cool.

6. With one corner of egg roll wrapper facing you, place ⅓ cup shrimp mixture just below center of wrapper. Cover remaining wrappers with a damp paper towel until ready to use. Fold bottom corner over filling. Moisten remaining edges of wrapper with water. Fold side corners toward center over filling. Roll spring roll up tightly, pressing at tip to seal. Repeat.

7. In an electric skillet or deep-fryer, heat oil to 375°. Fry spring rolls, a few at a time, for 3-5 minutes or until golden brown, turning occasionally. Drain on paper towels. Serve with sauce.

Red Pepper & Feta Dip

PREP/TOTAL TIME: 5 MINUTES **MAKES:** 1½ CUPS

- 1 package (8 ounces) cream cheese, softened
- 1 tablespoon 2% milk
- ½ cup chopped roasted sweet red peppers
- ½ cup crumbled feta cheese
  Baked pita chips

1. In a large bowl, beat cream cheese and milk until smooth; gently stir in red peppers and feta cheese. Serve with pita chips.

"My husband and I sampled a version of this dip as we dined out in the islands of the Great Barrier Reef. You can roast your own red peppers or use a jar of roasted red peppers."

—**MELODY LANDAICHE** LAFAYETTE, COLORADO
Teacher, Jefferson Academy Elementary School
Broomfield, Colorado

"I am an assistant at the Student Transition Center at Lake Havasu High School, and have been in the special education field for 29 years. What I really like most about my job is being able to take my students into the community each day and provide job training for them. When I'm not working, I enjoy baking with my two granddaughters."

—**PAT MOWERY** LAKE HAVASU CITY, ARIZONA
Staff, Lake Havasu High School, Lake Havasu City, Arizona

Smoky Chipotle Orange Dip

Letting the dip sit for two hours allows the flavors to meld. It is not only good with chips; fruit slices would also benefit from the smoky kick. People ask for the recipe as soon as they taste it.

—**PAT MOWERY** LAKE HAVASU CITY, ARIZONA

PREP: 10 MINUTES + CHILLING **MAKES:** 1¼ CUPS

- ½ **cup sour cream**
- ½ **cup mayonnaise**
- ½ **cup orange marmalade**
- 1 **tablespoon adobo sauce**
- ¾ **teaspoon ground cumin**
  Tortilla chips

1. In a small bowl, combine the first five ingredients. Cover and chill for at least 2 hours. Serve with chips.

Champagne Fruit Punch

Toast the happy couple at your next bridal shower with a fun and fruity drink! It's the perfect refreshment on a summer's day.

—KELLY TRAN SALEM, OREGON

Teacher, Hammond Elementary School, Salem, Oregon

PREP/TOTAL TIME: 10 MINUTES
MAKES: 16 SERVINGS (¾ CUP EACH)

- 2 **cups fresh or frozen raspberries**
- 1 **can (12 ounces) frozen orange juice concentrate, thawed**
- 1 **can (12 ounces) frozen cherry pomegranate juice concentrate, thawed**
- 1 **can (6 ounces) unsweetened pineapple juice, chilled**
- 1 **medium lemon, thinly sliced**
- 1 **bottle (1 liter) club soda, chilled**
- 1 **bottle (750 milliliters) Champagne or white sparkling grape juice, chilled**

1. In a punch bowl, combine the first five ingredients. Slowly stir in club soda and Champagne. Serve immediately.

Artichoke-Spinach Pinwheels

This is my type of holiday recipe. You can assemble them, freeze the unbaked pinwheels and bake them directly from the freezer. What convenience!

—**DONNA LINDECAMP** MORGANTON, NORTH CAROLINA
Teacher, Walter Johnson Middle School, Morganton, North Carolina

PREP: 20 MINUTES + CHILLING **BAKE:** 20 MINUTES
MAKES: 2 DOZEN

- 1 **can (14 ounces) water-packed artichoke hearts, rinsed, drained and chopped**
- 1 **package (10 ounces) frozen chopped spinach, thawed and squeezed dry**
- ½ **cup grated Parmesan cheese**
- ½ **cup mayonnaise**
- ½ **teaspoon onion powder**
- ½ **teaspoon garlic powder**
- ½ **teaspoon pepper**
- 1 **package (17.3 ounces) frozen puff pastry, thawed**

1. In a small bowl, combine the first seven ingredients. Unfold puff pastry. Spread the artichoke mixture over each sheet to within ½ in. of edges. Roll up jelly-roll style. Wrap in plastic; freeze for 30 minutes.

2. Using a serrated knife, cut each roll into 12 slices. Place cut side down on greased baking sheets. Bake at 400° for 18-22 minutes or until golden brown.

"I love Christmas so much that I decorate in October. I don't care for eggnog, but it's such a tradition at Christmastime that I created an eggnog that even I like! One sip of this beverage and I promise you will love eggnog forever."
—**DEBBIE HOLCOMBE** BRUNSWICK, GEORGIA

Chocolate Eggnog

PREP: 15 MINUTES **COOK:** 15 MINUTES + CHILLING
MAKES: 2 QUARTS (⅔ CUP EACH)

- 6 **eggs**
- ⅔ **cup sugar**
- 4 **cups 2% chocolate milk, divided**
- 3 **cups chocolate ice cream**
- 1 **teaspoon vanilla extract**
- ½ **teaspoon ground nutmeg**
- 1 **cup heavy whipping cream**
  Optional toppings: additional whipped cream, ground nutmeg and/or chocolate curls

1. In a small heavy saucepan, whisk eggs and sugar until blended; stir in 2 cups chocolate milk. Cook and stir over medium heat for 12-15 minutes or until mixture is just thick enough to coat a spoon and a thermometer reads at least 160°. Do not allow to boil. Immediately transfer to a large bowl.

2. Stir in the ice cream, vanilla and nutmeg until ice cream is melted. Add remaining chocolate milk. In a small bowl, beat cream until soft peaks form; stir into eggnog mixture. Transfer to a pitcher.

3. Refrigerate, covered, until cold. Stir just before serving. If desired, serve with toppings.

"Dill and garlic go well with the tang of feta in this cheese ball...in fact, I think it tastes like a million bucks. It's super easy to do and since the recipe makes two, it's ideal for gatherings."
—**KELLY YEAGER** HAHNVILLE, LOUISIANA
Teacher, St. Philip Neri School, Metairie, Louisiana

Feta Cheese Balls

PREP: 20 MINUTES + CHILLING
MAKES: 2 CHEESE BALLS (1¼ CUPS EACH)

- 2 **packages (8 ounces each) cream cheese, softened**
- 3 **tablespoons olive oil**
- 1 **cup (4 ounces) crumbled feta cheese**
- 5 **green onions, chopped**
- 3 **garlic cloves, minced**
- 1 **tablespoon dill weed**
- 2 **teaspoons dried oregano**
- ¾ **teaspoon coarsely ground pepper**
  Bagel chips

1. In a large bowl, beat the cream cheese and oil until smooth. Stir in feta cheese, onions, garlic, dill, oregano and pepper. Cover and refrigerate for at least 1 hour.

2. Shape cheese mixture into two balls. Wrap each in plastic; refrigerate for at least 1 hour. Serve with bagel chips.

Cheese-Trio Artichoke & Spinach Dip

No appetizer spread is complete without one amazing dip, and this is it. Creamy, cheesy and chock-full of veggies, it will quickly become your new go-to appetizer.

—DIANE SPEARE KISSIMMEE, FLORIDA

PREP: 20 MINUTES **COOK:** 2 HOURS **MAKES:** 4 CUPS

- 1 **cup chopped fresh mushrooms**
- 1 **tablespoon butter**
- 2 **garlic cloves, minced**
- 1½ **cups mayonnaise**
- 1 **package (8 ounces) cream cheese, softened**
- 1 **cup plus 2 tablespoons grated Parmesan cheese, divided**
- 1 **cup (4 ounces) shredded part-skim mozzarella cheese, divided**
- 1 **can (14 ounces) water-packed artichoke hearts, rinsed, drained and chopped**
- 1 **package (10 ounces) frozen chopped spinach, thawed and squeezed dry**
- ¼ **cup chopped sweet red pepper**
  Toasted French bread baguette slices

1. In a large skillet, saute mushrooms in butter until tender. Add garlic; cook 1 minute longer.

2. In a large bowl, combine the mayonnaise, cream cheese, 1 cup Parmesan cheese and ¾ cup mozzarella cheese. Add the mushroom mixture, artichokes, spinach and red pepper.

3. Transfer to a 3-qt slow cooker. Sprinkle with the remaining cheeses. Cover and cook on low for 2-3 hours or until heated through. Serve with the baguette slices.

Shrimp Salsa

For a salsa with lots of texture, color and mouthwatering taste, look no further! A medley of chopped shrimp, avocado, tomato, cucumber, onion and cilantro is tossed in lime juice and perked up with a blend of mild spices.

—ELIZA NOVOA-GONZALEZ HENDERSON, NEVADA

PREP/TOTAL TIME: 30 MINUTES **MAKES:** 8 CUPS

- 1 **pound peeled and deveined cooked medium shrimp, chopped**
- 5 **medium tomatoes, seeded and chopped**
- 2 **medium ripe avocados, peeled and chopped**
- 1 **medium cucumber, peeled and chopped**
- 1 **cup minced fresh cilantro**
- ⅓ **cup chopped sweet onion**
- ⅓ **cup orange juice**
- ¼ **cup key lime juice**
- 2 **tablespoons lime juice**
- 1 **teaspoon salt**
- 1 **teaspoon garlic powder**
- 1 **teaspoon garlic salt**
- 1 **teaspoon coarsely ground pepper**
  Tostones or tortilla chips

1. In a large bowl, combine the first 13 ingredients. Serve immediately with tostones or chips.

"As an elementary school music teacher and choir director, I get to share my love of creative expression with students through music. Outside of the classroom, I enjoy being creative in the kitchen by preparing and improvising different recipes."

—**JERRI GRADERT** LINCOLN, NEBRASKA

Teacher, Kahoa Elementary School, Lincoln, Nebraska

Gingered Cran-Orange Salsa over Cream Cheese

Fresh cranberries make an unusual but sensational salsa, which is great in the fall when cranberries are readily available. The brilliant red color will attract partygoers to this appetizer.

—**JERRI GRADERT** LINCOLN, NEBRASKA

PREP/TOTAL TIME: 20 MINUTES **MAKES:** 8 SERVINGS

- 1 **package (8 ounces) cream cheese, softened**
- 1½ **cups fresh cranberries, rinsed and patted dry**
- 1 **cup fresh cilantro leaves**
- 6 **tablespoons sugar**
- 1½ **teaspoons chopped seeded jalapeno pepper**
- ¾ **teaspoon minced fresh gingerroot**
- ¼ **cup chopped pecans**
- 3 **tablespoons thinly sliced green onions, divided**
- 1 **tablespoon orange juice**
  Assorted crackers or baked pita chips

1. Place cream cheese on a rimmed serving plate.

2. In a food processor, combine the cranberries, cilantro, sugar, jalapeno and ginger; cover and pulse until finely chopped. Stir in the pecans, 2 tablespoons green onions and orange juice. Spoon over cream cheese; sprinkle with remaining green onion. Serve with crackers.

Editor's Note: *Wear disposable gloves when cutting hot peppers; the oils can burn skin. Avoid touching your face.*

"I have been teaching for 30 years, and currently teach fourth grade. I like to bring my love of cooking into the classroom whenever I can. Once, when we were frying wontons for Chinese New Year, another teacher thought she smelled smoke and told the principal. The principal calmly responded, 'That must be Terry cooking again.' Since then, the incident has been fondly remembered as our Chinese Fire Drill."

—TERRY SKIBISKI BARRINGTON, ILLINOIS
Teacher, Hough Street School, Barrington, Illinois

Canadian Meatballs

Whenever there is a brunch at school, I always make these meatballs, and everyone looks forward to sampling them. They make about five dozen so they are ideal for potlucks.

—TERRY SKIBISKI BARRINGTON, ILLINOIS

PREP: 50 MINUTES **BAKE:** 15 MINUTES
MAKES: 5 DOZEN

- 2 **eggs, lightly beaten**
- ½ **cup evaporated milk**
- 1 **cup dry bread crumbs**
- 1 **cup (4 ounces) shredded cheddar cheese**
- ⅔ **cup finely chopped onion**
- 1 **pound bulk pork sausage**
- 1 **pound bulk spicy pork sausage**

MAPLE SAUCE

- 2 **tablespoons cornstarch**
- 1 **cup chili sauce**
- 1 **cup maple syrup**
- 2 **tablespoons Worcestershire sauce**
- 2 **teaspoons maple flavoring**

1. In a large bowl, combine eggs, milk, bread crumbs, cheese and onion. Crumble sausages over mixture and mix well. With wet hands, shape into 1-in. balls.

2. Place meatballs on a greased rack in a shallow baking pan. Bake, uncovered, at 400° for 15-20 minutes or until a thermometer reads 160°. Drain onto paper towels.

3. Meanwhile, in a large skillet, whisk the sauce ingredients until smooth. Bring to a boil. Cook and stir for 1-2 minutes or until thickened. Add meatballs; stir to coat.

Spicy Cheese Crackers

Crisp and flaky with a touch of zip...it's no wonder the crackers disappear in no time. They are a favorite at every gathering. These are great to make en masse and freeze to be pulled out later!

—DONNA LINDECAMP MORGANTON, NORTH CAROLINA
Teacher, Walter Johnson Middle School
Morgantown, North Carolina

PREP/TOTAL TIME: 30 MINUTES **MAKES:** 32 CRACKERS

- 1½ **cups (6 ounces) shredded extra-sharp cheddar cheese**
- ¾ **cup all-purpose flour**
- ½ **teaspoon kosher salt**
- ¼ **teaspoon crushed red pepper flakes**
- ¼ **cup cold butter, cubed**
- 1 **to 2 tablespoons half-and-half cream**

1. Place the cheese, flour, salt and pepper flakes in a food processor; process until blended. Add butter; pulse until butter is the size of peas. While pulsing, add just enough cream to form moist crumbs.

2. On a lightly floured surface, roll dough to ⅛-in. thickness. Cut with a floured 3-in. holiday-shaped cookie cutter. Place 2 in. apart on greased baking sheets. Reroll scraps and repeat.

3. Bake at 350° for 13-17 minutes or until golden brown. Remove from pans to wire racks to cool completely. Store in an airtight container.

Marinated Antipasto Medley

Each year during the winter holiday season, the faculty and staff at my school have a Goodies Day where we bring all manner of tasty things to share with everyone. These marinated bites were gone before the first lunch period!

—**LAURIE HUDSON** WESTVILLE, FLORIDA

PREP: 20 MINUTES + CHILLING **MAKES:** 9 SERVINGS

- 8 ounces Colby-Monterey Jack cheese, cut into ½-inch cubes
- 1 jar (10 ounces) pimiento-stuffed olives, drained
- 1 jar (16 ounces) cocktail onions, drained
- 1 cup grape tomatoes
- 6 ounces pepperoni, cut into ½-inch cubes

DRESSING
- ¼ cup olive oil
- 2 tablespoons cider vinegar
- ½ teaspoon sugar
- ¼ teaspoon salt
- ¼ teaspoon dried basil
- ¼ teaspoon dried oregano
- ⅛ teaspoon garlic powder
- ⅛ teaspoon pepper
- ⅛ teaspoon Louisiana-style hot sauce

1. In a large bowl, combine the first five ingredients. In a small bowl, whisk the dressing ingredients; pour over vegetable mixture and toss to coat. Cover and refrigerate for at least 3 hours. Stir before serving. Serve with a slotted spoon.

Caramel-Toffee Apple Dip

PREP/TOTAL TIME: 15 MINUTES **MAKES:** 4¼ CUPS

- 1 carton (12 ounces) whipped cream cheese
- 1¼ cups caramel apple dip
- 1 package (8 ounces) milk chocolate English toffee bits
- Apple wedges

1. Spread cream cheese into a serving dish. Layer with apple dip and sprinkle with toffee bits. Serve with apple wedges.

“The apple wedges fanned out along the rim make for a very festive, eye-catching piece. I have never had anyone try this who doesn't absolutely love it. I'm asked every year to bring it to all fall social events.”

—**ANGIE HILLMAN** COTTONWOOD, ARIZONA
Teacher, Cottonwood Middle School, Cottonwood, Arizona

"Not only do the flavors of chocolate, marshmallow and peanuts taste great together, this easy recipe reminds me of being up north at the cabin with my family. It makes a fast batch of cute and fun treats."
—JAMIE MCMAHON COLOGNE, MINNESOTA
Teacher, Minnesota River Valley Special Ed Cooperative, Jordan, Minnesota

Backwoods Bonfire Bark

PREP: 10 MINUTES **COOK:** 5 MINUTES + STANDING
MAKES: ABOUT 1½ POUNDS

- 1 **pound semisweet chocolate, chopped**
- 1½ **cups honey bear-shaped crackers**
- 1½ **cups miniature marshmallows**
- ¾ **cup dry roasted peanuts**

1. Place the chocolate in a microwave-safe bowl. Microwave on high for 1 minute; stir. Microwave 1 minute longer in 20-second intervals until melted; stir until smooth.

2. Spread the chocolate to ¼-in. thickness on a waxed paper-lined baking sheet. Immediately sprinkle the crackers, marshmallows and peanuts over chocolate; press in lightly.

3. Refrigerate until firm. Break or cut into pieces. Store in an airtight container.

Sparkling Fruit Punch

My golden-color punch takes just a few minutes to stir up. The recipe makes enough to serve a group.

—ANITA GEOGHAGAN WOODSTOCK, GEORGIA

PREP: 10 MINUTES + FREEZING
MAKES: 16 SERVINGS (¾ CUP)

  3 **orange slices, halved**
    Fresh or frozen cranberries
2½ cups unsweetened pineapple juice
1½ cups ginger ale

2 **bottles (750 milliliters each) brut Champagne, chilled**
1 **bottle (375 milliliters) sweet white wine, chilled**
1 **can (12 ounces) frozen lemonade concentrate, thawed**

1. Line the bottom of a 4½-cup ring mold with orange slices and cranberries. Combine pineapple juice and ginger ale; pour over fruit. Freeze until solid.

2. Just before serving, unmold ice ring into a punch bowl. Gently stir in the remaining ingredients.

Pineapple Shrimp Spread

PREP/TOTAL TIME: 15 MINUTES **MAKES:** 1½ CUPS

- 1 cup chopped cooked peeled shrimp
- ½ cup unsweetened crushed pineapple, drained
- ½ cup reduced-fat mayonnaise
- ¼ cup chopped pecans
- 2 tablespoons minced fresh parsley
- 1 tablespoon finely chopped onion
- 1 tablespoon lemon juice
- ½ teaspoon salt
- ⅛ teaspoon hot pepper sauce
  Celery sticks and/or crackers

1. In a small bowl, combine the first nine ingredients. Refrigerate until serving. Serve with celery sticks and/or crackers.

"My aunt used to bring this dish to family gatherings. It brings back childhood memories for me. Today, it's my go-to appetizer for celebrating with others."

—JODI TOMPKINS ELDON, MISSOURI
Teacher, Eldon Public Schools, Eldon, Missouri

Huevos Diablos

You'll think these eggs really do have a bit of devil's heat in them. For a milder version, remove the ribs and seeds from the jalapeno. My brother-in-law, Tom, is the official deviled egg-maker in our family. I created this recipe for him so that he could step outside of the box occasionally.

—**LINDA ROSS** WILLIAMSPORT, PENNSYLVANIA

PREP/TOTAL TIME: 30 MINUTES **MAKES:** 2 DOZEN

- 12 **hard-cooked eggs**
- 6 **tablespoons minced fresh cilantro, divided**
- 6 **tablespoons mayonnaise**
- 2 **green onions, thinly sliced**
- ¼ **cup sour cream**
- 1 **jalapeno pepper, seeded and minced**
- 1½ **teaspoons grated lime peel**
- 1 **teaspoon ground cumin**
- ¼ **teaspoon salt**
- ⅛ **teaspoon pepper**

1. Cut eggs in half lengthwise. Remove yolks; set whites aside. In a small bowl, mash the yolks. Add 3 tablespoons cilantro, mayonnaise, onions, sour cream, jalapeno, lime peel, cumin, salt and pepper; mix well. Stuff or pipe into egg whites. Refrigerate until serving. Garnish with remaining cilantro.

Hot Apple Pie Sipper

PREP: 10 MINUTES + FREEZING **MAKES:** 6 SERVINGS

- ¼ cup butter, softened
- ⅓ cup packed brown sugar
- 2 teaspoons ground cinnamon
- 1 teaspoon ground nutmeg
- ¼ teaspoon ground cloves
- 1 pint vanilla ice cream, softened
- 4 cups hot apple cider or unsweetened apple juice
  Brandy, optional

1. In a large bowl, cream the butter, brown sugar, cinnamon, nutmeg and cloves until light and fluffy. Beat in ice cream. Cover and freeze until firm.

2. For each serving, place ⅓ cup ice cream mixture in a mug; add ⅔ cup cider. Stir in brandy if desired.

❝If you love apple pie, this tasty beverage was created just for you. The spiced ice cream gives the sweet cider a smooth, creamy texture. Make it an adult drink by stirring in a little brandy.❞

—**CONNIE YOUNG** PONY, MONTANA
Teacher, Harrison Public School, Harrison, Montana

"You might say teaching is in my blood. According to my grandmother's calculations, I'm the 10th teacher in the family during her lifetime. For the past three years, I've been the academic support teacher at Pequea Elementary. My favorite thing to do in the classroom is story-telling. It is an incredibly interesting way to teach the students without them knowing it!"

—**ELLEN FINGER** LANCASTER, PENNSYLVANIA
Teacher, Pequea Elementary School, Willow Street, Pennsylvania

Teacher's Caviar

I love the fresh flavors, colors and convenience of this dish. It adds fun to a workday lunch without adding inches to the waistline or putting a dent in the food budget. This can be served immediately or chilled in the morning and eaten at lunch time. I think it's delicious with baked tortilla chips or spooned over grilled chicken.

ELLEN FINGER LANCASTER, PENNSYLVANIA

PREP/TOTAL TIME: 25 MINUTES **MAKES:** 8 CUPS

- 2 **cans (15 ounces each) black beans, rinsed and drained**
- 2 **medium tomatoes, seeded and chopped**
- 1½ **cups frozen corn, thawed**
- 1 **medium ripe avocado, peeled and cubed**
- 1 **can (8 ounces) unsweetened pineapple chunks, drained and quartered**
- 1 **medium sweet orange pepper, chopped**
- 6 **green onions, thinly sliced**
- ½ **cup minced fresh cilantro**
- ⅓ **cup lime juice**
- 2 **tablespoons olive oil**
- 2 **tablespoons honey**
- ½ **teaspoon salt**
- ⅛ **teaspoon cayenne pepper**
  Baked tortilla chip scoops

1. In a large bowl, combine the first eight ingredients.

2. In a small bowl, whisk the lime juice, oil, honey, salt and cayenne. Pour over the bean mixture; toss to coat. Serve with baked chips.

Mediterranean Artichoke and Red Pepper Roll-Ups

I just love these roll-ups. They are so easy to make and are quite tasty, too. Sometimes I just enjoy them as is, without the sauce.

—**DONNA LINDECAMP** MORGANTON, NORTH CAROLINA

PREP/TOTAL TIME: 30 MINUTES **MAKES:** 2 DOZEN

- 1 **can (14 ounces) water-packed artichoke hearts, rinsed, drained and finely chopped**
- 4 **ounces cream cheese, softened**
- ⅓ **cup grated Parmesan cheese**
- ¼ **cup crumbled feta cheese**
- 2 **green onions, thinly sliced**
- 3 **tablespoons prepared pesto**
- 8 **flour tortillas (8 inches), warmed**
- 1 **jar (7½ ounces) roasted sweet red peppers, drained and cut into strips**

SAUCE
- 1 **cup (8 ounces) sour cream**
- 1 **tablespoon minced chives**

1. In a small bowl, combine the artichokes, cream cheese, Parmesan cheese, feta cheese, green onions and pesto until blended. Spread ¼ cup mixture over each tortilla; top with red peppers and roll up tightly.

2. Place 1 in. apart on a greased baking sheet. Bake at 350° for 12-15 minutes or until heated through. Cut into thirds. Meanwhile, in a small bowl, combine sour cream and chives. Serve with rolls.

Shallot-Blue Cheese Dip

Perfect party fare, this five-ingredient dip is a treat on baked potatoes, too.

—ALISA PIRTLE BROWNS VALLEY, CALIFORNIA

PREP: 10 MINUTES **COOK:** 30 MINUTES + CHILLING
MAKES: 2 CUPS

1½ **cups thinly sliced shallots**
 1 **tablespoon canola oil**
 ¾ **cup reduced-fat mayonnaise**
 ¾ **cup reduced-fat sour cream**
1½ **cups (6 ounces) crumbled blue cheese**
 Assorted fresh vegetables

1. In a large skillet, saute shallots in oil until softened. Reduce heat to medium-low; cook for 25-30 minutes or until deep golden brown, stirring occasionally. Cool to room temperature.

2. In a small bowl, combine mayonnaise and sour cream. Stir in blue cheese and caramelized shallots. Cover and refrigerate for at least 2 hours. Serve with vegetables.

Sparkling Party Punch

PREP/TOTAL TIME: 5 MINUTES
MAKES: 17 SERVINGS (¾ CUP EACH)

- **1 can (46 ounces) unsweetened pineapple juice, chilled**
- **3 cups apricot nectar or juice, chilled**
- **1 liter diet lemon-lime soda, chilled**
  Pineapple sherbet, optional

1. In a punch bowl, combine the pineapple juice, apricot nectar and soda. Top with scoops of sherbet if desired. Serve immediately.

66 This has been my signature punch for years, and the much-requested favorite at our annual Christmas party. It's sparkly, fruity, frothy (if you add the sherbet) and so simple! 99

—**JAN WITTEVEEN** NORBORNE, MISSOURI

Crab Soup with Sherry

PREP: 15 MINUTES **COOK:** 30 MINUTES
MAKES: 6 SERVINGS

- 1 **pound fresh or frozen crabmeat, thawed**
- 6 **tablespoons sherry or chicken broth**
- 1 **small onion, grated**
- ¼ **cup butter, cubed**
- ¼ **cup all-purpose flour**
- ½ **teaspoon salt**
- 2 **cups 2% milk**
- 2 **chicken bouillon cubes**
- 3 **cups half-and-half cream**
- 2 **tablespoons minced fresh parsley**

1. In a small bowl, combine the crabmeat and sherry; set aside.

2. In a large saucepan, saute onion in butter until tender. Stir in flour and salt until blended; gradually add the milk and bouillon. Bring to a boil; cook and stir for 2 minutes or until thickened. Stir in cream and crab mixture; heat through. Sprinkle servings with parsley.

Soups, Sides & Salads

66Everybody loves this rich, comforting soup that's a tradition in the South. It is brimming with crab and has a smooth, creamy texture. 99

REGINA HUGGINS SUMMERVILLE, SOUTH CAROLINA
Staff, Newington Elementary School, Summerville, South Carolina

Hot and Sour Soup

We've tried several recipes for this soup and couldn't find one that resembled the one we liked at a restaurant. So I made my own, and I must say it's on par with what you'll find when dining out. Use regular or hot chili sauce, according to your taste.

—VERA LEITOW MANCELONA, MICHIGAN
Volunteer, Mancelona Schools, Mancelona, Michigan

PREP: 20 MINUTES **COOK:** 25 MINUTES
MAKES: 6 SERVINGS (ABOUT 2 QUARTS)

- ¾ **pound pork tenderloin, cut into 1½-inch x ¼-inch strips**
- 1 **tablespoon olive oil**
- ½ **pound sliced fresh mushrooms**
- 6 **cups chicken broth**
- ¼ **cup soy sauce**
- 2 **tablespoons chili garlic sauce**
- ¾ **teaspoon pepper**
- 1 **package (14 ounces) extra-firm tofu, drained and cut into ¼-inch cubes**
- 1 **can (8 ounces) bamboo shoots, drained**
- 1 **can (8 ounces) sliced water chestnuts, drained**
- ½ **cup white vinegar**
- ⅓ **cup cornstarch**
- ⅓ **cup cold water**
- 2 **teaspoons sesame oil**
   Finely chopped green onions

1. In a Dutch oven, brown pork in oil until no longer pink; remove meat and keep warm. Add mushrooms; saute until tender. Set aside and keep warm.

2. Add the broth, soy sauce, chili garlic sauce and pepper to the pan. Bring to a boil. Reduce heat; cover and simmer for 10 minutes. Return the meat and mushrooms to the pan. Stir in the tofu, bamboo shoots, water chestnuts and vinegar. Simmer, uncovered, for 10 minutes.

3. In a small bowl, combine the cornstarch and water until smooth; gradually stir into soup. Bring to a boil; cook and stir for 2 minutes or until thickened. Remove from the heat; stir in sesame oil. Garnish with onions.

Fiesta Corn Salad

This recipe is special because I was able to take a delectable, but somewhat complicated appetizer recipe and turn it into a salad that's easy to make and transport. Adjust the jalapeno and chipotles to suit your taste for spicy heat.

—RICHI REYNOLDS SCOTTSBORO, ALABAMA

PREP: 30 MINUTES **BAKE:** 25 MINUTES
MAKES: 12 SERVINGS (¾ CUP EACH)

TAMALE CROUTONS

- 3 cups frozen corn, divided
- ⅔ cup butter, softened
- ⅓ cup sugar
- ¼ teaspoon salt
- 1 cup masa harina
- ¼ cup all-purpose flour

CHIPOTLE RANCH DRESSING

- ¼ cup buttermilk
- ¼ cup mayonnaise
- 1 teaspoon buttermilk ranch salad dressing mix
- 1 teaspoon minced chipotle peppers in adobo sauce

SALAD

- 6 cans (7 ounces each) white or shoepeg corn, drained
- 2 cups grape tomatoes, chopped
- 1 can (10 ounces) diced tomatoes and green chilies, well drained
- 1 small red onion, chopped
- ½ cup chopped peeled jicama
- ¼ cup minced fresh cilantro
- ¼ cup lime juice
- 1 jalapeno pepper, seeded and minced
- 4 medium ripe avocados, peeled and cubed
- ¾ cup shredded Mexican cheese blend

1. Place 2 cups corn in food processor; cover and process until finely chopped. Add the butter, sugar and salt; cover and process until blended. Stir in the masa harina and flour until a soft dough forms; fold in the remaining corn. Using wet hands, press dough into a greased 15-in. x 10-in. x 1-in. baking pan.

2. Bake at 400° for 20 minutes. Score the dough into 1-in. squares. Bake 4-6 minutes longer or until golden brown. Immediately cut along the scored lines; cool in pan on a wire rack.

3. In a small bowl, combine the dressing ingredients. In a large bowl, combine the corn, tomatoes, onion, jicama, cilantro, lime juice and jalapeno. Pour dressing over salad and toss to coat; gently stir in avocados. Sprinkle with cheese and croutons. Serve immediately.

Editor's Note: *Wear disposable gloves when cutting hot peppers; the oils can burn skin. Avoid touching your face.*

❝ I've been an educator for 34 years, and the last 25 of those years I've been teaching kindergarten at Brownwood Elementary —a school with tremendous community involvement. This year, in November, we had an American Heritage Day celebration. The entire school participated. It was a wonderful learning experience for students.❞

—RICHI REYNOLDS SCOTTSBORO, ALABAMA
Teacher, Brownwood Elementary School, Scottsboro, Alabama

Halibut Chowder

I have a passion for cooking and entertaining. Several times a year I invite both my retired and current teaching friends to a dinner party with their spouses. I've served this halibut chowder at those parties and it was a big hit.

—**TERESA LUECK** ONAMIA, MINNESOTA

PREP: 25 MINUTES **COOK:** 30 MINUTES
MAKES: 12 SERVINGS (3 QUARTS)

- 4 **celery ribs, chopped**
- 3 **medium carrots, chopped**
- 1 **large onion, chopped**
- ½ **cup butter, cubed**
- ½ **cup all-purpose flour**
- ¼ **teaspoon white pepper**
- 2 **cups 2% milk**
- 1 **can (14½ ounces) chicken broth**
- ¼ **cup water**
- 1 **tablespoon chicken base**
- 3 **medium potatoes, peeled and chopped**
- 1 **can (15¼ ounces) whole kernel corn, drained**
- 3 **bay leaves**
- 2 **cups half-and-half cream**
- 2 **tablespoons lemon juice**
- 1 **pound halibut or other whitefish fillets, cut into 1-inch pieces**
- 1 **cup salad croutons**
- ¾ **cup grated Parmesan cheese**
- ½ **cup minced chives**

1. In a large saucepan, saute celery, carrots and onion in butter until tender. Stir in flour and pepper until blended; gradually add milk, broth, water and chicken base. Bring to a boil; cook and stir for 2 minutes or until thickened.

2. Add the potatoes, corn and bay leaves. Return to a boil. Reduce heat; cover and simmer for 15-20 minutes or until potatoes are tender.

3. Stir in cream and lemon juice; return to a boil. Add halibut. Reduce heat; simmer, uncovered, for 7-11 minutes or until fish flakes easily. Discard bay leaves.

4. Garnish servings with croutons, cheese and chives.

Editor's Note: *Look for chicken base near the broth and bouillon.*

Sausage Stuffing Muffins

PREP: 45 MINUTES **BAKE:** 20 MINUTES
MAKES: 1½ DOZEN

- 1 **pound bulk pork sausage**
- 4 **celery ribs, chopped**
- 2 **medium onions, chopped**
- ¼ **cup butter, cubed**
- 1 **package (14 ounces) crushed corn bread stuffing**
- 2 **medium apples, peeled and chopped**
- 1 **package (5 ounces) dried cranberries**
- 1 **cup chopped pecans**
- 1 **teaspoon salt**
- 1 **teaspoon pepper**
- 2 **to 3 cups reduced-sodium chicken broth**
- 2 **eggs**
- 2 **teaspoons baking powder**

1. In a large skillet, cook sausage over medium heat until no longer pink; drain. Transfer to a large bowl; set aside.

2. In the same skillet, saute celery and onions in butter until tender. Transfer to the bowl; add the stuffing, apples, cranberries, pecans, salt and pepper. Stir in enough broth to reach desired moistness. Whisk eggs and baking powder; add to stuffing mixture.

3. Spoon into 18 greased muffin cups. Bake at 375° for 20-25 minutes or until lightly browned. Cool for 10 minutes. Run a knife around edges of muffin cups to loosen. Serve immediately.

❝This recipe puts stuffing into a muffin form for a special presentation. I made these when I cooked my first Thanksgiving dinner. You can also bake the stuffing in a greased baking dish.❞

—**TRICIA BIBB** HARTSELLE, ALABAMA
Teacher, Hartselle Junior High School, Hartselle, Alabama

Grilled Sweet Potato Wedges

I love when an entire meal can be cooked outside on the grill and I don't need to heat up the kitchen on hot days. These tasty fries meet that requirement.

—**NATALIE KNOWLTON** KAMAS, UTAH

PREP/TOTAL TIME: 30 MINUTES
MAKES: 8 SERVINGS

- 4 **large sweet potatoes, peeled and cut into ½-inch wedges**
- ½ **teaspoon garlic salt**
- ¼ **teaspoon pepper**

DIPPING SAUCE
- ½ **cup reduced-fat mayonnaise**
- ½ **cup fat-free plain yogurt**
- 1 **teaspoon ground cumin**
- ½ **teaspoon seasoned salt**
- ½ **teaspoon paprika**
- ½ **teaspoon chili powder**

1. Place potatoes in a large saucepan and cover with water. Bring to a boil. Reduce heat; cover and simmer for 4-5 minutes or until crisp-tender. Drain; pat dry with paper towels. Sprinkle potatoes with garlic salt and pepper.

2. Grill, covered, over medium heat for 10-12 minutes or until tender, turning once. In a small bowl, combine the mayonnaise, yogurt and seasonings. Serve with sweet potatoes.

"I've been the Family and Consumer Science teacher at Treasure Mountain Junior High for two years. My favorite part of teaching at Treasure is our involvement with our sister school in Uganda, Africa. To raise money for that school, we held a hunger banquet where my Food and Nutrition classes prepared dinner for nearly 300 guests. At home, my husband and I love to try new dishes. It's a definite perk that I can test out some of those recipes with my students!"

—**NATALIE KNOWLTON** KAMAS, UTAH
Teacher, Treasure Mountain Junior High, Park City, Utah

Cranberry Ambrosia Salad

My paternal grandmother made this fluffy and fruity salad for Christmas dinner. I'm not sure how many batches she made, as there were nearly 50 aunts, uncles and cousins in our family. I still make the recipe in memory of her, and it's still just as good as I remember.

—JANET HURLEY SHELL ROCK, IOWA
Teacher, Shell Rock Elementary, Shell Rock, Iowa

PREP: 20 MINUTES + CHILLING
MAKES: 9 SERVINGS

1   **pound fresh or frozen cranberries**
1   **can (20 ounces) crushed pineapple, drained**
1   **cup sugar**
2   **cups miniature marshmallows**
1   **cup heavy whipping cream, whipped**
½ **cup chopped pecans**

1. In a food processor, cover and process cranberries until coarsely chopped. Transfer to a large bowl; stir in pineapple and sugar. Cover and refrigerate overnight.

2. Just before serving, fold in the marshmallows, whipped cream and pecans.

> "I love tomatoes, and these are healthy and versatile. You can use them in sandwiches, omelets and to top broiled chicken."
> —**JULIE TILNEY (GOMEZ)** DOWNEY, CALIFORNIA
> *Teacher, Paramount Unified School District, Paramount, California*

Slow-Roasted Tomatoes

PREP: 20 MINUTES **BAKE:** 3 HOURS + COOLING
MAKES: 4 CUPS

- 20 **plum tomatoes (about 5 pounds)**
- ¼ **cup olive oil**
- 5 **teaspoons Italian seasoning**
- 2½ **teaspoons salt**

1. Cut tomatoes into ½-in. slices. Brush with oil; sprinkle with Italian seasoning and salt.

2. Place on racks coated with cooking spray in foil-lined 15-in. x 10-in. x 1-in. baking pans. Bake, uncovered, at 325° for 3 to 3½ hours or until tomatoes are deep brown around the edges and shriveled. Cool for 10-15 minutes. Serve warm or at room temperature.

3. Store in an airtight container in the refrigerator for up to 1 week or freeze for up to 3 months. Bring tomatoes to room temperature before using.

Quinoa and Black Bean Salad

Here's a good-for-you dish that can be served either cold, as a side salad for eight people, or warm, as an entree for four. The lime vinaigrette adds a nice punch of flavor to this wonderful dish.

—**YVONNE COMPTON** ELKTON, OREGON

PREP: 20 MINUTES **COOK:** 15 MINUTES
MAKES: 8 SERVINGS

- 1 **cup vegetable broth**
- 1 **cup water**
- 1 **cup quinoa, rinsed**
- 1 **medium sweet orange pepper, chopped**
- 1 **small red onion, chopped**
- 1 **garlic clove, minced**
- 1 **can (15 ounces) black beans, rinsed and drained**
- 1 **cup frozen corn, thawed**
- 2 **cups cherry tomatoes, halved**
- ¼ **cup olive oil**
- 2 **tablespoons lime juice**
- 1 **teaspoon balsamic vinegar**
- ½ **teaspoon salt**
- ¼ **teaspoon pepper**
- ¼ **teaspoon chili powder**
- 1 **medium ripe avocado, peeled and cubed**
- 2 **tablespoons minced fresh cilantro**

1. In a small saucepan, bring broth and water to a boil. Add quinoa. Reduce heat; cover and simmer for 12-16 minutes or until liquid is absorbed. Remove from the heat; fluff with a fork.

2. In a large nonstick skillet coated with cooking spray, cook the orange pepper, onion and garlic for 2 minutes. Stir in beans and corn; cook 2-3 minutes longer or until onion is tender. Remove from the heat; cool for 5 minutes. Stir in the tomatoes.

3. In a small bowl, whisk the oil, lime juice, vinegar, salt, pepper and chili powder. Pour over tomato mixture; toss to coat.

4. Spoon quinoa onto a serving platter. Top with tomato mixture, avocado and cilantro.

Editor's Note: *Look for quinoa in the cereal, rice or organic food aisle.*

"I'm a native Australian and taught there for 15 years before moving to Elkton (population 180) some 20 years ago. I teach kindergarten, and my teaching philosophy can be summed up in these words: 'Each stage of development is complete in itself. A 3-year-old is not an incomplete 5-year-old. The child is not an incomplete adult. Never are we simply on our way! Always, we have arrived.'"

—**YVONNE COMPTON** ELKTON, OREGON
Teacher, Elkton Charter School, Elkton, Oregon

Fiesta Corn Chip Salad

Whenever I bring this corn salad to a gathering, the recipe is always requested! It's quick, easy and great alongside just about any main course.

—MANDY MCKINNON NORTH CANTON, OHIO

PREP/TOTAL TIME: 10 MINUTES
MAKES: 10 SERVINGS

- 2 cans (15¼ ounces each) whole kernel corn, drained
- 2 cups (8 ounces) shredded Mexican cheese blend
- 1 medium sweet red pepper, chopped
- 1 cup mayonnaise
- ⅛ teaspoon salt
- ⅛ teaspoon pepper
- 1 package (9¼ ounces) chili cheese-flavored corn chips, crushed

1. In a large bowl, combine the corn, cheese, red pepper, mayonnaise, salt and pepper. Chill until serving. Just before serving, stir in corn chips.

Cranberry Broccoli Slaw

Perk up any cookout with this fun broccoli slaw. This super-easy salad is ready in minutes.

—ALLISON STRAIN LANCASTER, CALIFORNIA

PREP/TOTAL TIME: 15 MINUTES
MAKES: 16 SERVINGS (¾ CUP EACH)

- 1 package (14 ounces) coleslaw mix
- 4 cups fresh broccoli florets
- 1 cup dried cranberries
- ½ cup chopped walnuts
- ½ cup raisins
- ⅓ cup chopped red onion
- 6 bacon strips, cooked and crumbled
- 1 cup reduced-fat mayonnaise
- ¼ cup sugar
- 1 tablespoon cider vinegar

1. In a large bowl, combine the first seven ingredients. In a small bowl, whisk the mayonnaise, sugar and vinegar. Pour over cabbage mixture; toss to coat. Refrigerate until serving.

Greek Salad with Green Grapes

Prepared with ingredients traditionally associated with Greece, this healthy and colorful salad offers a delightful combination of flavors. It's outstanding for any entree, but goes especially well with lamb or pork dishes prepared in a Mediterranean style.

—HOLLY HEUPEL COLORADO SPRINGS, COLORADO
Teacher, Foothills Elementary, Colorado Springs, Colorado

PREP/TOTAL TIME: 25 MINUTES
MAKES: 9 SERVINGS

- 1 **package (5 ounces) spring mix salad greens**
- 3½ **cups torn romaine**
- 1 **large cucumber, chopped**
- 1 **cup green grapes**
- ½ **cup cherry tomatoes, halved**
- ½ **cup chopped walnuts**
- 1 **cup (4 ounces) crumbled feta cheese**
- 1 **can (3.8 ounces) sliced ripe olives, drained**

GREEK YOGURT VINAIGRETTE
- ¾ **cup white wine vinegar**
- 2 **tablespoons plain Greek yogurt**
- 2 **tablespoons honey**
- 2 **teaspoons snipped fresh dill**
- ⅛ **teaspoon salt**
- ⅛ **teaspoon pepper**
- 7 **tablespoons olive oil**

1. In a large bowl, combine first eight ingredients.

2. In a small bowl, whisk the vinegar, yogurt, honey, dill, salt and pepper. Gradually add the oil in a steady stream until combined. Pour over salad; toss to coat.

Editor's Note: *If Greek yogurt is not available in your area, line a strainer with a coffee filter and place over a bowl. Place ¼ cup plain yogurt in prepared strainer; refrigerate overnight. Discard liquid from bowl; proceed as directed.*

French Onion Soup

In my opinion, the key to a delicious French onion soup is a dark, savory broth, which you traditionally get from beef broth. But to make a vegetarian version with the same robust taste using vegetable broth is more difficult. To achieve the earthy tones I'm looking for, I've used a few nontraditional ingredients in this recipe.

—PAUL DEBENEDICTIS READING, MASSACHUSETTS

PREP: 30 MINUTES **COOK:** 1 HOUR 20 MINUTES
MAKES: 6 SERVINGS

- 3 **pounds yellow onions**
- 1 **pound sweet onions, thinly sliced**
- 2 **tablespoons butter**
- 1 **tablespoon olive oil**
- 1 **teaspoon dried thyme**
- 1 **teaspoon brown sugar**
- 1 **teaspoon balsamic vinegar**
- 1 **tablespoon all-purpose flour**
- 1 **can (14½ ounces) vegetable broth**
- 1 **can (12 ounces) beer or 12 ounces vegetable broth**
- ¼ **cup white wine or additional vegetable broth**
- 2 **tablespoons reduced-sodium soy sauce**
- 1 **tablespoon Worcestershire sauce**
- 2 **teaspoons brandy**
- ½ **teaspoon coarsely ground pepper**
- ¼ **teaspoon salt**
- ⅛ **teaspoon cayenne pepper**
- 6 **slices French bread (1 inch thick)**
- 6 **slices Swiss cheese**

1. In a Dutch oven, saute onions in butter and oil until tender. Reduce heat to medium-low; cook for 1 hour or until golden brown, stirring occasionally. Stir in the thyme, brown sugar and vinegar.

2. Combine flour and broth until blended. Gradually stir into onion mixture. Stir in the beer, wine, soy sauce, Worcestershire sauce, brandy, pepper, salt and cayenne. Bring to a boil. Reduce heat; cover and simmer for 10 minutes.

3. Meanwhile, place bread on a baking sheet. Broil 4 in. from the heat for 2 minutes on each side or until toasted. Top each with a cheese slice; broil 2-3 minutes longer or until cheese is melted and lightly browned. Ladle the soup into bowls; garnish with the toast.

"During the day, I moonlight as 'Mr. D,' a fun-loving and dedicated first and second grade teacher. I find that working with 6-, 7-, and 8-year-olds is much like cooking. It involves thinking outside the box, being quick on one's feet, putting out fires, and keeping a sense of creativity! After school, I share my love of cooking with my wife and brothers."

—PAUL DEBENEDICTIS READING, MASSACHUSETTS
Teacher, Lincoln Elementary School, Winchester, Massachusetts

"I have taught elementary school in Las Vegas for over 20 years. One of the best parts of teaching is knowing that you're helping to sculpt our youth and give them a firm foundation for learning. My goal is to make learning fun and meaningful to my students, and to instill in them how important and special each of them is to me and to society."

—NICHOLE FISCHER LAS VEGAS, NEVADA
Teacher, Thompson Elementary, Las Vegas, Nevada

Reuben Pasta Salad

I have German heritage and I brought this German-influenced salad to my neighbor's Octoberfest party. A house full of teachers all gave it an A+!

—NICHOLE FISCHER LAS VEGAS, NEVADA

PREP/TOTAL TIME: 30 MINUTES
MAKES: 16 SERVINGS (¾ CUP EACH)

- 4 **cups uncooked egg noodles**
- ⅓ **cup packed brown sugar**
- ¼ **cup olive oil**
- ¼ **cup Dijon mustard**
- 2 **tablespoons cider vinegar**
- 1½ **teaspoons caraway seeds**
- 6 **cups coleslaw mix**
- 8 **ounces sliced deli corned beef, cut into strips**
- ¼ **cup shredded Swiss cheese**

1. In a large saucepan, cook noodles according to package directions.

2. In a small saucepan over low heat, combine the brown sugar, oil, mustard, vinegar and caraway seeds. Cook and stir for 3-5 minutes or until heated through.

3. Drain the noodles. In a large bowl, combine the coleslaw mix, noodles, corned beef and warm dressing; toss to coat. Sprinkle with cheese. Serve warm or at room temperature.

Tossed Salad with Cilantro Vinaigrette

This is not a salad that you'll see everywhere. It features a unique mix of veggies tossed with romaine. Everybody asks for seconds after they've tried it.

—LARI MONTESINO ELKHART, INDIANA
Teacher, Riverview Elementary, Elkhart, Indiana

PREP/TOTAL TIME: 25 MINUTES
MAKES: 16 SERVINGS (¾ CUP EACH)

- ⅓ **cup olive oil**
- ¼ **cup minced fresh cilantro**
- ¼ **cup lime juice**
- ⅛ **teaspoon salt**
- 8 **cups torn romaine**
- 1 **medium zucchini, chopped**
- 1 **medium cucumber, chopped**
- 1 **medium sweet yellow pepper, chopped**
- 5 **to 10 radishes, sliced**

1. In a small bowl, whisk the oil, cilantro, lime juice and salt.

2. In a large bowl, combine the romaine, zucchini, cucumber, yellow pepper and radishes. Drizzle with dressing; toss to coat. Serve immediately.

Creamy Turnip Soup

PREP: 20 MINUTES **COOK:** 20 MINUTES
MAKES: 9 SERVINGS (2¼ QUARTS)

- 1 **medium onion, chopped**
- 2 **tablespoons butter**
- 3 **garlic cloves, minced**
- ½ **cup white wine or reduced-sodium chicken broth**
- 3 **pounds turnips, peeled and cut into 1-inch cubes**
- 1 **carton (32 ounces) reduced-sodium chicken broth**
- 1 **medium potato, peeled and cubed**
- 1 **cup half-and-half cream**
- ½ **teaspoon salt**
- ½ **teaspoon ground nutmeg**
- 3 **cups fresh baby spinach**
- ½ **teaspoon olive oil**

1. In a Dutch oven, saute onion in butter until tender. Add garlic; cook 1 minute longer. Stir in wine. Bring to a boil; cook until liquid is reduced by half.

2. Add the turnips, broth and potato. Bring to a boil. Reduce heat; simmer, uncovered, for 20-25 minutes or until vegetables are tender. Cool slightly.

3. In a food processor, process soup in batches until smooth. Return all to pan. Stir in the cream, salt and nutmeg; heat through. Meanwhile, in a large nonstick skillet, saute spinach in oil until tender. Garnish soup with spinach.

❝In nearby Wardsboro, Vermont, they have a fall festival where one of the entrees is this delicious turnip soup. It reheats wonderfully in a slow cooker and is perfect to serve for my school's monthly teacher luncheons.❞

—**LIZ WHEELER** WILMINGTON, VERMONT

> "I love jicama dipped in citrus and sprinkled with salt and jalapenos. So when I needed to bring a salad to a 4th of July picnic, I decided to use this crunchy vegetable as the star of the salad."
> —**JAN LYSAK-RUIZ** YUCAIPA, CALIFORNIA
> *Staff, Ridgeview Elementary, Yucaipa, California*

Confetti Jicama Salad

PREP: 35 MINUTES + CHILLING
MAKES: 6 SERVINGS

- ½ medium jicama, peeled and julienned
- 1⅓ cups julienned seedless cucumber
- 1 each small sweet red, orange and yellow peppers, julienned
- ½ cup thinly sliced red onion
- 3 green onions, chopped

DRESSING

- ⅓ cup minced fresh cilantro
- 1 jalapeno pepper, seeded and finely chopped
- 2 tablespoons lime juice
- 2 tablespoons orange juice concentrate
- 2 tablespoons olive oil
- 1 garlic clove, minced
- 1 teaspoon sugar
- ½ teaspoon salt
- ¼ teaspoon pepper
- ⅛ teaspoon cayenne pepper

1. In a large bowl, combine the jicama, cucumber, peppers and onions.

2. In a small bowl, whisk the cilantro, jalapeno, lime juice, juice concentrate, oil, garlic and seasonings. Pour over salad; toss to coat. Cover and refrigerate for at least 1 hour. Stir before serving.

Edtor's Note: *Wear disposable gloves when cutting hot peppers; the oils can burn skin. Avoid touching your face.*

"Totally scrumptious and packed with nutrition, this salad was my response to friends who asked how they could incorporate kale into their diets without sacrificing taste. It is also wonderful made with collard or mustard greens, prepared in the same fashion as the kale, or with a mix of spinach and arugula or watercress."

—**ELIZABETH WARREN** OKLAHOMA CITY, OKLAHOMA

Bacon Kale Salad with Honey-Horseradish Vinaigrette

PREP: 35 MINUTES **MAKES:** 8 SERVINGS

- 10 kale leaves, stems removed and thinly sliced
- ¼ cup loosely packed basil leaves, thinly sliced
- ½ cup alfalfa sprouts
- 4 bacon strips, cooked and crumbled
- ½ cup crumbled feta cheese
- ½ medium ripe avocado, peeled and thinly sliced
- 1 hard-cooked egg, chopped
- 1 cup grape tomatoes, chopped

VINAIGRETTE
- ⅓ cup olive oil
- 3 tablespoons lemon juice
- 2 tablespoons prepared horseradish
- 2 tablespoons honey
- 1½ teaspoons garlic powder
- 1½ teaspoons spicy brown mustard
- ¼ teaspoon crushed red pepper flakes
- ⅛ teaspoon pepper
  Dash salt

1. Divide the kale and basil among eight salad plates. Top each with the sprouts, bacon, cheese, avocado, egg and tomatoes.

2. In a small bowl, whisk the vinaigrette ingredients. Drizzle over salads; serve immediately.

Black-Eyed Pea Spinach Salad

PREP/TOTAL TIME: 20 MINUTES
MAKES: 16 SERVINGS (¾ CUP EACH)

- ¼ **cup olive oil**
- ¼ **cup red wine vinegar**
- 4 **teaspoons Dijon mustard**
- 1 **teaspoon salt**
- 1 **teaspoon pepper**
- 2 **cans (15½ ounces each) black-eyed peas, rinsed and drained**
- 3 **medium tomatoes, seeded and chopped**
- ½ **cup thinly sliced red onion**
- 1 **package (9 ounces) fresh spinach**
- ½ **cup chopped pecans, toasted**
- 6 **bacon strips, cooked and crumbled**

1. In a large bowl, whisk the first five ingredients. Stir in the peas, tomatoes and onion. Cover and refrigerate until serving.

2. Place the spinach and vegetable mixture in a large serving bowl; toss gently. Sprinkle with the pecans and bacon.

66Here's a Southern take on a classic spinach salad with black-eyed peas and pecans. It is always a hit with my guests.99

—**DEBBIE INGLE** WINFIELD, ALABAMA
Teacher, Hubbertville School, Fayette, Alabama

Sesame Spaghetti Salad with Peanuts

I love the sweet and spicy combination of the Asian-style sauce in this dish—and that it can be made a day ahead!

—LEANN FUJIMOTO NORMAL, ILLINOIS

PREP/TOTAL TIME: 30 MINUTES
MAKES: 10 SERVINGS

- 1 package (1 pound) spaghetti
- ⅓ cup sesame oil
- ¼ cup canola oil
- 1 teaspoon crushed red pepper flakes
- ¼ cup reduced-sodium soy sauce
- 3 tablespoons honey
- 1½ teaspoons kosher salt
- ½ cup dry roasted peanuts, chopped
- ¼ cup minced fresh cilantro
- 2 tablespoons sesame seeds, toasted

1. Cook spaghetti according to package directions.

2. Meanwhile, in a small saucepan over medium heat, heat the sesame oil, canola oil and pepper flakes until oil is fragrant. Remove from the heat. Stir in the soy sauce, honey and salt; set aside.

3. Drain spaghetti and rinse in cold water; transfer to a large bowl. Add the peanuts, cilantro, sesame seeds and oil mixture; toss to coat. Chill until serving.

"I have taught math and science on the Einstein team at Chiddix Jr. High School for nearly my entire teaching career. I have been honored with the Illinois Math and Science Academy's 1999 Caring to Challenge Award, and recognized as a 2007 Turner N. Wiley Teacher of the Year. In addition to teaching, I coach volleyball for the Illini Elite Volleyball Club. Whether teaching or coaching, I live by the philosophy: 'Children don't care what you know until they know that you care!'"

—LEANN FUJIMOTO NORMAL, ILLINOIS
Teacher, Chiddix Junior High, Normal, Illinois

> "A good friend of mine makes these scones and shares them with me. They are so good! You can see the flecks of cheese, ham and green onions."
>
> —**FELICITY LA RUE** PALMDALE, CALIFORNIA
> *Teacher, Lake Los Angeles Elementary School, Palmdale, California*

Ham and Cheddar Scones

PREP: 25 MINUTES **BAKE:** 20 MINUTES
MAKES: 1 DOZEN

- **3 cups all-purpose flour**
- **½ cup sugar**
- **2 tablespoons baking powder**
- **½ teaspoon salt**
- **2 cups heavy whipping cream**
- **1 cup diced fully cooked ham**
- **½ cup diced cheddar cheese**
- **4 green onions, thinly sliced**

1. In a large bowl, combine the flour, sugar, baking powder and salt. Stir in cream just until moistened. Stir in the ham, cheese and onions. Turn onto a floured surface; knead 10 times.

2. Transfer dough to a greased baking sheet. Pat into a 9-in. circle. Cut into 12 wedges, but do not separate. Bake at 400° for 20-25 minutes or until golden brown. Serve warm.

"During the school year, J.F. Kennedy High regularly plans staff social events where food is always a central part. I'm always happy to provide a dish. Many of my recipes have been complimented, which is why I decided to share some of them with *Taste of Home*. It's my way to give back to the school some of the blessings I have received by being part of such a wonderful school family."
—**MADELINE ETZKORN** BURIEN, WASHINGTON
Staff, J.F.Kennedy High School, Burien, Washington

Swiss Sweet Onion Casserole

I think this is a great side dish for barbecued chicken or ribs. Sweet onions are available most of the year, so don't substitute another type of onion...the dish will not be quite as fantastic!
—**MADELINE ETZKORN** BURIEN, WASHINGTON

PREP: 30 MINUTES **BAKE:** 1 HOUR
MAKES: 6 SERVINGS

- ½ cup uncooked long grain rice
- 8 cups halved sliced sweet onions
- 2 tablespoons butter
- 1 cup (4 ounces) shredded Swiss cheese
- ½ cup half-and-half cream
- ½ teaspoon salt
- ⅛ teaspoon ground nutmeg

1. Cook rice according to the package directions.

2. In a large skillet, saute onions in butter until tender. Remove from the heat; stir in the cooked rice, cheese, cream, salt and nutmeg. Pour into a greased 8-in. square baking dish.

3. Bake, uncovered, at 325° for 1 to 1¼ hours or until golden brown.

Spicy Cucumber Salad

Salting the cucumbers makes them crisp and crunchy for the salad. The soy sauce and sesame oil dressing is a wonderful change from the usual vinegar- or mayonnaise-coated cukes. I made this for a faculty picnic one year and it was really a hit.

—KELLY GARDNER ALTON, ILLINOIS
Teacher, East Alton-Wood River High School, Wood River, Illinois

PREP: 15 MINUTES + STANDING
MAKES: 5 SERVINGS

- 3   medium cucumbers, peeled, halved, seeded and sliced
- ½   teaspoon salt
- 2   tablespoons rice vinegar
- 2   tablespoons soy sauce
- 1   tablespoon sesame oil
- 1½ teaspoons sugar
- 1½ teaspoons red curry paste

1. Place cucumbers in a strainer over a plate; sprinkle with salt and toss. Let stand for 30 minutes. Rinse and drain well.

2. Transfer cucumbers to a large bowl. In a small bowl, whisk the vinegar, soy sauce, oil, sugar and curry paste; pour over cucumbers and toss to coat. Chill until serving. Serve with a slotted spoon.

Crunchy Apple Salad

Whenever our staff celebrates a birthday or a special occasion, "Mary's Apple Salad" is always at the top of the wish list! The ingredients can also be prepared the day before and put together in a flash for our teachers' 20-minute lunchtime.

—MARY ROBERTSON LOUISVILLE, KENTUCKY
Teacher, Malcolm B. Chancey Elementary, Louisville, Kentucky

PREP/TOTAL TIME: 30 MINUTES
MAKES: 16 SERVINGS (1 CUP EACH)

    2 packages (5 ounces each) spring mix salad greens
    2 large apples, chopped
    2 cups bagel chips, coarsely crushed
 1½ cups honey-roasted peanuts
    1 cup (4 ounces) crumbled blue cheese

DRESSING
    ⅓ cup sugar
    ⅓ cup canola oil
    ¼ cup cider vinegar
    1 tablespoon poppy seeds
 1¼ teaspoons dried minced onion
    1 teaspoon Worcestershire sauce
    ½ teaspoon salt
    ¼ teaspoon paprika
    ⅛ teaspoon pepper

1. In a large salad bowl, combine the first five ingredients. In a small bowl, whisk the dressing ingredients. Drizzle over salad; toss to coat.

"Even self-avowed carnivores won't miss the meat in this zippy dish. It's chock-full of healthy ingredients that will keep you feeling satisfied. This is a variation of a chicken-lentil soup that I make for my vegan friends."
—**LAURIE STOUT-LETZ** BOUNTIFUL, UTAH
Teacher, Eisenhower Junior High School, Taylorsville, Utah

Southwest Vegetarian Lentil Soup

PREP: 25 MINUTES **COOK:** 7 HOURS
MAKES: 6 SERVINGS (2 QUARTS)

- 3 cups vegetable broth
- 1 large onion, chopped
- 1 can (10 ounces) mild diced tomatoes and green chilies, undrained
- 1 cup mild salsa
- 1 cup dried lentils, rinsed
- 1 cup frozen corn
- 1 can (8 ounces) tomato sauce
- 1 can (4 ounces) chopped green chilies
- 3 garlic cloves, minced
- 1½ teaspoons chili powder
- 1 teaspoon ground cumin
- ½ teaspoon celery salt
- ½ teaspoon paprika
- ⅛ teaspoon cayenne pepper
- 1 package (16 ounces) firm tofu, drained and cut into ¼-inch cubes
- 1 can (4¼ ounces) chopped ripe olives
- 3 green onions, sliced

1. In a 3- or 4-qt. slow cooker, combine the first 14 ingredients. Cover and cook on low for 8-10 hours or until lentils are tender. Sprinkle with tofu, olives and green onions.

Italian Wedding Soup

PREP: 30 MINUTES **COOK:** 40 MINUTES
MAKES: 9 SERVINGS (2¼ QUARTS)

- 2 eggs, lightly beaten
- ½ cup dry bread crumbs
- ¼ cup minced fresh parsley
- 2 tablespoons grated Parmesan cheese
- 1 tablespoon raisins, finely chopped
- 3 garlic cloves, minced
- ¼ teaspoon crushed red pepper flakes
- ½ pound lean ground beef (90% lean)
- ½ pound bulk spicy pork sausage
- 2 cartons (32 ounces each) reduced-sodium chicken broth
- ½ teaspoon pepper
- 1½ cups cubed rotisserie chicken
- ⅔ cup uncooked acini di pepe pasta
- ½ cup fresh baby spinach, cut into thin strips
  Shredded Parmesan cheese, optional

1. In a large bowl, combine the first seven ingredients. Crumble beef and sausage over mixture and mix well. Shape into ½-in. balls.

2. In a Dutch oven, brown meatballs in small batches; drain. Add the broth and pepper; bring to a boil. Reduce heat; simmer, uncovered, for 10 minutes. Stir in chicken and pasta; cook 5-7 minutes longer or until pasta is tender. Stir in spinach; cook until wilted. Sprinkle with shredded Parmesan cheese if desired.

"You don't have to be Italian to love this easy-to-make soup! It's a hit with everyone who tries it and makes a great meal with hot crusty Italian bread or garlic bread."

—MARY SHEETZ CARMEL, INDIANA
Staff, Prairie Trace Elementary, Carmel, Indiana

Dill and Chive Bread

Store-bought chive and onion cream cheese is such an effortless way to give plain bread dough a punch. I love how easy and wonderful this bread is.

—**DAWN HIGGS** EAST MOLINE, ILLINOIS
Teacher, Cambridge Elementary School, Cambridge, Illinois

PREP: 15 MINUTES **BAKE:** 3 HOURS
MAKES: 1 LOAF (1½ POUNDS, 16 SLICES)

- ¾ cup water (70° to 80°)
- ½ cup spreadable chive and onion cream cheese
- 2 tablespoons sugar
- 2 teaspoons dill weed
- 1¼ teaspoons salt
- 3 cups all-purpose flour
- 1 package (¼ ounce) active dry yeast

1. In bread machine pan, place all ingredients in order suggested by manufacturer. Select basic bread setting. Choose crust color and loaf size if available. Bake according to bread machine directions (check dough after 5 minutes of mixing; add 1 to 2 tablespoons of water or flour if needed).

"As a lead teacher, I encourage educators to incorporate the magnet theme into their lessons. In this position, I am the spokesperson for programs offered, and a tour guide and representative to the community. The best part of this position is the flexibility to work with different groups of students and to see the impact of our environmental programs on students."
—**SUSAN FERRELL** TAMPA, FLORIDA

Teacher, Dowdell Middle Magnet School, Tampa, Florida

Easy Gazpacho

I really enjoy gazpacho a lot. Sometimes I make this soup on Sunday evening and then take it to school for lunch all week. The crunchy vegetables in the tomato base just add a healthy item to my menu.

—**SUSAN FERRELL** TAMPA, FLORIDA

PREP: 25 MINUTES + CHILLING **MAKES:** 4 SERVINGS

- 2 **cups Clamato juice**
- 3 **plum tomatoes, seeded and finely chopped**
- ½ **cup finely chopped green pepper**
- ½ **cup finely chopped seeded cucumber**
- ½ **cup finely chopped celery**
- ¼ **cup finely chopped onion**
- 2 **tablespoons olive oil**
- 2 **tablespoons red wine vinegar**
- 2 **teaspoons minced fresh parsley**
- 1 **teaspoon minced chives**
- 1 **garlic clove, minced**
- ½ **teaspoon pepper**
- ½ **teaspoon Worcestershire sauce**
- ¼ **teaspoon salt**
   Salad croutons, optional

1. In a large bowl, combine Clamato juice, tomatoes, green pepper, cucumber, celery, onion, oil, vinegar, parsley, chives, garlic, pepper, Worcestershire sauce and salt. Cover and refrigerate for at least 4 hours. Serve with croutons if desired.

Grilled Zucchini with Onions

PREP/TOTAL TIME: 20 MINUTES **MAKES:** 4 SERVINGS

- 6 **small zucchini, halved lengthwise**
- 4 **teaspoons olive oil, divided**
- 2 **green onions, thinly sliced**
- 2 **tablespoons lemon juice**
- ½ **teaspoon salt**
- ⅛ **teaspoon crushed red pepper flakes**

1. Drizzle zucchini with 2 teaspoons oil. Grill, covered, over medium heat for 8-10 minutes or until tender, turning once.

2. Place in a large bowl. Add the green onions, lemon juice, salt, pepper flakes and remaining oil; toss to coat.

❝Wondering what to do with all of your vegetable garden zucchini? Tired of the same old bread and cupcakes? My grill recipe is a great change of pace— with the added bonus of being healthy.❞

—**ALIA SHUTTLEWORTH** AUBURN, CALIFORNIA

Jazzed-Up French Bread

PREP: 10 MINUTES **GRILL:** 30 MINUTES + STANDING
MAKES: 10 SERVINGS

- 2 **cups (8 ounces) shredded Colby-Monterey Jack cheese**
- ⅔ **cup mayonnaise**
- 6 **green onions, chopped**
- 1 **loaf (1 pound) French bread, halved lengthwise**

1. In a small bowl, combine the cheese, mayonnaise and onions. Spread over cut sides of bread and reassemble loaf. Wrap in a double thickness of heavy-duty foil (about 28 in. x 18 in.); seal tightly.

2. Grill, covered, over indirect medium heat for 25-30 minutes or until cheese is melted, turning once. Let stand for 5 minutes before cutting into slices.

"Fire up the grill right away for this tasty French bread. It takes seconds to prepare and then cooks away over indirect heat, giving you plenty of time to assemble the rest of the meal."

—LORI LECROY EAST TAWAS, MICHIGAN

"This is one of my stand-by side dishes, which can complement most meat and meatless entrees. It is special enough for company and quick enough for weeknights."

—JACQUELINE OGLESBY SPRUCE PINE, NORTH CAROLINA
Teacher, West McDowell Junior High, Marion, North Carolina

Pecan Rice Pilaf

PREP: 15 MINUTES **COOK:** 20 MINUTES
MAKES: 9 SERVINGS

- 1 **cup chopped pecans**
- 5 **tablespoons butter, divided**
- 1 **small onion, chopped**
- 2 **cups uncooked long grain rice**
- 1 **carton (32 ounces) chicken broth**
- 3 **tablespoons minced fresh parsley, divided**
- ½ **teaspoon salt**
- ¼ **teaspoon dried thyme**
- ⅛ **teaspoon pepper**
- 1 **cup shredded carrots**

1. In a large saucepan, saute pecans in 2 tablespoons butter until toasted; remove from pan and set aside.

2. In the same pan, saute onion in remaining butter until tender. Add the rice; cook and stir for 3-4 minutes or until the rice is lightly browned. Stir in the broth, 2 tablespoons parsley, salt, thyme and pepper. Bring to a boil. Reduce heat; cover and simmer for 10 minutes.

3. Add carrots; simmer 3-5 minutes longer or until rice is tender. Stir in toasted pecans and remaining parsley. Fluff with a fork.

"I have been a parent volunteer at Sierra Hills School since 2007. As a volunteer, I have been involved in everything from being 'cooking mom,' to making the classroom quilt and helping coordinate the Lunch Time Running Club."

—ALIA SHUTTLEWORTH AUBURN, CALIFORNIA
Volunteer, Sierra Hills School, Meadow Vista, California

Roasted Vegetable Pasta Salad

I can't make this dish without printing up enough copies of the recipe to hand out at my book club and potlucks!

—ALIA SHUTTLEWORTH AUBURN, CALIFORNIA

PREP: 30 MINUTES **BAKE:** 35 MINUTES
MAKES: 9 SERVINGS

- ⅓ cup lemon juice
- ⅓ cup olive oil
- ½ teaspoon kosher salt
- ½ teaspoon pepper

ROASTED VEGETABLES

- 1 small eggplant, peeled and cut into ¾-inch cubes
- 1 medium sweet red pepper, cut into 1-inch pieces
- 1 medium sweet yellow pepper, cut into 1-inch pieces
- 1 large red onion, cut into 1-inch pieces
- 6 garlic cloves, peeled and halved
- ½ cup olive oil
- ½ teaspoon kosher salt
- ½ teaspoon pepper

SALAD

- 1¼ cups uncooked orzo pasta
- 4 green onions, finely chopped
- 15 fresh basil leaves, thinly sliced
- ¼ cup pine nuts, toasted
- 12 ounces feta cheese, cut into ¾-inch cubes

1. In a bowl, whisk first four ingredients; set aside.

2. In a large bowl, combine eggplant, and next seven ingredients; toss to coat. Transfer to a 15-in. x 10-in. x 1-in. baking pan. Bake at 425° for 35-40 minutes or until vegetables are tender. Cool to room temperature.

3. Cook orzo according to package directions; drain.

4. In a large serving bowl, combine roasted vegetables, pasta, green onions, basil and pine nuts. Drizzle with dressing; toss to coat. Add cheese; toss gently.

Sausage & Bean Soup

PREP/TOTAL TIME: 30 MINUTES
MAKES: 6 SERVINGS (2 QUARTS)

- 1 **pound bulk hot Italian sausage**
- 2 **cans (15½ ounces each) great northern beans, rinsed and drained**
- 1 **package (16 ounces) coleslaw mix**
- 1 **jar (24 ounces) garlic and herb spaghetti sauce**
- 3 **cups water**

1. In a Dutch oven, cook the sausage over medium heat until no longer pink; drain. Stir in the remaining ingredients. Bring to a boil. Reduce heat; simmer, uncovered, for 16-20 minutes or until the flavors are blended.

❝The unusual blend of sausage and beans with coleslaw makes this soup for a cold winter night the definition of complete comfort food. The recipe doubles easily, so serve a crowd and pair with crusty bread and a tossed salad.❞

—**STACEY BENNETT** LOCUST GROVE, VIRGINIA

Tangy Beef Chili

Blue cheese is an unusual ingredient to add to chili, but it adds a creamy, tangy accent. People will be asking you for the secret ingredient!

—LUANN MANER TAYLOR, ARIZONA
Administration, Taylor Intermediate School, Taylor, Arizona

PREP: 15 MINUTES **COOK:** 35 MINUTES
MAKES: 6 SERVINGS

- 1 **pound lean ground beef (90% lean)**
- 1 **small green pepper, chopped**
- 1 **small onion, chopped**
- 1 **can (15 ounces) ranch-style beans (pinto beans in seasoned tomato sauce)**
- 2 **cans (14½ ounces each) no-salt-added diced tomatoes, undrained**
- 4 **teaspoons chili powder**
- 1¼ **teaspoons ground cumin**
- ½ **teaspoon pepper**
- 6 **wedges The Laughing Cow light blue cheese**

1. In a large saucepan, cook the beef, green pepper and onion over medium heat until the meat is no longer pink; drain.

2. Stir in the beans, tomatoes, chili powder, cumin and pepper. Bring to a boil. Reduce heat; cover and simmer for 15 minutes or until the flavors are blended. Top with cheese.

> "With a medley of barley, beef and vegetables, this thick soup is more like a stew and just brimming with flavor and texture. Every spoonful will warm you from head to toe on cold winter evenings."
> —**RACHEL KOHNEN** POMEROY, IOWA

Beef & Barley Soup

PREP: 50 MINUTES **COOK:** 2 HOURS
MAKES: 8 SERVINGS (2½ QUARTS)

- 4 **bacon strips, diced**
- 2 **pounds beef stew meat, cut into 1-inch cubes**
- 4 **medium carrots, chopped**
- 2 **medium onions, chopped**
- ½ **pound sliced baby portobello mushrooms**
- 1 **cup dry red wine or beef broth**
- 8 **cups beef broth, divided**
- 4 **teaspoons spicy brown mustard**
- 1 **teaspoon dried thyme or 4 fresh thyme sprigs, chopped**
- 1 **bay leaf**
- 1 **cup medium pearl barley**
- ¼ **teaspoon salt**
- ¼ **teaspoon pepper**

1. In a Dutch oven, cook bacon over medium heat until crisp. Using a slotted spoon, remove to paper towels. Brown beef in drippings. Remove and set aside.

2. In the same pan, saute the carrots, onions and mushrooms until tender. Add wine, stirring to loosen browned bits from pan. Stir in 4 cups broth, mustard, thyme, bay leaf and beef. Bring to a boil. Reduce heat; cover and simmer for 1 hour or until beef is tender.

3. Stir in the barley, salt, pepper and remaining broth. Return to a boil. Reduce heat; cover and simmer for 1 hour or until the barley is tender. Discard bay leaf. Stir in bacon.

Roasted Green Vegetable Medley

PREP: 15 MINUTES **BAKE:** 20 MINUTES
MAKES: 13 SERVINGS

- 2 **cups fresh broccoli florets**
- 1 **pound thin fresh green beans, trimmed and cut into 2-inch pieces**
- 10 **small fresh mushrooms, halved**
- 8 **fresh Brussels sprouts**
- 2 **medium carrots, cut into ¼-inch slices**
- 1 **medium onion, cut into ¼-inch slices**
- 3 **to 5 garlic cloves, peeled and thinly sliced**
- 4 **tablespoons olive oil, divided**
- ½ **cup grated Parmesan cheese**
- 3 **tablespoons fresh basil leaves, cut into thin strips, optional**
- 2 **tablespoons minced fresh parsley**
- 2 **tablespoons lemon juice**
- 3 **teaspoons grated lemon peel**
- ¼ **teaspoon salt**
- ¼ **teaspoon pepper**

1. Place vegetables and garlic in a large bowl; drizzle with 2 tablespoons oil. Toss well. Place in a single layer in two 15-in. x 10-in. x 1-in. baking pans coated with cooking spray.

2. Bake, uncovered, at 425° for 20-25 minutes or until tender, stirring occasionally.

3. Meanwhile, in a small bowl, combine the cheese, basil if desired, parsley, lemon juice, lemon peel, salt, pepper and remaining oil. Transfer vegetables to a large serving bowl. Add the Parmesan mixture; toss to coat.

> ❝I have cooked a lot of dishes—from family favorites to gourmet—but I had never roasted vegetables as a side until lately. Now, this is my preferred way to cook them! I've adapted this recipe to use my favorite vegetables, but almost any kind can be cooked this way. ❞

—**SUZAN CROUCH** GRAND PRAIRIE, TEXAS
Teacher, Colin Powell Elementary, Grand Prairie, Texas

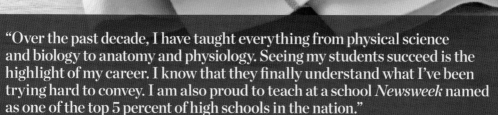

Mediterranean Pasta Salad

My mom always encouraged us to try different foods. She made it her mission in life to expose us to new recipes with a unique flavor combination. This salad reminds me of my mom in the way it makes eating exciting.

—**CHRISTINE GREEN** CONWAY, SOUTH CAROLINA

PREP: 35 MINUTES **COOK:** 20 MINUTES
MAKES: 18 SERVINGS (¾ CUP EACH)

- 1 **package (12 ounces) tricolor spiral pasta**
- 2½ **cups quartered and thinly sliced cucumbers**
- 1¼ **cups grape tomatoes, halved**
- 1 **jar (5¾ ounces) pimiento-stuffed olives, drained and halved**
- ½ **cup chopped green pepper**
- ½ **cup chopped sweet yellow pepper**
- 2 **tablespoons capers, drained**
- 1 **cup (4 ounces) crumbled feta cheese**
- 6 **slices provolone cheese, chopped**
- 1 **cup shredded Parmesan cheese, divided**
- ¼ **pound hard salami, cubed**
- 1 **cup Italian salad dressing**

1. Cook pasta according to package directions. Drain pasta and rinse in cold water.

2. In a large bowl, combine the cucumbers, tomatoes, olives, peppers, capers and pasta. Stir in the feta and provolone cheeses, ½ cup Parmesan cheese and salami. Add dressing; toss to coat. Sprinkle with remaining Parmesan cheese.

Herbed Tomato Bisque

This would be great to chase away the chill on a stormy night. This creamy tomato soup has a hint of sweetness from honey and great herb flavor.

—JOSH PERKINS, MAPLE GROVE, MINNESOTA

PREP: 20 MINUTES **COOK:** 35 MINUTES
MAKES: 8 SERVINGS (2 QUARTS)

- 1 **medium onion, finely chopped**
- ¼ **cup butter, cubed**
- ¼ **cup all-purpose flour**
- 1 **teaspoon dill weed**
- 1 **teaspoon dried oregano**
- 3 **cups chicken broth**
- 3 **cans (14½ ounces each) diced tomatoes, undrained**
- ¼ **cup minced fresh parsley**
- 2 **tablespoons honey**
- ¾ **teaspoon salt**
- ¾ **teaspoon white pepper**
- 1½ **cups half-and-half cream**

1. In a large saucepan, saute onion in butter until tender. Stir in the flour, dill and oregano until blended; gradually add broth. Bring to a boil; cook and stir for 2 minutes or until thickened.

2. Stir in the tomatoes, parsley, honey, salt and pepper. Return to a boil. Reduce heat; simmer, uncovered, for 15 minutes. Stir in cream; heat through.

Pasta & Sun-Dried Tomato Salad

The beauty of orzo pasta is that it can be served warm or cold—an ideal dish for casual picnics and cookouts.

—DAWN WILLIAMS SCOTTSBORO, ALABAMA

PREP: 20 MINUTES **COOK:** 15 MINUTES
MAKES: 8 SERVINGS

- 1 **can (49 ounces) reduced-sodium chicken broth**
- 1 **package (16 ounces) orzo pasta**
- ¼ **cup chopped oil-packed sun-dried tomatoes plus**
- 2 **teaspoons oil from the jar**
- 1 **garlic clove, minced**
- ¾ **teaspoon salt**
- ¼ **teaspoon pepper**
- ⅓ **cup shredded Parmesan cheese**
- 4 **fresh basil leaves, thinly sliced**
    Optional toppings: crumbled feta cheese and
       canned garbanzo beans

1. In a large saucepan, bring broth to a boil. Stir in orzo; return to a boil. Cook for 8-10 minutes or until tender, stirring occasionally.

2. Drain the orzo; transfer to a large bowl. (Discard broth or save for another use.) Stir in the tomatoes, oil from sun-dried tomatoes, garlic, salt and pepper; cool the orzo completely.

3. Add Parmesan cheese and basil; toss to combine. Cover and refrigerate until serving. Serve with the toppings if desired.

Crunchy Cool Coleslaw

This recipe is my version of the Honey Roasted Peanut Slaw at Lucille's Smokehouse BBQ, which I love. I think it's a pretty close match!

—ELAINE HOFFMANN SANTA ANA, CALIFORNIA

PREP/TOTAL TIME: 30 MINUTES
MAKES: 16 SERVINGS

- 2 **packages (16 ounces each) coleslaw mix**
- 2 **medium Honey Crisp apples, julienned**
- 1 **large carrot, shredded**
- ¾ **cup chopped red onion**
- ½ **cup chopped green pepper**
- ½ **cup cider vinegar**
- ⅓ **cup canola oil**
- 1½ **teaspoons sugar**
- ½ **teaspoon celery seed**
- ½ **teaspoon salt**
- ½ **cup coarsely chopped dry roasted peanuts or cashews**

1. In a large bowl, combine the first five ingredients. In a small bowl, whisk the vinegar, oil, sugar, celery seed and salt.

2. Just before serving, pour dressing over salad; toss to coat. Sprinkle with peanuts.

Favorite Mashed Sweet Potatoes

PREP/TOTAL TIME: 20 MINUTES **MAKES:** 8 SERVINGS

- 6 **medium sweet potatoes, peeled and cubed**
- 3 **tablespoons orange juice**
- 2 **tablespoons brown sugar**
- 2 **tablespoons maple syrup**
- ¼ **teaspoon pumpkin pie spice**

1. Place potatoes in a Dutch oven and cover with water. Bring to a boil. Reduce heat; cover and cook for 10-15 minutes or until tender. Drain. Mash potatoes with remaining ingredients.

❝My family begs me to make this recipe at Thanksgiving and Christmas. They like it because pumpkin pie spice enhances the flavor of the sweet potatoes. I like the fact that it can be made a day ahead and warmed before serving.❞

SENJA MERRILL, SANDY, UTAH
Teacher, Ridgecrest Elementary School, Cottonwood Heights, Utah

> "This vegetarian soup has a wonderful Middle Eastern flavor. It's also low in calories and fat, which makes it great for those of us watching our weight."
> —**RITA COMBS** VALDOSTA, GEORGIA
> *Parent Teacher Organization Officer, Sallas Mahone Elementary School, Valdosta, Georgia*

Spicy Couscous & Tomato Soup

PREP: 15 MINUTES **COOK:** 40 MINUTES
MAKES: 7 SERVINGS

- 2 medium sweet yellow peppers, chopped
- 1 medium red onion, chopped
- 2½ teaspoons olive oil
- 3 garlic cloves, minced
- 6 cups vegetable broth
- 6 plum tomatoes, chopped
- 1½ teaspoons ground cumin
- 1½ teaspoons ground coriander
- ½ teaspoon ground cinnamon
- ½ teaspoon cayenne pepper
- ¼ teaspoon pepper
- ½ cup uncooked couscous

1. In a Dutch oven, saute peppers and onion in oil until tender. Add garlic; cook 1 minute longer. Stir in the broth, tomatoes, cumin, coriander, cinnamon, cayenne and pepper. Bring to a boil. Reduce the heat; cover and simmer for 20-25 minutes or until flavors are blended.

2. Stir in couscous; cover and cook 4-6 minutes longer or until couscous is tender.

Italian Sausage Soup

This hearty and warming soup makes a comforting dinner. The herbs make the kitchen smell incredible! You can use lower-calorie turkey sausage for the Italian sausage if you like. I recommend adding 2 teaspoons olive oil to the sausage while cooking to prevent sticking.

—KENDRA VAN DOREN CLYDE, OHIO

PREP: 35 MINUTES **COOK:** 25 MINUTES
MAKES: 11 SERVINGS (2¾ QUARTS)

- 1 pound Italian turkey sausage links, casings removed
- 1 large onion, chopped
- 1 medium carrot, chopped
- 1 celery rib, chopped
- 2 cartons (32 ounces each) reduced-sodium chicken broth
- 1 can (14½ ounces) diced tomatoes, undrained
- 1 can (8 ounces) tomato sauce
- 1 garlic clove, minced
- 1 teaspoon dried oregano
- ½ teaspoon dried rosemary, crushed
- ½ teaspoon dried basil
- ¼ teaspoon dried thyme
- ¼ teaspoon fennel seed, crushed
- 1 bay leaf
- ¾ cup uncooked orzo pasta
  Grated Parmesan cheese, optional

1. In a Dutch oven coated with cooking spray, cook the sausage, onion, carrot and celery over medium heat until meat is no longer pink; drain.

2. Add the broth, tomatoes, tomato sauce, garlic, seasonings and bay leaf. Bring to a boil. Stir in orzo; cook, uncovered, for 8-10 minutes or until pasta is tender. Discard bay leaf. Sprinkle servings with Parmesan cheese if desired.

66As the principal at Bataan Memorial Elementary School, I feel honored that I get the opportunity to influence and interact with my students on a daily basis. There is never a boring day. And as a K-2 principal, I get a lot of hugs every day!99

—KENDRA VAN DOREN CLYDE, OHIO
Administrator, Bataan Memorial Elementary School
Port Clinton, Ohio

"I've been the Superintendent of Schools in McPherson County, Nebraska, for the past four years. I most enjoy collaborating with the board of education, staff and parents to lead school improvement. Watching students grow toward their full potential is truly rewarding."

—**JOE SHERWOOD** TRYON, NEBRASKA

Administrator, McPherson County Schools, Tryon, Nebraska

Baked Greek Ratatouille

When I lived in Florida, a friend's wife served a beautiful and delicious side dish with eggplant and later shared the recipe with me. While I've made her version many times with great success, I was inspired by the movie *Ratatouille* to modify the dish to this recipe.

—**JOE SHERWOOD** TRYON, NEBRASKA

PREP: 30 MINUTES + CHILLING **BAKE:** 45 MINUTES
MAKES: 13 SERVINGS (¾ CUP EACH)

- 1 **small eggplant**
- 2 **small zucchini**
- 2 **small yellow summer squash**
- 4 **plum tomatoes**
- 1 **large sweet onion**
- ½ **cup butter, melted**
- ½ **cup minced fresh parsley**
- 3 **garlic cloves, minced**
- ½ **teaspoon salt**
- ½ **teaspoon each dried thyme, oregano, tarragon and basil**
- ½ **teaspoon dried rosemary, crushed**
- ½ **teaspoon pepper**
- 1 **cup (4 ounces) shredded part-skim mozzarella cheese**

1. Cut vegetables into ¼-in. thick slices. In a greased 13-in. x 9-in. baking dish, layer the eggplant, zucchini, squash, tomatoes and onion. In a small bowl, combine the butter, parsley, garlic and seasonings; pour over vegetables. Cover and refrigerate overnight. Remove from the refrigerator 30 minutes before baking. Bake, uncovered, at 375° for 35 minutes. Sprinkle with cheese. Bake 10-15 minutes longer or until cheese is melted. Serve with a slotted spoon.

Baked Cranberry Peach Sauce

This ruby red peach sauce is just fantastic and so versatile!
It would be great on ham, pork or turkey. Or as a topping
on waffles, pound cake or ice cream.

—KIMBERLY SWIMMER PHOENIX, ARIZONA
Teacher, Mountain Pointe High School, Phoenix, Arizona

PREP: 10 MINUTES **BAKE:** 35 MINUTES
MAKES: 16 SERVINGS (¼ CUP EACH)

5 **cups fresh or frozen cranberries, thawed**
1 **cup flaked coconut**
1 **cup chopped peeled fresh or frozen peaches,
   thawed**
1 **cup orange marmalade**
¾ **cup sugar**
½ **cup water**

1. In a large bowl, combine all ingredients. Pour into a
greased 13-in. x 9-in. baking dish. Bake, uncovered, at
350° for 35-40 minutes or until cranberries are tender.
Serve warm or cold. Refrigerate leftovers.

Portobello Risotto with Mascarpone

PREP: 20 MINUTES **COOK:** 25 MINUTES
MAKES: 6 SERVINGS

- 1½ cups water
- 1 can (14 ounces) reduced-sodium beef broth
- ½ cup chopped shallots
- 2 garlic cloves, minced
- 1 tablespoon canola oil
- 1 cup uncooked arborio rice
- 1 tablespoon minced fresh thyme or 1 teaspoon dried thyme
- ½ teaspoon salt
- ½ teaspoon pepper
- ½ cup white wine or additional reduced-sodium beef broth
- 1 cup sliced baby portobello mushrooms, chopped
- ¼ cup grated Parmesan cheese
- ½ cup mascarpone cheese

1. In a large saucepan, heat water and broth and keep warm. In a large saucepan, saute shallots and garlic in oil for 2-3 minutes or until shallots are tender. Add the rice, thyme, salt and pepper; cook and stir for 2-3 minutes. Reduce heat; stir in wine. Cook and stir until all of the liquid is absorbed.

2. Add heated broth, ½ cup at a time, stirring constantly. Allow the liquid to absorb between additions. Cook just until risotto is creamy and rice is almost tender. (Cooking time is about 20 minutes.)

3. Add mushrooms and Parmesan cheese; stir gently until cheese is melted. Garnish each serving with a heaping tablespoon of mascarpone. Serve immediately.

❝The portobello mushrooms in this creamy classic add a beefy flavor. Each serving is topped with soft, buttery mascarpone cheese, which makes it extra special.❞

—**CARMELLA RYAN** ROCKVILLE CENTRE, NEW YORK
Staff, Francis F. Wilson Elementary School
Rockville Centre, New York

Easy Colcannon

This tasty and traditional Irish recipe for buttery potatoes and cabbage is good any time of year.

—PAM KENNEDY LUBBOCK, TEXAS
Teacher, Christ the King Cathedral School, Lubbock, Texas

PREP/TOTAL TIME: 30 MINUTES **MAKES:** 8 SERVINGS

  1½ **pounds medium red potatoes, cut into 1-inch cubes**
  7½ **cups chopped cabbage**
  8 **green onions, chopped**
  1 **cup fat-free milk**
  ⅓ **cup reduced-fat butter**
  ¾ **teaspoon salt**
  ¼ **teaspoon pepper**

1. Place the potatoes in a Dutch oven; cover with water. Bring to a boil. Cover and cook over medium heat for 12-15 minutes or until potatoes are almost tender, adding the cabbage during the last 5 minutes of cooking.

2. Meanwhile, in a small saucepan, combine green onions and milk. Bring to a boil. Reduce heat; simmer, uncovered, for 5-6 minutes or until onions are soft.

3. Drain potato mixture. Mash with milk mixture, butter, salt and pepper.

Chive Horseradish Sauce

Smoked salmon gets a delicious treatment when paired with a creamy horseradish sauce. I also use this for a special touch to rare roast beef sandwiches served for teacher appreciation luncheons. People always compliment it for having just the right amount of "bite."

—**CONNIE FICKES** YORK, PENNSYLVANIA
Teacher, York Suburan School District, York, Pennsylvania

PREP/TOTAL TIME: 5 MINUTES **MAKES:** 1½ CUPS

1½ cups sour cream
3 tablespoons prepared horseradish
2 tablespoons minced chives
2 teaspoons lemon juice
¼ teaspoon salt
  Smoked salmon or lox
  Pumpernickel bread slices

1. In a small bowl, combine sour cream, horseradish, chives, lemon juice and salt. Refrigerate until serving. Serve with salmon and pumpernickel bread.

"You can prepare this casserole the night before and refrigerate it. Then simply reheat it in the microwave for a quick and easy side. It's a favorite of parents and teachers at my school's holiday luncheons."
—**KRIS CAMPION** MARSHALL, MINNESOTA
Teacher, Marshall High School, Marshall, Minnesota

Tarragon Mashed Potato Casserole

PREP: 35 MINUTES + CHILLING **COOK:** 15 MINUTES
MAKES: 9 SERVINGS

- 10 **medium potatoes, peeled and quartered**
- 1 **package (8 ounces) cream cheese, softened**
- 1 **cup (8 ounces) sour cream**
- ¼ **cup butter, cubed**
- 1 **teaspoon pepper**
- ¾ **teaspoon salt**
- ½ **teaspoon garlic powder**
- ½ **teaspoon dried tarragon**
- ¼ **teaspoon paprika, optional**

1. Place potatoes in a large saucepan and cover with water. Bring to a boil. Reduce heat; cover and simmer for 15-20 minutes or until tender. Drain.

2. In a large bowl, beat cream cheese and sour cream until smooth. Add potatoes; beat until light and fluffy. Beat in the butter, pepper, salt, garlic powder, tarragon and paprika if desired. Spoon into a greased 2-qt. microwave-safe dish. Cover and refrigerate overnight.

3. Remove from the refrigerator 30 minutes before microwaving. Microwave, uncovered, on high for 10 minutes, stirring once. Microwave 4-6 minutes longer or until heated through.

Editor's Note: *This recipe was tested in a 1,100-watt microwave.*

Three Potato Salad

We love this creamy salad because it has sweet potatoes in it. When I bring it to parties, people are always commenting on how good it is and asking for the recipe.

—JILL FOX WELLINGTON, OHIO

PREP: 30 MINUTES **COOK:** 20 MINUTES + CHILLING
MAKES: 10 SERVINGS

- 3 **medium potatoes, peeled and cubed**
- 3 **medium red potatoes, cubed**
- 1 **large sweet potato, peeled and cubed**
- 6 **green onions, chopped**
- 1 **celery rib, chopped**
- ⅓ **cup chopped green pepper**
- ¼ **cup seeded chopped cucumber**
- 1 **cup mayonnaise**
- 2 **teaspoons white vinegar**
- 1 **teaspoon salt**
- 1 **teaspoon dill weed**
- ½ **teaspoon pepper**
- 8 **bacon strips, cooked and crumbled**

1. Place potatoes in a Dutch oven; cover with water. Bring to a boil. Reduce heat; cover and cook for 10-15 minutes or until tender. Drain and cool.

2. In a large bowl, combine the potatoes, green onions, celery, green pepper and cucumber. In a small bowl, combine the mayonnaise, vinegar, salt, dill and pepper. Pour over salad and toss to coat. Cover and refrigerate for 4 hours or overnight. Sprinkle with bacon.

Sue's Cream of Baked Potato Soup

With a garnish of shredded cheese and crumbled, cooked bacon, this rich, velvety soup feels like something you'd get at a restaurant. Serve it with crusty bread and a crisp salad.

—SUE SHEPARD TERRYTOWN, LOUISIANA

PREP: 1¼ HOURS **COOK:** 20 MINUTES
MAKES: 7 SERVINGS

- 3 medium potatoes
- 6 bacon strips, chopped
- 1 large onion, chopped
- 3 garlic cloves, minced
- 1 can (14½ ounces) chicken broth
- 1 can (10¾ ounces) condensed cream of chicken soup, undiluted
- 1 can (5 ounces) evaporated milk
- 1 package (8 ounces) process cheese (Velveeta), cubed
- 1 cup 2% milk
- ¼ cup butter, cubed
- 1 teaspoon dried basil
- ⅛ teaspoon pepper
  Shredded cheddar cheese

1. Scrub and pierce potatoes. Bake at 400° for 50-60 minutes or until tender.

2. Meanwhile, in a large saucepan, cook bacon over medium heat until crisp. Remove to paper towels with a slotted spoon; drain, reserving 2 tablespoons of the drippings. Set aside bacon.

3. Saute onion in drippings until tender. Add garlic; cook 1 minutes longer. Stir in the broth, soup and evaporated milk. Bring to a gentle boil. Remove the pulp from potatoes; stir into soup mixture. Discard potato shells.

4. Cool slightly. In a blender, process half of the soup until smooth. Return to pan. Add the process cheese, 2% milk, butter, basil and pepper; cook and stir until cheese is melted. Sprinkle servings with cheddar cheese and bacon.

“I have held my position as the administrative assistant for Christ the King Parish Elementary School for 30 years. While my job responsibilities vary, my most important duty is taking care of the students by showing them the love they need and deserve. ”

—SUE SHEPARD TERRYTOWN, LOUISIANA
Staff, Christ the King School, Terrytown, Louisiana

Breakfast Biscuit Cups

PREP: 30 MINUTES **BAKE:** 20 MINUTES
MAKES: 8 SERVINGS

- ⅓ **pound bulk pork sausage**
- 1 **tablespoon all-purpose flour**
- ⅛ **teaspoon salt**
- ½ **teaspoon pepper, divided**
- ¾ **cup plus 1 tablespoon 2% milk, divided**
- ½ **cup frozen cubed hash brown potatoes, thawed**
- 1 **tablespoon butter**
- 2 **eggs**
- ⅛ **teaspoon garlic salt**
- 1 **can (16.3 ounces) large refrigerated flaky biscuits**
- ½ **cup shredded Colby-Monterey Jack cheese**

1. In a large skillet, cook the sausage over medium heat until no longer pink; drain. Stir in the flour, salt and ¼ teaspoon pepper until blended; gradually add ¾ cup milk. Bring to a boil; cook and stir for 2 minutes or until thickened. Remove from the heat and set aside.

2. In another large skillet over medium heat, cook potatoes in butter until tender. Whisk the eggs, garlic salt and remaining milk and pepper; add to skillet. Cook and stir until almost set.

3. Press each biscuit onto the bottom and up the sides of eight ungreased muffin cups. Spoon the egg mixture, half of the cheese and sausage into cups; sprinkle with remaining cheese.

4. Bake at 375° for 18-22 minutes or until golden brown. Cool for 5 minutes before removing from pan. Serve immediately or allow to cool completely. Tightly wrap individual biscuit cups in foil; freeze for up to 3 months.

To use one frozen biscuit cup: Unwrap; microwave on high for 50-60 seconds or until heated through.

> ❝The first time I made these biscuit cups, my husband and his assistant basketball coach came in as I was pulling them out of the oven. They loved them!❞

—DEBRA CARLSON COLUMBUS JUNCTION, IOWA
Teacher, Columbus Community High School, Columbus Junction, Iowa

Deep-Fried Rice Balls

PREP: 35 MINUTES + CHILLING **COOK:** 5 MINUTES/BATCH
MAKES: 12 SERVINGS

4½ cups water
2 cups uncooked long grain rice
2 tablespoons butter
1 teaspoon salt
½ teaspoon pepper
4 eggs, beaten
⅓ cup grated Parmesan cheese
2 tablespoons dried parsley flakes
1¾ cups seasoned bread crumbs
Oil for deep-fat frying

1. In a large saucepan, bring the water, rice, butter, salt and pepper to a boil. Reduce heat; cover and simmer for 15-18 minutes or until liquid is absorbed and rice is tender. Cool slightly.

2. In a large bowl, combine the eggs, cheese, parsley and rice. Cover and refrigerate for 20 minutes. Place bread crumbs in a shallow bowl. Shape ½ cupfuls of rice mixture into balls; roll in bread crumbs.

3. In a deep-fat fryer or electric skillet, heat oil to 375°. Fry rice balls, a few at a time, for 2-3 minutes or until golden brown. Drain on paper towels.

"My mother moved in with us about eight years ago and started making this side dish. Now that she is in her 90s, I've taken over the duty of making these unique rice balls. Everyone in our family is thrilled to see them when they are placed on the table."

—ELIZABETH BLAKE CHESAPEAKE, VIRGINIA
Staff, Fairfield Elementary School, Virginia Beach, Virginia

Sweet Corn and Potato Gratin

This tasty side combines great garlic and onion flavor, and kids love the nice crispy topping, too!

—JENNIFER OLSON PLEASANTON, CALIFORNIA
Teacher, Irvington High School, Fremont, California

PREP: 30 MINUTES **BAKE:** 45 MINUTES + STANDING
MAKES: 8 SERVINGS

- 1　**medium onion, thinly sliced**
- 2　**tablespoons butter**
- 2　**tablespoons all-purpose flour**
- 2　**garlic cloves, minced**
- 1　**teaspoon salt**
- ½　**teaspoon pepper**
- 1　**cup whole milk**
- 2　**pounds medium Yukon Gold potatoes, peeled and cut into ⅛-inch slices**
- 2　**cups fresh or frozen corn**
- 1　**can (8¼ ounces) cream-style corn**
- ¾　**cup panko (Japanese) bread crumbs**
- 1　**tablespoon butter, melted**

1. In a large saucepan, saute onion in butter until tender. Stir in the flour, garlic, salt and pepper until blended; gradually add milk. Stir in potatoes. Bring to a boil. Reduce heat; cook and stir for 8-10 minutes or until potatoes are crisp-tender.

2. Stir in corn and cream-style corn. Transfer to an 8-in. square baking dish coated with cooking spray.

3. In a small bowl, combine bread crumbs and butter; sprinkle over potatoes. Bake at 350° for 45-50 minutes or until golden brown and potatoes are tender. Let stand for 10 minutes before serving.

Cornucopia Salad

PREP: 30 MINUTES **COOK:** 5 MINUTES
MAKES: 8 SERVINGS

- ½ cup sliced almonds
- 3 tablespoons sugar
- 4 cups torn leaf lettuce
- 4 cups torn romaine
- 2 celery ribs, chopped
- 4 green onions, chopped
- ¼ cup dried cranberries
- 1 can (11 ounces) mandarin oranges, drained
- 1 medium apple, chopped

VINAIGRETTE
- ¼ cup canola oil
- 2 tablespoons sugar
- 2 tablespoons rice vinegar
- 1 tablespoon minced fresh parsley
- ½ teaspoon salt
- ¼ teaspoon pepper
- ½ cup crumbled blue cheese, optional

1. In a small heavy skillet over medium-low heat, stir the almonds and sugar until sugar is melted and almonds are coated. Cool on waxed paper. Break apart and set aside.

2. In a large bowl, combine the lettuce, romaine, celery, onions and cranberries. Add oranges and apple.

3. In a small bowl, whisk the oil, sugar, vinegar, parsley, salt and pepper. Drizzle over salad; toss to coat. Sprinkle with almonds and blue cheese if desired.

❝I first enjoyed this salad at a church potluck and it has since become a Thanksgiving tradition at my house. I've made some adjustments to the original recipe to please my vegetarian friends, but for a complete meal, add three cooked, shredded chicken breasts to the salad mix.❞

—**CHERYL PETERMAN** PRESCOTT, ARIZONA
Teacher, Granville Elementary, Prescott Valley, Arizona

"I have been an educator for eight years and I currently teach third grade. You might say my classroom is a zoo—there are three classroom pets! The three pets are used for hands-on science learning. They are a Chilean rose-hair tarantula, a corn snake and a ball python. Parents allow their children in my class to babysit the animals during school breaks. Very few parents want to babysit the tarantula, but all the kids want to take it home!"

—JASON JOHNSON WEST VALLEY CITY, UTAH
Teacher, Hillside Elementary, West Valley City, Utah

Harvest Pumpkin Soup

Dazzling golden orange, this soup will brighten any day. I especially enjoy it on a cool autumn night.

—JASON JOHNSON WEST VALLEY CITY, UTAH

PREP: 35 MINUTES **COOK:** 35 MINUTES
MAKES: 10 SERVINGS (2½ QUARTS)

- 6 **medium carrots, shredded**
- 1 **large sweet onion, finely chopped**
- 2 **celery ribs, finely chopped**
- 3 **tablespoons butter**
- 1 **medium apple, peeled and shredded**
- 5 **garlic cloves, minced**
- 1 **can (29 ounces) solid-pack pumpkin**
- 1 **can (14½ ounces) chicken broth**
- ¼ **cup minced fresh parsley**
- 2 **teaspoons dried thyme**
- 1 **teaspoon salt**
- 1 **teaspoon brown sugar**
- 1 **teaspoon ground cumin**
- ½ **teaspoon ground nutmeg**
- ½ **teaspoon ground ginger**
- ¼ **teaspoon pepper**
- 2 **cups 2% milk**
- 1 **cup heavy whipping cream**
  Salted pumpkin seeds or pepitas

1. In a Dutch oven, saute carrots, onion and celery in butter for 4 minutes. Add the apple and garlic; cook 2 minutes longer or until vegetables are tender.

2. Stir in the pumpkin, broth, parsley and seasonings. Bring to a boil. Reduce heat; cover and simmer for 20 minutes. Add milk and cream. Cool slightly. In a blender, process soup in batches until smooth. Return all to pan and heat through. Garnish servings with a sprinkling of pumpkin seeds.

Sicilian Brussels Sprouts

I love to make this dish because the flavors jumping around in your mouth keep you coming back bite after bite! Other nuts can be used in place of the pine nuts.

—MARSHA GILLETT YUKON, OKLAHOMA

PREP: 30 MINUTES **BAKE:** 20 MINUTES
MAKES: 12 SERVINGS

- 12 **ounces pancetta, diced**
- 2 **pounds fresh Brussels sprouts, halved**
- 6 **tablespoons capers, drained**
- ¼ **cup olive oil**
- 3 **tablespoons Champagne wine vinegar**
- 1 **teaspoon lemon juice**
- ¼ **teaspoon salt**
- ¼ **teaspoon pepper**
- ¾ **cup golden raisins**
- ½ **cup pine nuts, toasted**
- 1 **teaspoon grated lemon peel**

1. In a large ovenproof skillet, cook the pancetta over medium heat until browned. Remove to paper towels with a slotted spoon.

2. Add Brussels sprouts to pan; cook and stir until lightly browned. Remove from the heat. Stir in the capers, oil, vinegar, lemon juice, salt and pepper.

3. Bake, uncovered, at 350° for 15-20 minutes or until caramelized, stirring occasionally. Add the raisins, pine nuts, lemon peel and pancetta; toss to coat.

Turkey-Sweet Potato Soup

This yummy soup brings the tastes and aroma of Thanksgiving to my table all year long.

—RADINE KELLOGG FAIRVIEW, ILLINOIS

PREP: 20 MINUTES **COOK:** 30 MINUTES
MAKES: 4 SERVINGS

- 2 cups water
- 2 teaspoons sodium-free chicken bouillon granules
- 2 medium sweet potatoes, cubed
- 1 can (14¾ ounces) cream-style corn
- 1 tablespoon minced fresh sage
- ¼ teaspoon pepper
- 1 tablespoon cornstarch
- 1 cup 2% milk
- 2 cups cubed cooked turkey breast

1. In a large saucepan, bring water and bouillon to a boil. Add sweet potatoes. Reduce heat; cover and cook for 10-15 minutes or until potatoes are tender. Stir in the corn, sage and pepper; heat through. Combine cornstarch and milk until smooth. Stir into pan. Bring to a boil; cook and stir for 2 minutes or until thickened. Stir in turkey; heat through.

Cajun Shrimp

PREP/TOTAL TIME: 25 MINUTES
MAKES: 4 SERVINGS

- 2 garlic cloves, minced
- 3 tablespoons butter
- ½ cup amber beer or beef broth
- 1 teaspoon pepper
- 1 teaspoon Worcestershire sauce
- ½ teaspoon salt
- ½ teaspoon dried thyme
- ½ teaspoon dried rosemary, crushed
- ½ teaspoon crushed red pepper flakes
- ¼ teaspoon cayenne pepper
- ⅛ teaspoon dried oregano
- 1 pound uncooked large shrimp, peeled and deveined

1. In a large skillet, saute garlic in butter for 1 minute. Add the beer and seasonings. Bring to a boil. Reduce heat to medium-high. Add shrimp; cook and stir for 3-4 minutes or until shrimp turn pink.

Entrees

66There is plenty of sauce with these savory shrimp. You can serve them over linguine, beans or rice for an inviting dinner. I usually have some bread on the side to soak up the flavorful sauce.99

—MARK OPPE NORTH POLE, ALASKA
Teacher, Hutchison High School, Fairbanks, Alaska

> "Corned beef gets a touch of sweetness with a maple syrup glaze. Even people who say they don't care for corned beef will ask for seconds when served this one. This recipe was passed down from my great-grandmother."
>
> **—GAYLE MACKLIN** VAIL, ARIZONA
> *Teacher, Corona Foothills Middle School, Vail, Arizona*

Maple-Glazed Corned Beef

PREP: 25 MINUTES **COOK:** 2½ HOURS
MAKES: 12 SERVINGS

- 2 **corned beef briskets with spice packets (3 pounds each)**
- 1 **large sweet onion, sliced**
- 12 **garlic cloves, peeled and halved**
- ¼ **cup kosher salt**
- ¼ **cup whole peppercorns**
- 8 **bay leaves**
- 2 **tablespoons dried basil**
- 2 **tablespoons dried oregano**
- 4 **quarts water**
- 3 **cups beef broth**
- ¼ **cup maple syrup**
- ⅓ **cup packed brown sugar**

1. Place briskets and contents of the spice packets in a stockpot. Add onion, garlic, salt, peppercorns, bay leaves, basil and oregano. Pour in water and beef broth. Bring to a boil. Reduce heat; cover and simmer for 2½ to 3 hours or until meat is tender.

2. Transfer meat to a broiler pan. Brush with maple syrup; sprinkle with brown sugar. Broil 4-6 in. from the heat for 2-3 minutes or until beef is glazed. Thinly slice across the grain.

Pepperoni Lasagna Roll-Ups

Tastes like pizza, looks like manicotti and everyone loves it! The dish works great for teacher meetings and potlucks because the roll-ups can be made well in advance, it travels well and is way easier than stuffing filling into manicotti noodles!

—JAMIE MILLER MAPLE GROVE, MINNESOTA

PREP: 45 MINUTES **BAKE:** 55 MINUTES
MAKES: 16 SERVINGS

- 16 uncooked lasagna noodles
- ½ pound bulk Italian sausage
- ½ pound sliced baby portobello mushrooms
- ¼ cup chopped sweet onion
- 1 jar (24 ounces) tomato basil pasta sauce
- 1½ teaspoons brown sugar
- 1½ teaspoons fennel seed, crushed
- ½ teaspoon dried tarragon
- 1⅛ teaspoons salt, divided
- ⅛ teaspoon crushed red pepper flakes, optional
- 1 package (3½ ounces) sliced pepperoni
- 2½ cups (10 ounces) shredded part-skim mozzarella cheese
- 2½ cups part-skim ricotta cheese
- 2 cups grated Parmesan cheese, divided
- 2 eggs, lightly beaten
- 6 tablespoons minced fresh parsley, divided
- 3 tablespoons minced fresh basil or 1 tablespoon dried basil
- ½ teaspoon pepper

1. Cook noodles according to the package directions.

2. Meanwhile, in a Dutch oven, cook the sausage, mushrooms and onion over medium heat until meat is no longer pink; drain and transfer to a large bowl. Stir in the pasta sauce, brown sugar, fennel seed, tarragon, ⅛ teaspoon salt and pepper flakes if desired.

3. In the same pan, cook pepperoni for 4-5 minutes or until lightly browned; remove to paper towels to drain.

4. In another large bowl, combine the mozzarella, ricotta, 1 cup Parmesan, eggs, 4 tablespoons parsley, basil, pepper and remaining salt.

5. Drain noodles. Spread 1 cup meat sauce in a greased 13-in. x 9-in. baking dish. Spread ¼ cup cheese mixture over each noodle; top with 3 or 4 pepperoni slices. Carefully roll up; place seam side down in prepared dish. Top with remaining meat sauce; sprinkle with remaining Parmesan.

6. Cover and bake at 350° for 55-60 minutes or until bubbly. Sprinkle with remaining parsley before serving.

❝As a parent volunteer, I contribute in various ways in both the library and my daughter's kindergarten class. As part of the WAY (We Appreciate You) committee, I contribute food to a monthly teachers' lunch called First Fridays. The teachers love it.❞

—JAMIE MILLER MAPLE GROVE, MINNESOTA
Volunteer, Heritage Christian Academy, Maple Grove, Minnesota

Cranberry BBQ Pulled Pork

Cranberry sauce adds a yummy twist on traditional pulled pork. My family can't get enough of it! The pork cooks to tender perfection in the slow cooker, which also makes this dish conveniently portable.

—**CARRIE WIEGAND** MT. PLEASANT, IOWA
Staff, Mount Pleasant Christian School, Mt. Pleasant, Iowa

PREP: 20 MINUTES **COOK:** 9 HOURS **MAKES:** 14 SERVINGS

- 1   boneless pork shoulder roast (4 to 6 pounds)
- ⅓   cup cranberry juice
- 1   teaspoon salt

SAUCE
- 1   can (14 ounces) whole-berry cranberry sauce
- 1   cup ketchup
- ⅓   cup cranberry juice
- 3   tablespoons brown sugar
- 4½ teaspoons chili powder
- 2   teaspoons garlic powder
- 1   teaspoon onion powder
- ½   teaspoon salt
- ¼   teaspoon ground chipotle pepper
- ½   teaspoon liquid smoke, optional
- 14 hamburger buns, split

1. Cut roast in half. Place in a 4-qt. slow cooker. Add cranberry juice and salt. Cover and cook on low for 8-10 hours or until meat is tender.

2. Remove roast and set aside. In a small saucepan, combine the cranberry sauce, ketchup, cranberry juice, brown sugar, seasonings and liquid smoke if desired. Cook and stir over medium heat for 5 minutes or until slightly thickened.

3. Skim fat from cooking juices; set aside ½ cup juices. Discard remaining liquid. When cool enough to handle, shred pork with two forks and return to the slow cooker.

4. Stir in sauce mixture and reserved cooking juices. Cover and cook on low for 1 hour or until heated through. Serve on buns.

White Chicken Chili

PREP: 25 MINUTES **COOK:** 1 HOUR
MAKES: 7 SERVINGS

- 2 cans (14½ ounces each) chicken broth
- 3 bone-in chicken breast halves (8 ounces each), skin removed
- 1 large onion, chopped
- 2 garlic cloves, minced
- 1 teaspoon ground cumin
- 1 teaspoon dried oregano
- ½ teaspoon salt
- ¼ teaspoon cayenne pepper
- 2 cans (15½ ounces each) great northern beans, rinsed and drained
- 1½ cups frozen white corn
- ⅓ cup lime juice
  Sour cream, shredded white cheddar cheese and/or minced fresh cilantro, optional

1. In a large saucepan, combine the first eight ingredients. Bring to a boil. Reduce heat; cover and simmer for 35-40 minutes or until a thermometer reads 170°. Remove chicken from broth; allow to cool.

2. Remove meat from bones; discard bones. Cube chicken and return to pan. Mash half of the beans. Add all of the beans, corn and lime juice to chicken mixture. Return to a boil. Reduce heat; cover and simmer for 15-20 minutes or until flavors are blended.

3. Serve with the sour cream, cheese and cilantro if desired.

1. Cut peppers in half lengthwise and discard seeds. Place peppers, cut sides down, on an ungreased 15-in. x 10-in. x 1-in. baking pan. Brush with 1 tablespoon butter; sprinkle with pepper and salt. Bake, uncovered, at 350° for 10-15 minutes or until tender.

2. Meanwhile, in a large skillet, saute onion and celery in remaining butter until tender. Stir in the cream cheese until melted. Add the shrimp, cheese blend, rice, lemon juice and seasonings; heat through. Spoon into pepper halves.

3. Place on an ungreased 15-in. x 10-in. x 1-in. baking pan. Combine topping ingredients; sprinkle over peppers. Bake, uncovered, at 350° for 10-15 minutes or until topping is golden brown.

Editor's Note: *Wear disposable gloves when cutting hot peppers; the oils can burn skin. Avoid touching your face.*

Shrimp-Stuffed Poblano Peppers

PREP: 35 MINUTES **BAKE:** 10 MINUTES
MAKES: 8 SERVINGS

- 4 large poblano peppers
- 2 tablespoons butter, melted, divided
- 1 teaspoon coarsely ground pepper
- ½ teaspoon kosher salt
- 1 small onion, finely chopped
- 2 celery ribs, chopped
- 4 ounces cream cheese, softened
- 1 pound chopped cooked peeled shrimp
- 1¾ cups shredded Mexican cheese blend
- 1½ cups cold cooked rice
- 2 tablespoons lemon juice
- 2 teaspoons dried cilantro flakes
- ½ teaspoon onion powder
- ½ teaspoon garlic powder

TOPPING
- 1 cup panko (Japanese) bread crumbs
- ¼ cup grated Parmesan cheese
- 2 tablespoons butter, melted

❝I created this dish for my mother when she moved back to our hometown. Since my mom really enjoys shrimp and slightly spicy food, I decided to create shrimp-stuffed poblanos to surprise her. She was delighted with the creation.❞

—**TINA GARCIA-ORTIZ** TAMPA, FLORIDA
Staff, Lanier Elementary School, Tampa, Florida

Grilled Salmon Kyoto

The men in my family went on a fishing trip to Alaska and brought home an abundance of fish. The cooks in the family swapped fish recipes so we could experiment with different ways to prepare the bounty. My mom shared this recipe with us, and it has become a favorite.

—SANDY ZIMMERMAN PIERRE, SOUTH DAKOTA
Staff, Jefferson Elementary School, Pierre, South Dakota

PREP: 15 MINUTES + MARINATING **GRILL:** 5 MINUTES
MAKES: 4 SERVINGS

- ⅓ cup reduced-sodium soy sauce
- ¼ cup thawed orange juice concentrate
- 2 tablespoons canola oil
- 2 tablespoons tomato sauce
- 1 tablespoon finely chopped green onion
- 1 garlic clove, minced
- 1 teaspoon lemon juice
- ½ teaspoon minced fresh gingerroot
- ½ teaspoon prepared mustard
- 4 salmon steaks or fillets (1 inch thick)

1. In a small bowl, whisk the first nine ingredients until well blended. Pour ½ cup marinade into a large resealable plastic bag. Add the salmon; seal bag and turn to coat. Refrigerate for up to 1 hour. Set aside remaining marinade for basting.

2. Drain salmon and discard marinade. Moisten a paper towel with cooking oil; using long-handled tongs, lightly coat the grill rack. Grill salmon, covered, over high heat or broil 3-4 in. from the heat for 3 minutes. Turn; grill or broil 2-7 minutes longer or until fish flakes easily with a fork, basting occasionally with reserved marinade.

"As the data specialist at Okatie Elementary School, I meet and greet new enrollees, maintain the student records and information database and handle state reporting. I truly enjoy my job and put as much dedication into it as I do my second love, cooking. At work and at home, I have my tasters, critics and supporters who guide me with my love of cooking."

—**LISA NELSON** BLUFFTON, SOUTH CAROLINA
Staff, Okatie Elementary School, Okatie, South Carolina

Bayou Okra Sausage Stew

My husband and I worked on this recipe together. We make a big pot and freeze it to enjoy all winter long. We also have added sauteed shrimp for a delicious addition to this stew.

—**LISA NELSON** BLUFFTON, SOUTH CAROLINA

PREP: 20 MINUTES **COOK:** 20 MINUTES
MAKES: 9 SERVINGS

- 1 **pound smoked sausage, halved lengthwise and cut into ¼-inch slices**
- 2 **large onions, chopped**
- 1 **large green pepper, chopped**
- 8 **green onions, sliced**
- 1 **cup minced fresh parsley**
- ¼ **cup olive oil**
- 6 **garlic cloves, minced**
- 1 **cup white wine**
- 1 **can (28 ounces) diced tomatoes, undrained**
- 1 **package (16 ounces) frozen sliced okra**
- 1 **can (8 ounces) tomato sauce**
- 2 **tablespoons soy sauce**
- 1 **tablespoon Louisiana-style hot sauce**
  Hot cooked rice

1. In a Dutch oven, saute the first five ingredients in oil until the vegetables are tender. Add garlic; cook 1 minute longer. Add wine, stirring to loosen browned bits from pan.

2. Stir in the tomatoes, okra, tomato sauce, soy sauce and hot sauce; bring to a boil. Reduce heat; simmer, uncovered, for 4-5 minutes or until okra is tender. Serve with rice.

Eggs Benedict Brunch Braid

PREP: 45 MINUTES **BAKE:** 20 MINUTES
MAKES: 8 SERVINGS

- 3 **egg yolks**
- 1 **tablespoon lemon juice**
- ¼ **teaspoon salt**
- ¼ **teaspoon Dijon mustard**
  Dash cayenne pepper
- ½ **cup unsalted butter, melted**

BRAID

- 1 **tablespoon unsalted butter**
- 6 **eggs**
- ½ **teaspoon salt**
- ¼ **teaspoon pepper**
- 1 **sheet frozen puff pastry, thawed**
- 6 **slices Canadian bacon**
- 2 **tablespoons minced chives, divided**
- 1 **teaspoon water**

1. In a blender, combine the first five ingredients. Cover and process on high. While processing, gradually add butter in a steady stream until combined. Set aside.

2. In a large skillet, melt butter over medium-high heat. Whisk five eggs, salt and pepper; add to skillet. Cook and stir until barely set; stir in sauce.

3. On a lightly greased baking sheet, roll out pastry into a 12-in. x 10-in. rectangle. Layer the Canadian bacon and egg mixture down the center of rectangle; sprinkle with 1 tablespoon chives.

4. On each long side, cut ½-in.-wide strips. Starting at one end, fold alternating strips at an angle across filling; pinch ends to seal. Whisk remaining egg and water; brush over braid.

5. Bake at 375° for 20-25 minutes or until the braid is golden brown and the eggs are completely set. Let stand for 5 minutes before cutting. Sprinkle with remaining chives.

"Here's a great make-ahead brunch entree to serve during the holidays and at potlucks. It has all the ingredients of a classic eggs Benedict encased in puff pastry. You can refrigerate the assembled braid overnight or freeze it for up to two weeks. Cover tightly with plastic wrap so the pastry doesn't dry out. Before baking, brush strudel with egg wash. Add 20 minutes to baking time if the strudel is frozen."

—**SARAH STROHL** COMMERCE TOWNSHIP, MICHIGAN
Volunteer, Loon Lake Elementary, Wixom, Michigan

Beef Stew with Sesame Seed Biscuits

Warm and hearty comfort food is what this dinner is all about. It has it all: homemade biscuits, tender meat and an assortment of veggies.

—**LINDA BACCI** LIVONIA, NEW YORK

PREP: 20 MINUTES + SIMMERING **BAKE:** 30 MINUTES
MAKES: 5 SERVINGS

- 1 **pound beef stew meat, cut into 1-inch cubes**
- 2 **tablespoons olive oil**
- 1½ **cups chopped onions**
- 1 **cup chopped celery**
- 1 **garlic clove, minced**
- 1 **tablespoon all-purpose flour**
- 1½ **cups water**
- 1 **cup diced tomatoes**
- ½ **cup Burgundy wine or beef broth**
- ⅓ **cup tomato paste**
- 1 **tablespoon sugar**
- ¾ **teaspoon salt**
- ½ **teaspoon Worcestershire sauce**
- ¼ **teaspoon pepper**
- 2 **cups cubed peeled potatoes**
- 2 **cups sliced fresh carrots**
- 1 **can (4 ounces) mushroom stems and pieces, drained**
- ¼ **cup sour cream**

SESAME SEED BISCUITS

- 1¼ **cups all-purpose flour**
- 2 **teaspoons baking powder**
- ½ **teaspoon salt**
- ¼ **cup shortening**
- ¾ **cup sour cream**
- 2 **tablespoons 2% milk**
- 1 **tablespoon sesame seeds**

1. In a Dutch oven, brown the beef in oil in batches. Remove and keep warm. In the same pan, saute the onions and celery until tender. Add the garlic; cook 1 minute longer.

2. Stir in flour until blended. Gradually add water; stir in the tomatoes, wine, tomato paste, sugar, salt, Worcestershire sauce, pepper and beef. Bring to a boil. Reduce heat; cover and simmer for 1¼ hours.

3. Add potatoes and carrots; cook for 30-45 minutes longer or until beef and vegetables are tender. Stir in mushrooms and sour cream. Transfer to a greased 13-in. x 9-in. baking dish.

4. For biscuits, in a large bowl, combine the flour, baking powder and salt. Cut in shortening until mixture resembles coarse crumbs. Stir in sour cream just until moistened.

5. Turn onto a lightly floured surface; knead 8-10 times. Roll out to ½-in. thickness; cut with a floured 2-in. biscuit cutter. Brush with milk; sprinkle with sesame seeds. Arrange over stew.

6. Bake at 400° for 30-35 minutes or until biscuits are golden brown.

"Even though Manor Intermediate School houses more than 700 students, I think the school has a warm, family feel about it. We are more than just a group of teachers and staff! As school secretary, the best part of my job is being able to help parents, students and our great staff on a daily basis."

—**LINDA BACCI** LIVONIA, NEW YORK
Staff, Manor Intermediate School, Honeoye Falls, New York

Pesto Grilled Cheese Sandwiches

What my daughter always says about my cooking is that I make the ordinary better. That is what this recipe is about: an old favorite with a new twist. This is fabulous on raisin walnut or raisin bread.

—ARLENE REAGAN LIMERICK, PENNSYLVANIA
Teacher, Limerick Elementary School, Royersford, Pennsylvania

PREP/TOTAL TIME: 10 MINUTES **MAKES:** 4 SERVINGS

- 8 **slices walnut-raisin bread**
- 3 **to 4 tablespoons prepared pesto**
- 8 **slices provolone and mozzarella cheese blend**
- 8 **slices tomato**
- ¼ **cup butter, softened**

1. Spread four slices of bread with pesto. Layer with cheese and tomato; top with remaining bread. Butter outsides of sandwiches.

2. In a large skillet over medium heat, toast sandwiches for 2-3 minutes on each side or until golden brown and cheese is melted.

> "Pork chops are a great, versatile cut and cook up quickly, making them ideal for busy weeknight meals. But turning out tender chops can be tricky. Browning them first, then finishing them in this tangy, slightly sweet sauce results in perfectly cooked chops."
> —**SUSAN BENTLEY** BURLINGTON, NEW JERSEY
> *Staff, Burlington City High School, Burlington, New Jersey*

Pork Chops with Honey-Mustard Sauce

PREP/TOTAL TIME: 30 MINUTES **MAKES:** 4 SERVINGS

- ¾ **teaspoon garlic powder, divided**
- ½ **teaspoon salt**
- ¼ **teaspoon pepper**
- 4 **boneless pork loin chops (6 ounces each)**
- 1 **tablespoon olive oil**
- ½ **cup white wine or chicken broth**
- ¼ **cup chicken broth**
- 2 **tablespoons Dijon mustard**
- 1 **tablespoon honey**
- ½ **cup heavy whipping cream**

1. Combine ½ teaspoon garlic powder, salt and pepper; sprinkle over pork chops. In a large skillet, brown pork chops in oil. Remove and keep warm.

2. Remove skillet from heat and add wine, stirring to loosen browned bits from pan. Bring to a boil; cook until liquid is reduced by half. Reduce heat to medium. Whisk in broth, mustard, honey and remaining garlic powder; cook and stir for 1 minute. Whisk in cream; cook and stir for 4-6 minutes or until thickened.

3. Return pork chops and juices to the skillet. Cover and cook for 3-5 minutes or until a thermometer reads 145°. Let stand for 5 minutes before serving.

Broccoli Quiche

My mother passed down this quiche recipe to me. She has been making it for over 30 years. You can serve it for brunch, lunch and even dinner. Any leftover quiche can be frozen and reheated in the microwave.

—BRIDGET CORBETT VALDOSTA, GEORGIA

PREP: 30 MINUTES **BAKE:** 35 MINUTES + STANDING
MAKES: 6 SERVINGS

- 1 refrigerated pie pastry
- 1 package (9 ounces) frozen broccoli cuts, thawed and chopped
- 1 small onion, finely chopped
- 2 tablespoons butter
- 1 cup heavy whipping cream
- 3 eggs
- ½ cup mayonnaise
- 1 tablespoon all-purpose flour
- 1 tablespoon chicken broth
- ½ teaspoon salt
- ⅛ teaspoon ground nutmeg
- ⅛ teaspoon pepper
- 1½ cups (6 ounces) shredded cheddar cheese

1. Unroll pastry into a 9-in. deep-dish pie plate; flute edges. Line unpricked pastry with a double thickness of heavy-duty foil. Bake at 450° for 8 minutes. Remove foil; bake 5 minutes longer. Cool on a wire rack.

2. In a large skillet, saute broccoli and onion in butter until onion is tender. Remove from the heat. In a large bowl, whisk the cream, eggs, mayonnaise, flour, broth, salt, nutmeg and pepper; stir in the cheese and broccoli mixture. Pour into crust.

3. Bake at 350° for 35-40 minutes or until a knife inserted near the center comes out clean. Let stand for 10 minutes before cutting.

❝I've been teaching kindergarten reading, language arts and math for 10 years. The best part of my position is working with and teaching 5- and 6-year-olds, many of whom have never been to school before. The greatest satisfaction comes from watching students grow into individuals who can read and write.❞

—BRIDGET CORBETT VALDOSTA, GEORGIA
Teacher, Lake Park Elementary School, Lake Park, Georgia

Caramel-Pecan French Toast Bake

For a sensational dish for a Sunday brunch, try this French toast. You make it up the night before, so you only need to bake it and make the syrup the following day.

—BRAD SHUE HARPER, KANSAS
Teacher, Harper Elementary School, Harper, Kansas

PREP: 20 MINUTES + CHLLING **BAKE:** 30 MINUTES
MAKES: 8 SERVINGS

- 1 **cup packed brown sugar**
- ½ **cup butter, cubed**
- 2 **tablespoons light corn syrup**
- 1 **cup chopped pecans, divided**
- 8 **slices French bread (¾ inch thick)**
- 6 **eggs**
- 1½ **cups 2% milk**
- 1½ **teaspoons ground cinnamon**
- 1 **teaspoon ground nutmeg**
- 1 **teaspoon vanilla extract**
- ¼ **teaspoon salt**

SAUCE
- ½ **cup packed brown sugar**
- ¼ **cup butter, cubed**
- 1 **tablespoon light corn syrup**

1. In a small saucepan, combine the brown sugar, butter and corn syrup. Bring to a boil. Reduce heat; cook and stir for 3-4 minutes or until thickened. Pour into a greased 13-in. x 9-in. baking dish. Sprinkle with ½ cup pecans; top with bread slices.

2. In a large bowl, whisk the eggs, milk, cinnamon, nutmeg, vanilla and salt; pour evenly over the bread. Sprinkle with remaining pecans. Cover and refrigerate for 8 hours or overnight.

3. Remove from the refrigerator 30 minutes before baking. Bake, uncovered, at 350° for 30-35 minutes or until a knife inserted near the center comes out clean.

4. Meanwhile, in a small saucepan, combine sauce ingredients. Bring to a boil. Reduce heat; cook and stir for 2 minutes or until thickened. Serve with the French toast.

"I love pumpkin and my husband loves chili. So I combined both loves into a dish we would both be happy to have. It has also become a big hit with the rest of my family, and they are always delighted to see it at suppertime."
—CATHERINE WALMSLEY PHOENIX, ARIZONA

Pumpkin Turkey Chili

PREP: 20 MINUTES **COOK:** 1¾ HOURS
MAKES: 6 SERVINGS (2¼ QUARTS)

- 1 pound ground turkey
- 1 medium sweet yellow pepper, chopped
- 1 medium onion, chopped
- 3 garlic cloves, minced
- 2 teaspoons olive oil
- 2 cups chicken broth
- 1 can (15 ounces) kidney beans, rinsed and drained
- 1 can (15 ounces) black beans, rinsed and drained
- 1 can (15 ounces) solid-pack pumpkin
- 1 can (15 ounces) tomato sauce
- 4 medium tomatoes, chopped
- ⅔ cup chili sauce
- 3 tablespoons brown sugar
- 1 tablespoon dried oregano
- 1 tablespoon dried parsley flakes
- 1 teaspoon dried tarragon
- ¾ teaspoon salt
- ¾ teaspoon pepper
  Dash crushed red pepper flakes
  Dash cayenne pepper

1. In a Dutch oven, cook the turkey, yellow pepper, onion and garlic in oil over medium heat until meat is no longer pink; drain. Stir in remaining ingredients. Bring to a boil. Reduce heat; simmer, uncovered, for 1½ hours or until chili reaches desired thickness.

Italian Grilled Cheese Sandwiches

PREP/TOTAL TIME: 25 MINUTES **MAKES:** 4 SERVINGS

- 8 slices Italian bread
- 4 tablespoons prepared pesto
- 4 slices provolone cheese
- 4 slices part-skim mozzarella cheese
- 5 teaspoons olive oil
  Marinara sauce, warmed, optional

1. Spread four bread slices with pesto. Layer with cheeses; top with remaining bread. Spread outsides of sandwiches with oil.

2. In a large skillet over medium heat, toast sandwiches for 3-4 minutes on each side or until cheese is melted. Serve with marinara if desired.

Spicy Coconut Chicken Strips

My family has always enjoyed Thai food, but we really love chicken curry. Since we have a 2-year-old son, I wanted to make something that he would eat. His favorite food is chicken strips, so I started making the strips with some curry flavor. Now my family prefers these even more than my chicken curry.

—DANIEL FOX QUEEN CREEK, ARIZONA
Teacher, Eduprize Charter School, Queen Creek, Arizona

PREP: 25 MINUTES **COOK:** 5 MINUTES/BATCH
MAKES: 4 SERVINGS (⅔ CUP SAUCE)

- 2 eggs
- ½ cup coconut milk
- 2 tablespoons red curry paste
- 1 tablespoon cornstarch
- 1 cup flaked coconut
- 1 cup all-purpose flour
- 4 teaspoons chili powder
- 12 chicken tenderloins
  Oil for deep-fat frying

PEANUT DIPPING SAUCE
- ¼ cup chunky peanut butter
- ¼ cup coconut milk
- 3 tablespoons 2% milk
- 4½ teaspoons reduced-sodium soy sauce
- 3 garlic cloves, minced
- 1 tablespoon minced fresh cilantro
- 1 tablespoon brown sugar
- 1 tablespoon lime juice

1. In a shallow bowl, whisk the eggs, coconut milk, curry paste and cornstarch until smooth. In another shallow bowl, combine the coconut, flour and chili powder. Dip chicken in egg mixture, then coat with coconut mixture.

2. In an electric skillet or deep fryer, heat oil to 375°. Fry chicken, a few strips at a time, for 2-3 minutes on each side or until golden brown. Drain on paper towels.

3. In a microwave-safe bowl, combine the sauce ingredients. Cover and microwave on high for 45 seconds or until heated through, stirring once. Serve with chicken.

1 teaspoon celery seed
1 teaspoon ground ginger
½ teaspoon mixed pickling spices
¼ teaspoon ground allspice
¼ teaspoon pepper
¼ cup cornstarch
½ cup water

1. In a large skillet, brown meat in oil on all sides. Transfer meat and drippings to a 5-qt. slow cooker. In a large bowl, combine the vinegar, onion, sugar, soup mix, carrot, bouillon, Worcestershire sauce and seasonings; pour over roast. Cover and cook on low for 6-8 hours or until tender.

2. Remove the meat to a serving platter; keep warm. Strain the cooking juices, discarding the vegetables and seasonings.

3. Skim fat from cooking juices; transfer juices to a large saucepan. Bring to a boil. Combine cornstarch and water until smooth; gradually stir into the pan. Bring to a boil; cook and stir for 2 minutes or until thickened. Serve with beef.

> **"**As the school secretary at Miami Elementary, I find a lot of enjoyment in my day-to-day interactions with students. The students also provide a good dose of laughter. At the start of one school year I asked a student which bus he rode. He answered, 'The yellow one.'**"**
>
> —**LAURA EHLERS** LAFAYETTE, INDIANA
> *Staff, Miami Elementary School, Lafayette, Indiana*

Special Sauerbraten

After simmering in the slow cooker for hours, the rump roast is fork-tender and has taken on the flavors of the sauce. My family looks forward to having this home-style meal. I serve it with mashed potatoes and corn.

—**LAURA EHLERS** LAFAYETTE, INDIANA

PREP: 25 MINUTES **COOK:** 6 HOURS
MAKES: 6 SERVINGS

1 beef rump roast or bottom round roast (3 to 4 pounds), cut in half
1 tablespoon olive oil
1½ cups cider vinegar
1 medium onion, chopped
⅔ cup packed brown sugar
1 envelope onion soup mix
⅓ cup shredded carrot
2 tablespoons beef bouillon granules
1 tablespoon Worcestershire sauce
1 bay leaf
1 garlic clove, minced
1 teaspoon salt

Pasta Arrabbiata (Angry Pasta)

I learned how to make this while I was in Italy one summer. You can add more or less crushed red pepper to decide how "angry" you would like your pasta.

—**STACIE GOMM** PROVIDENCE, UTAH

PREP: 15 MINUTES **COOK:** 25 MINUTES
MAKES: 6 SERVINGS

- ½ **pound bacon strips, chopped**
- 2 **garlic cloves, minced**
- ⅓ **cup olive oil**
- 3 **cans (15 ounces each) tomato puree**
- 6 **fresh basil leaves, thinly sliced**
- ½ **to 1 teaspoon crushed red pepper flakes**
- 3 **cups uncooked penne pasta**
  Grated Parmesan cheese

1. In a large skillet, cook bacon over medium heat until crisp. Remove to paper towels with a slotted spoon; discard drippings.

2. In the same skillet, saute the garlic in olive oil for 1 minute. Add the tomato puree, basil, pepper flakes and bacon. Bring to a boil. Reduce heat and simmer for 15 minutes to allow flavors to blend; stir occasionally.

3. Meanwhile, cook pasta according to the package directions; drain. Serve with sauce; sprinkle with Parmesan cheese.

Skillet-Roasted Lemon Chicken with Potatoes

PREP: 20 MINUTES **BAKE:** 25 MINUTES
MAKES: 4 SERVINGS

- 1 **tablespoon olive oil, divided**
- 1 **medium lemon, thinly sliced**
- 4 **garlic cloves, minced and divided**
- ¼ **teaspoon grated lemon peel**
- ½ **teaspoon salt, divided**
- ¼ **teaspoon pepper, divided**
- 8 **boneless skinless chicken thighs (4 ounces each)**
- ¼ **teaspoon dried rosemary, crushed**
- 1 **pound fingerling potatoes, halved lengthwise**
- 8 **cherry tomatoes**

1. Grease a 10-inch cast-iron skillet with 1 teaspoon oil. Arrange lemon slices in a single layer in skillet.

2. Combine 1 teaspoon oil, 2 minced garlic cloves, lemon peel, ¼ teaspoon salt and ⅛ teaspoon pepper; rub over chicken. Place over lemon.

3. In a large bowl, combine rosemary and remaining oil, garlic, salt and pepper. Add potatoes and tomatoes; toss to coat. Arrange over chicken. Bake, uncovered, at 450° for 25-30 minutes or until chicken is no longer pink and potatoes are tender.

Sunday Paella

My adult children adore this recipe and look forward to eating it when they come over for lunch on Sundays after church. I do some preparation for this recipe before leaving for church and finish when we return home. That is why we call it Sunday Paella.

—LINDA RHOADS LEBANON, MISSOURI

PREP: 25 MINUTES **COOK:** 40 MINUTES
MAKES: 8 SERVINGS

- 1½ **pounds boneless skinless chicken breasts, cubed**
- 3 **tablespoons canola oil**
- 1 **pound smoked sausage, cut into ¼-inch slices**
- 1 **small onion, chopped**
- 1½ **cups uncooked long grain rice**
- 2 **teaspoons Italian seasoning**
- ¼ **teaspoon ground turmeric**
- ¼ **teaspoon pepper**
- 3 **cups chicken broth**
- 1½ **pounds uncooked medium shrimp, peeled and deveined**
- 1 **can (28 ounces) diced tomatoes, undrained**
- 1½ **cups frozen peas, thawed**
- 1 **tablespoon sugar**

1. In a Dutch oven, cook and stir chicken in oil over medium heat until no longer pink. Add sausage and onion; cook 3-4 minutes longer. Add the rice, Italian seasoning, turmeric and pepper; cook and stir for 3-4 minutes or until rice is lightly browned.

2. Add broth. Bring to a boil. Reduce heat; cover and simmer for 14-18 minutes or until rice is almost tender. Stir in the shrimp, tomatoes, peas and sugar; cover and cook for 10-15 minutes or until shrimp turn pink, stirring occasionally.

“In addition to being the administrative assistant to the principal, I am a mother and a grandmother who loves to cook Sunday lunch for my family every weekend. My husband, Jim, bakes amazing cookies for everyone and I love to cook the meal, so we make a great team.”

—LINDA RHOADS LEBANON, MISSOURI
Staff, Hillcrest School, Lebanon, Missouri

1 jar (15 ounces) Alfredo sauce, warmed
8 bacon strips, cooked and crumbled
¼ cup grated Parmesan cheese

1. Place one slice mozzarella cheese and ham on each turkey cutlet. Roll up each from a short side and secure with toothpicks.

2. Place bread crumbs and eggs in separate shallow bowls. In another shallow bowl, combine the flour, salt and pepper. Dip turkey in the flour mixture, eggs, then bread crumbs.

3. In a large skillet, brown turkey in oil in batches. Place in a greased 13-in. x 9-in. baking dish. Bake, uncovered, at 350° for 20-25 minutes or until turkey juices run clear. Discard toothpicks.

4. Spoon Alfredo sauce over turkey. Sprinkle with bacon and Parmesan cheese.

> I took my background in advertising-marketing and medical transcription to the education field in 2005. Besides clerical support, I'm responsible for making school purchases, maintaining the purchasing budget, coordinating graduation and acting as co-adviser to the sophomore class. Being involved with young people keeps me energized, inspires me to be the best I can be and teaches me to embrace change.

—**SANDY KOMISAREK** SWANTON, OHIO
Staff, Rossford High School, Rossford, Ohio

Turkey Cordon Bleu with Alfredo Sauce

For our annual Kentucky Derby party I wanted to create a twist on a traditional Kentucky Hot Brown sandwich. The turkey is tender and flavorful, full of smoky ham and melted cheese, but the crispy bacon really sets the dish off.

—**SANDY KOMISAREK** SWANTON, OHIO

PREP: 30 MINUTES **BAKE:** 20 MINUTES
MAKES: 8 SERVINGS

8 slices part-skim mozzarella cheese
8 thin slices deli honey ham
8 turkey breast cutlets
2 cups panko (Japanese) bread crumbs
2 eggs, lightly beaten
½ cup all-purpose flour
½ teaspoon salt
¼ teaspoon pepper
¼ cup canola oil

Sizzle & Smoke Flat Iron Steaks

Smoked paprika and chipotle pepper give this version of blackened steak a spicy Southwestern flair. To cool things off, add a salad of leafy greens with fruit and cheeses.

—DENISE POUNDS HUTCHINSON, KANSAS

PREP/TOTAL TIME: 20 MINUTES **MAKES:** 4 SERVINGS

1½ teaspoons smoked paprika
1 teaspoon salt
1 teaspoon ground chipotle pepper
½ teaspoon pepper

1¼ pounds beef flat iron steaks or top sirloin steak (¾ inch thick)
2 tablespoons butter
Lime wedges, optional

1. Combine seasonings; rub over steaks. In a large skillet, cook beef in butter over medium-high heat for 30 seconds on each side. Reduce heat to medium; cook steaks for 5-7 minutes on each side or until meat reaches desired doneness (for medium-rare, a thermometer should read 145°; medium, 160°; well-done, 170°).

2. Cut into slices; serve with lime wedges if desired.

"I teach kindergarten in the very room where I attended kindergarten. One of my favorite things about teaching is watching a child read for the first time. Their excitement and eagerness to read at this level is amazing, and I am so blessed that I get to lead the children through this walk."

—**KIMBERLY KNUPPENBURG** MENOMONEE FALLS, WISCONSIN
Teacher, Grace Evangelical Lutheran School, Menomonee Falls, Wisconsin

Thai Chicken Pizza

This is a recipe I make for my friends on "girls' night." It is simple to make but full of flavor.

—**KIMBERLY KNUPPENBURG**

PREP/TOTAL TIME: 25 MINUTES **MAKES:** 6 SERVINGS

- 1 prebaked 12-inch pizza crust
- ⅔ cup Thai peanut sauce
- 2 tablespoons reduced-sodium soy sauce
- 2 tablespoons creamy peanut butter
- 1 cup shredded cooked chicken breast
- 1 cup (4 ounces) shredded part-skim mozzarella cheese
- 3 green onions, chopped
- ½ cup bean sprouts
- ½ cup shredded carrot

1. Place the crust on an ungreased 12-in. pizza pan or baking sheet. In a small bowl, combine the peanut sauce, soy sauce and peanut butter. Add chicken; toss to coat. Spread over crust; sprinkle with cheese and onions.

2. Bake at 400° for 10-12 minutes or until cheese is melted. Top with bean sprouts and carrot.

Artichoke & Spinach Enchiladas

Surprise your gang with these delightful vegetarian enchiladas. The mushroom, artichoke and spinach filling is fantastic. My family loves it.

—JOAN KOLLARS NORFOLK, NEBRASKA

PREP: 30 MINUTES **BAKE:** 20 MINUTES
MAKES: 8 SERVINGS

- 3 **tablespoons butter**
- 3 **tablespoons all-purpose flour**
- 1 **can (14½ ounces) vegetable broth**
- 1 **can (8 ounces) tomato sauce**
- 1½ **teaspoons chili powder**
- ¾ **teaspoon ground cumin**

ENCHILADAS

- 1 **large onion, chopped**
- 3 **garlic cloves, minced**
- 2 **tablespoons olive oil**
- ½ **pound medium fresh mushrooms, quartered**
- 1 **can (14 ounces) water-packed artichoke hearts, rinsed, drained and chopped**
- 1 **package (10 ounces) frozen chopped spinach, thawed and squeezed dry**
- 1 **carton (15 ounces) ricotta cheese**
- 1 **cup (8 ounces) sour cream**
- 2 **cups (8 ounces) shredded Monterey Jack cheese, divided**
- 8 **whole wheat tortillas (8 inches), warmed**

1. In a small saucepan, melt butter. Stir in flour until smooth; gradually add broth. Bring to a boil; cook and stir for 2 minutes or until thickened. Stir in the tomato sauce, chili powder and cumin. Simmer, uncovered, for 6-8 minutes or until slightly thickened. Spread ¾ cup sauce into a greased 13-in. x 9-in. baking dish. Set aside remaining sauce.

2. In a large skillet, saute onion and garlic in oil until tender. Stir in mushrooms; cook 3 minutes longer. Add artichokes and spinach; cook for 4-5 minutes longer. Remove from the heat; stir in the ricotta cheese, sour cream and 1 cup Monterey Jack cheese.

3. Place ⅔ cup mushroom mixture down the center of each tortilla. Roll up and place seam side down in prepared dish. Pour reserved sauce over the top; sprinkle with remaining cheese.

4. Bake, uncovered, at 375° for 20-25 minutes or until heated through.

"My career at Northeast Community College Library began in 1999. Because we have a small staff, we all have been cross-trained to work in all areas. I also work in circulation and reference as needed. I find working in an academic environment is stimulating and rewarding. I enjoy meeting and working with students of all ages. There is never a dull moment!"

—JOAN KOLLARS NORFOLK, NEBRASKA
Staff, Northeast Community College, Norfolk, Nebraska

1. In a small saucepan, combine first five ingredients. Bring to a boil; cook until liquid is reduced to ½ cup. Set aside and keep warm.

2. Flatten pork to ½-in. thickness; sprinkle with ¼ teaspoon salt and ¼ teaspoon pepper. In a large skillet, brown pork in butter; remove and keep warm.

3. In the same skillet, saute shallot in drippings until tender. Add cream, reserved cherry mixture and remaining salt and pepper, stirring to dissolve browned bits from pan. Bring to a boil; cook until liquid is reduced to sauce consistency. Return pork to the pan; cook until no longer pink.

Pork Tenderloin with Dried Cherries

I love cherries, especially since I grew up in Michigan, and they pair so nicely with pork. Here's a wonderful skillet dish that takes just minutes to cook. It is fabulous for both weeknights and company dinners.

—**KATHY FOX** GOODYEAR, ARIZONA

PREP: 20 MINUTES **COOK:** 15 MINUTES
MAKES: 4 SERVINGS

- ¾ **cup chicken broth**
- ⅓ **cup dried tart cherries**
- ¼ **cup brandy**
- 1 **teaspoon minced fresh thyme or ¼ teaspoon dried thyme**
- ⅛ **teaspoon ground allspice**
- 1 **pork tenderloin (1 pound), cut into 1-inch slices**
- ½ **teaspoon salt, divided**
- ½ **teaspoon pepper, divided**
- 1 **tablespoon butter**
- 1 **shallot, minced**
- ¼ **cup heavy whipping cream**

❝I teach earth and space science and coach the girls' varsity soccer team at Estrella Foothills High School. I truly enjoy educating our youth and helping them succeed, either in the classroom or on the soccer field. The best part of my position is interacting with the students and seeing them light up with excitement when they understand something that I am teaching.❞

—**KATHY FOX** GOODYEAR, ARIZONA
Teacher, Estrella Foothills High School, Goodyear, Arizona

Turkey Potpie Cups

My children always look forward to turkey or chicken leftovers since I created this recipe. Refrigerated flaky biscuits make perfect individual potpie crusts.

—**KAREN WOODARD** MUSTANG, OKLAHOMA
Staff, Mustang North Middle School, Yukon, Oklahoma

PREP: 25 MINUTES **BAKE:** 20 MINUTES
MAKES: 8 SERVINGS

- 1 **tube (16.3 ounces) large refrigerated flaky biscuits**
- 3 **cups cubed cooked turkey**
- 3 **cups turkey gravy**
- 2¼ **cups frozen mixed vegetables**
- ½ **teaspoon salt**
- ½ **teaspoon pepper**
- 1 **cup French-fried onions**
- 2¼ **cups mashed potatoes**
- ⅓ **cup 2% milk**
- ½ **cup shredded cheddar cheese**

1. On a lightly floured surface, roll each biscuit into an 8-in. circle. Press onto the bottoms and up the sides of eight greased 8-oz. ramekins.

2. In a large saucepan, combine the turkey, gravy, vegetables, salt and pepper. Bring to a boil. Reduce heat; simmer, uncovered, for 5 minutes. Sprinkle onions into ramekins; top with turkey mixture. In a small bowl, combine potatoes and milk; spread over tops. Sprinkle with cheese.

3. Bake the potpies at 375° for 18-22 minutes or until golden brown.

"Everyone in the family will want a piece of this pie, and every cook will appreciate a helping hand from packaged beef roast and refrigerated pie pastry."

—**PATRICIA MYERS** MARYVILLE, TENNESSEE

Roast Beef Potpie

PREP: 30 MINUTES **BAKE:** 30 MINUTES
MAKES: 6 SERVINGS

- 10 **fresh baby carrots, chopped**
- 6 **small red potatoes, cubed**
- 1 **medium onion, chopped**
- 2 **tablespoons olive oil**
- 1 **package (17 ounces) refrigerated beef roast au jus, coarsely chopped**
- 2 **tablespoons minced fresh cilantro**
- ¼ **teaspoon salt**
- ¼ **teaspoon pepper**
- ⅓ **cup all-purpose flour**
- 2¼ **cups reduced-sodium beef broth**
- 1 **sheet refrigerated pie pastry**
- 1 **egg, beaten**

1. In a large skillet, saute the carrots, potatoes and onion in oil until crisp-tender. Add the beef roast, cilantro, salt and pepper. Combine flour and broth until smooth; gradually stir into the pan. Bring to a boil; cook and stir for 2 minutes or until thickened.

2. Transfer to a 9-in. deep-dish pie plate. Place pie pastry over filling. Trim, seal and flute edges. Cut slits in pastry; brush with egg. Bake at 375° for 30-35 minutes or until golden brown.

Ricotta Gnocchi with Spinach & Gorgonzola

Gnocchi are thick, soft dumpling-like pasta made from potatoes. In this special dish, the tender pillows of pasta are treated to a creamy white sauce that features butternut squash, spinach and Gorgonzola cheese.

—BRUD HOLLAND WATKINS GLEN, NEW YORK

PREP: 2 HOURS **COOK:** 10 MINUTES **MAKES:** 8 SERVINGS

- 3 **large potatoes**
- 3 **cups reduced-fat ricotta cheese**
- ¼ **cup grated Romano cheese**
- 2 **tablespoons olive oil**
- 1 **tablespoon kosher salt**
- 6 **eggs**
- 4½ **cups cake flour**
- 4 **quarts water**

SAUCE

- 2⅔ **cups cubed peeled butternut squash**
- ⅓ **cup thinly sliced fresh basil leaves**
- ⅓ **cup water**
- 2 **tablespoons plus 2 teaspoons olive oil**
- 2 **garlic cloves, peeled and thinly sliced**
- 1¼ **teaspoons kosher salt**
- ¾ **teaspoon pepper**
- 1⅓ **cups heavy whipping cream**
- ⅔ **cup crumbled Gorgonzola cheese**
- 1½ **pounds fresh spinach, coarsely chopped**

1. Scrub and pierce potatoes. Bake at 400° for 50-55 minutes or until tender. Peel potatoes; press through a potato ricer or strainer into a large bowl. Cool slightly.

2. Add the ricotta and Romano cheeses, oil and salt to potato pulp; beat on low speed until smooth. Beat in eggs, one at a time. Add flour; mix well. On a lightly floured surface, knead 10-12 times, forming a soft dough.

3. Divide dough into 16 portions. On a floured surface, roll each portion into a ½-in.-thick rope; cut into ¾-in. pieces. Press and roll each piece with a lightly floured fork.

4. In a Dutch oven, bring water to a boil. Cook gnocchi in batches for 30-60 seconds or until they float. Remove with a slotted spoon and keep warm.

5. In a large saucepan, combine the squash, basil, water, oil, garlic, salt and pepper. Bring to a boil. Cover and cook for 4-6 minutes or until squash is tender.

6. Stir in cream and Gorgonzola. Bring to a boil. Reduce heat; simmer, uncovered, for 2 minutes. Add spinach; cook until wilted. Serve with gnocchi.

“With kids at two different schools, I find myself doing double volunteer duty at Watkins Glen Middle School and Watkins Glen High School. But I don't mind. There's nothing like sharing your talents and life experiences with students and inspiring them to try new things. It's especially satisfying to hear them say, 'I can do that!'”

—BRUD HOLLAND WATKINS GLEN, NEW YORK
Volunteer, Watkins Glen Middle School, Watkins Glen, New York

1. Sprinkle the roast with salt and pepper. In an ovenproof Dutch oven, heat oil over medium heat. Brown roast on all sides. Remove from pan.

2. Add the celery, carrots and onion to the same pan; cook and stir until tender. Add the turnips, sweet potato and garlic; cook 1 minute longer.

3. Add wine, stirring to loosen browned bits from pan. Stir in the broth, vinegar and herbs. Return roast to pan; bring to a boil. Cover and bake at 325° for 2½ to 3 hours or until meat is tender.

4. Remove beef and vegetables; keep warm. Discard herbs from cooking liquid; skim fat. In a small bowl, mix the cornstarch and water until smooth; stir into the cooking liquid. Bring to a boil; cook and stir for 2 minutes or until thickened. Serve with the pot roast and vegetables.

Balsamic Braised Pot Roast

PREP: 30 MINUTES **BAKE:** 2½ HOURS
MAKES: 8 SERVINGS

- 1 **boneless beef chuck roast (3 to 4 pounds)**
- 1 **teaspoon salt**
- ½ **teaspoon pepper**
- 2 **tablespoons olive oil**
- 3 **celery ribs with leaves, cut into 2-inch pieces**
- 2 **medium carrots, cut into 1-inch pieces**
- 1 **medium onion, coarsely chopped**
- 3 **medium turnips, peeled and quartered**
- 1 **large sweet potato, peeled and cubed**
- 3 **garlic cloves, minced**
- 1 **cup dry red wine or beef broth**
- 1 **can (14½ ounces) beef broth**
- ½ **cup balsamic vinegar**
- 1 **bunch fresh thyme sprigs**
- 4 **fresh sage leaves**
- 2 **bay leaves**
- ¼ **cup cornstarch**
- ¼ **cup cold water**

"Pot roast seems like an easy, elegant way to prepare a relatively inexpensive cut of meat, but I have spent years perfecting this recipe. Believe it or not, there is an art to perfect pot roast, and every time I make this dish, parents and kids alike gobble it up. Even the children at my daughter's preschool clamor for more!"

—**KELLY ANDERSON** GLENDALE, CALIFORNIA

"This scrumptious pasta salad will shine as is, or double the vinaigrette and use half of it to marinate and grill chicken breasts. Slice and add to the salad for a hearty dish."

—BENICE SILVER CARMEL, INDIANA
Teacher, J. Everett Light Career Center, Indianapolis, Indiana

Spinach Penne Salad

PREP/TOTAL TIME: 30 MINUTES **MAKES:** 10 SERVINGS

- 1 package (16 ounces) uncooked whole wheat penne pasta

VINAIGRETTE

- ½ cup olive oil
- ½ cup white wine vinegar
- ⅓ cup grated Parmesan cheese
- 1 tablespoon Dijon mustard
- 2 garlic cloves, minced
- 1 teaspoon dried oregano
- ¼ teaspoon salt
- ¼ teaspoon pepper

SALAD

- 1 package (6 ounces) fresh baby spinach
- 3 medium tomatoes, seeded and chopped
- ¾ cup (6 ounces) crumbled feta cheese
- 4 green onions, thinly sliced
- ½ cup sliced ripe or Greek olives

1. In a Dutch oven, cook pasta according to package directions. Drain and rinse in cold water; drain again.

2. Meanwhile, in a small bowl, whisk the vinaigrette ingredients. In a large bowl, combine the pasta, spinach, tomatoes, feta cheese, onions and olives. Add vinaigrette; toss to coat. Serve immediately.

I'm Stuffed French Toast

PREP: 30 MINUTES **COOK:** 5 MINUTES
MAKES: 4 SERVINGS

- 2 **medium ripe bananas, sliced**
- 2 **tablespoons brown sugar**
- 1 **teaspoon banana or vanilla extract**
- 1 **package (8 ounces) reduced-fat cream cheese**
- 8 **slices oat bread (½ inch thick)**
- 2 **eggs**
- ⅔ **cup evaporated milk**
- 1¼ **teaspoons ground cinnamon**
- 1¼ **teaspoons vanilla extract**
- 1 **tablespoon butter**
- 1 **cup sliced fresh strawberries or frozen unsweetened sliced strawberries, thawed**
- ½ **cup fresh blueberries or frozen unsweetened blueberries**
- 1 **tablespoon sugar**
  Confectioners' sugar

1. In a large skillet coated with cooking spray, saute bananas with brown sugar. Stir in banana extract. In a small bowl, beat cream cheese until smooth. Add the banana mixture; beat well. Spread on four slices of bread; top with the remaining bread.

2. In a shallow bowl, whisk eggs, milk, cinnamon and vanilla. Dip both sides of sandwiches in egg mixture.

3. In a large skillet, toast sandwiches in butter for 2-3 minutes on each side or until golden brown.

4. Meanwhile, in a small saucepan, combine the berries and sugar; heat through. Serve with French toast; sprinkle with confectioners' sugar.

Coffee Roast Beef

PREP: 20 MINUTES **BAKE:** 2¼ HOURS
MAKES: 6 SERVINGS PLUS LEFTOVERS

- 1 **boneless beef chuck roast (5 pounds)**
- 2 **tablespoons olive oil**
- 1 **medium onion, chopped**
- 1 **garlic clove, minced**
- 1 **teaspoon dried oregano**
- 1 **teaspoon dried basil**
- ½ **teaspoon pepper**
- ¾ **teaspoon salt**
- 1 **cup strong brewed coffee**
- ¾ **cup plus ⅓ cup water, divided**
- ¾ **cup beef stock**
- 3 **tablespoons all-purpose flour**

1. In a Dutch oven, brown the roast in oil on all sides. Remove and set aside. Add onion to the pan; saute until tender. Add garlic and seasonings; cook 1 minute longer.

2. Add the coffee, ¾ cup water and stock; return roast to pan. Bring to a boil. Cover and bake at 325° for 2¼ to 2¾ hours or until meat is tender.

3. Remove the roast to a serving platter; keep warm. Combine flour and remaining water until smooth. Stir into pan. Bring to a boil; cook and stir for 2 minutes or until thickened.

4. Slice roast and serve with gravy.

> ❝I used to work in a coffee shop, so the idea of using coffee in a delicious entree just tickles me. The coffee adds a rich flavor to the gravy.❞
>
> —**APRIL GUNTERMAN** CENTERVILLE, OHIO
> *Teacher, Franklin City Schools, Franklin, Ohio*

1. In a small bowl, combine the first six ingredients. Pour ¾ cup marinade into a large resealable plastic bag. Add the chicken; seal bag and turn to coat. Refrigerate for at least 8 hours or overnight. Cover and refrigerate remaining marinade.

2. Drain chicken and discard marinade. Moisten a paper towel with cooking oil; using long-handled tongs, lightly coat the grill rack. Grill chicken, covered, over medium heat or broil 4 in. from the heat for 5 minutes. Turn; grill or broil 4-9 minutes longer or until a thermometer reads 170°, basting occasionally with reserved marinade.

> "I have been teaching fourth-grade language arts at Sabetha Elementary School for the past 23 years. I love to see kids get really excited about a good book. I like to share some of my favorite books with the students. I also like to cook, and always get a chuckle out of seeing a student at the grocery store. They are amazed to see their teacher comes there, too."
>
> —**KAREN AESCHLIMAN** SABETHA, KANSAS
> *Teacher, Sabetha Elementary School, Sabetha, Kansas*

Herbed Lemon Chicken

This is a sensational recipe for cooks on the go. You can put the chicken into the marinade the day before, and it will be ready to grill when you come home from work the next night. In the winter, I grill the chicken on my indoor electric grill. It's so easy and always turns out terrific.

—**KAREN AESCHLIMAN** SABETHA, KANSAS

PREP: 10 MINUTES + MARINATING **GRILL:** 10 MINUTES
MAKES: 6 SERVINGS

- 1 **cup mayonnaise**
- ¼ **cup lemon juice**
- 2 **tablespoons white wine or chicken broth**
- 1 **tablespoon garlic powder**
- 1 **tablespoon dried oregano**
- ¼ **teaspoon pepper**
- 6 **boneless skinless chicken breast halves (5 ounces each)**

Cheesy Mac & Cheese

Everyone comes home for dinner when I make this macaroni and cheese. It also receives great compliments at potlucks.

—DEBRA SULT CHANDLER, ARIZONA
Teacher, Wood Elementary School, Tempe, Arizona

PREP: 20 MINUTES **BAKE:** 30 MINUTES
MAKES: 8 SERVINGS

- 2 cups uncooked elbow macaroni
- 1 tablespoon all-purpose flour
- 1 cup heavy whipping cream
- 1 cup half-and-half cream
- ¼ cup sour cream
- 1 egg
- ½ teaspoon ground mustard
- ½ teaspoon cayenne pepper
- ¼ teaspoon salt
- ¼ teaspoon pepper
- ⅛ teaspoon ground nutmeg
- 8 ounces Monterey Jack cheese, cubed
- 8 ounces cheddar cheese, cubed
- 2 cups (8 ounces) shredded cheddar cheese

1. Cook macaroni according to package directions. Meanwhile, in a large bowl, whisk the flour, cream, half-and-half, sour cream, egg, mustard, cayenne, salt, pepper and nutmeg until smooth.

2. Drain pasta. Transfer to a greased 2½-qt. baking dish. Stir in cubed cheeses. Top with cream mixture. Sprinkle with shredded cheese.

3. Bake, uncovered, at 350° for 30-40 minutes or until bubbly and golden brown.

"Have your bacon cheeseburger from the inside out. Since everything is mixed into the patties, you'll get all the flavor in every bite. My family thinks they are just so yummy."
—TERESA EUKEN RED OAK, IOWA
Teacher, Washington Intermediate School, Red Oak, Iowa

Cheddar & Bacon Burgers

PREP/TOTAL TIME: 25 MINUTES **MAKES:** 8 SERVINGS

½ cup shredded cheddar cheese
½ cup crumbled cooked bacon
1 envelope onion soup mix
2 pounds ground beef
8 hamburger buns, split
 Lettuce leaves and tomato slices, optional

1. In a large bowl, combine the cheese, bacon and soup mix. Crumble beef over mixture and mix well. Shape into eight patties.

2. Grill burgers, covered, over medium heat or broil 4 in. from the heat for 5-7 minutes on each side or until a thermometer reads 160° and juices run clear. Serve on buns with lettuce and tomato if desired.

Curried Chicken Rice Salad

Since I usually make and serve this salad while my teacher friends and I are on summer break, I always associate this dish with relaxed good times! This recipe is best made ahead so that the flavors can mingle.

—PAMELA HESSELBART SYLVANIA, OHIO

PREP: 30 MINUTES + CHILLING **COOK:** 25 MINUTES
MAKES: 6 SERVINGS

- 1 **package (6.6 ounces) toasted almond rice pilaf**
- 2 **cups cubed cooked chicken**
- ¾ **cup diced celery**
- ½ **cup dried cranberries**
- ½ **cup golden raisins**
- ½ **cup mayonnaise**
- ⅓ **cup chutney**
- 3 **tablespoons sour cream**
- 2 **tablespoons lemon juice**
- 1 **teaspoon curry powder**
- 2 **medium apples, cubed**
- 8 **lettuce leaves**
- ¼ **cup sliced almonds, toasted**

1. Cook rice pilaf according to package directions; cool. In a large bowl, combine the chicken, celery, cranberries, raisins and rice.

2. In a small bowl, combine the mayonnaise, chutney, sour cream, lemon juice and curry powder; stir in apples. Add to rice mixture; toss to coat. Cover and refrigerate for at least 2 hours.

3. Serve on lettuce; garnish with almonds.

"I've been in the education field for 33 years and the third-grade teacher at Sylvan Elementary School for 27 years. Sylvan Elementary was built in the 1970s, and my father was a member of the school board. The best part of the job is getting to know young people of all backgrounds and cultures, ever diverse, and yet ever the same."

—PAMELA HESSELBART SYLVANIA, OHIO
Teacher, Sylvan Elementary School, Sylvania, Ohio

1. In a small bowl, combine the first five ingredients. Set aside.

2. Make a lengthwise slit down the center of each roast to within ½ in. of bottom. Open roast so it lies flat; cover with plastic wrap. Flatten slightly. Remove plastic wrap. Season with salt and pepper.

3. Arrange two sausage links in center of each roast. Close roasts; brush with mustard mixture. Wrap each roast with bacon. Tie several times with kitchen string; secure ends with toothpicks. Place on a rack in a shallow roasting pan. Pour broth and wine into roasting pan.

4. Bake, uncovered, at 400° for 40-50 minutes or until a thermometer inserted into the pork loin reads 145 °. Let stand for 5 minutes before slicing. Discard string and toothpicks.

Andouille-Stuffed Pork Loin

A faculty potluck favorite, this andouille-stuffed and bacon-wrapped pork loin is full of bold flavors, and yet is simple to prepare. This recipe may be prepared ahead, covered, refrigerated and baked when needed to provide a wonderful, warm entree.

—**JUDY ARMSTRONG** PRAIRIEVILLE, LOUISIANA

PREP: 30 MINUTES **BAKE:** 40 MINUTES
MAKES: 12 SERVINGS

- ¼ cup Dijon mustard
- 2 tablespoons apricot preserves
- 1 tablespoon minced fresh rosemary or 1 teaspoon dried rosemary, crushed
- 1 tablespoon minced fresh thyme or 1 teaspoon dried thyme
- 3 garlic cloves, minced
- 2 boneless pork loin roasts (2 pounds each)
- 1 teaspoon salt
- 1 teaspoon pepper
- 4 fully cooked andouille sausage links (about 1 pound)
- 12 bacon strips
- ½ cup chicken broth
- ½ cup white wine or additional chicken broth

❝Two weeks after I accepted the position of principal at St. Thomas More Catholic School, Hurricane Katrina hit Louisiana. That is when I realized just how caring and dedicated our faculty is. Within a week, and while schools were officially closed, the faculty came to help with displaced students and nursing home residents staying in our gym. That dedicated and caring spirit is part of what makes my job so enjoyable.❞

—**JUDY ARMSTRONG** PRAIRIEVILLE, LOUISIANA
*Administrator, St. Thomas More Catholic School
Baton Rouge, Louisiana*

"The word 'panini' refers to a sandwich that is pressed and toasted. I love making them for my fellow teachers and friends. For potlucks, I make several and cut them into fourths. The sandwiches work well as an appetizer for any occasion."

—MARTHA MUELLENBERG VERMILLION, SOUTH DAKOTA

Mediterranean Turkey Panini

PREP/TOTAL TIME: 25 MINUTES **MAKES:** 4 SERVINGS

- 4 **ciabatta rolls, split**
- 1 **jar (24 ounces) marinara or spaghetti sauce, divided**
- 1 **container (4 ounces) crumbled feta cheese**
- 1 **jar (7½ ounces) marinated quartered artichoke hearts, drained and chopped**
- 2 **plum tomatoes, sliced**
- 1 **pound sliced deli turkey**

1. Spread each ciabatta bottom with 2 tablespoons marinara sauce. Top with the cheese, artichokes, tomato and turkey. Spread each ciabatta top with 2 tablespoons marinara sauce; place over turkey.

2. Cook on a panini maker or indoor grill for 4-5 minutes or until cheese is melted. Place remaining marinara sauce in a small microwave-safe bowl; cover and microwave on high until heated through. Serve with sandwiches.

"Kids and adults alike will devour this quick pasta dinner. It's prepared at home, but tastes like restaurant fare. I like to pair it with a Caesar salad."
—**JULIE KAMLADE** SHELBY, NORTH CAROLINA
Teacher, Burns High School, Lawndale, North Carolina

Chicken Tortellini in Cream Sauce

PREP/TOTAL TIME: 30 MINUTES **MAKES:** 4 SERVINGS

- 1 **package (19 ounces) frozen cheese tortellini**
- 1 **cup fresh broccoli florets**
- 1 **garlic clove, minced**
- 2 **tablespoons butter**
- 1 **cup shredded Parmesan cheese**
- 1 **cup heavy whipping cream**
- ½ **teaspoon Italian seasoning**
- ¼ **teaspoon salt**
- ⅛ **teaspoon pepper**
- 1⅓ **cups cubed cooked chicken breast**
    Minced fresh basil, optional

1. In a large saucepan, cook tortellini according to the package directions, adding the broccoli during the last 5 minutes of cooking.

2. Meanwhile, in a large skillet, saute garlic in butter until tender. Stir in the cheese, cream and seasonings. Bring to a boil; reduce heat. Simmer, uncovered, for 7-9 minutes or until slightly thickened. Add the chicken; heat through.

3. Drain tortellini and broccoli; toss with chicken mixture. Sprinkle with basil if desired.

Creamy Clam Linguini

PREP: 10 MINUTES **COOK:** 25 MINUTES
MAKES: 8 SERVINGS

- 1 **pound linguine**
- 1 **medium onion, chopped**
- ¼ **cup butter, cubed**
- 2 **tablespoons olive oil**
- 4 **garlic cloves, minced**
- 3 **tablespoons all-purpose flour**
- 2 **cups chicken broth**
- 1 **cup clam juice**
- ½ **cup heavy whipping cream**
- 3 **cans (6½ ounces each) minced clams, drained**
- ½ **cup minced fresh parsley**
- ¼ **teaspoon dried oregano**
- ¼ **teaspoon chipotle hot pepper sauce**
- ⅛ **teaspoon salt**
- ⅛ **teaspoon pepper**
- ⅛ **teaspoon crushed red pepper flakes**
- ⅔ **cup grated Parmesan cheese**

1. Cook linguine according to the package directions.

2. Meanwhile, in a large saucepan, saute onion in butter and oil. Add garlic; saute for 1-2 minutes longer. Stir in flour until blended; gradually add the broth, clam juice and cream. Bring to a boil; cook and stir for 2 minutes or until thickened.

3. Add the clams and seasonings; cook and stir for 2-3 minutes or until heated through. Drain linguine. Add pasta and cheese to sauce; toss to coat.

"This is a fast but special entree that I made up when my sons were home. They loved it so much that they request it whenever they visit. You can use the juice from the canned clams, but bottled clam juice gives a better flavor."

—**MARGIE CLEVENGER** BOWLING GREEN, KENTUCKY
Teacher, T.C. Cherry Elementary School, Bowling Green, Kentucky

N'Orleans Shrimp with Beans & Rice

PREP/TOTAL TIME: 25 MINUTES **MAKES:** 4 SERVINGS

- ¼ **cup butter, softened**
- 1 **garlic clove, minced**
- ¾ **cup chopped red onion, divided**
- 1½ **pounds uncooked large shrimp, peeled and deveined**
- ¼ **cup chopped tomatoes**
- ¼ **cup minced fresh parsley**
- 1 **tablespoon lemon juice**
- 2½ **teaspoons Creole seasoning, divided**
- ½ **cup white wine or chicken broth**
- 3 **cups cooked long grain rice**
- 1 **can (16 ounces) kidney beans, rinsed and drained**

1. In a small bowl, combine butter and garlic.

2. In a skillet, saute ¼ cup onion in 3 tablespoons butter mixture. Add the shrimp, tomatoes, parsley, lemon juice and 1½ teaspoons Creole seasoning; cook 1 minute longer. Stir in wine. Bring to a boil; cook until liquid is almost evaporated and shrimp turn pink.

3. Meanwhile, in a large saucepan, saute remaining onion and Creole seasoning in remaining butter mixture. Add rice and beans; heat through. Serve with the shrimp.

Editor's Note: *The following spices may be substituted for 1 teaspoon Creole seasoning: ¼ teaspoon each salt, garlic powder and paprika; and a pinch each of dried thyme, ground cumin and cayenne pepper.*

❝Thirty minutes is all it takes to place this tasty shrimp dish on the table. It's quick for weeknight meals, but special enough for guests.❞

—**ELAINE HOLMES** BRANDON, FLORIDA
Teacher, Buckhorn Elementary School, Valrico, Florida

Chicken Portobello Stroganoff

Stroganoff used to be a dish of sauteed beef with sour cream in 19th century Russia. This modern chicken and portobello version is the result of having opened the fridge for dinner one night to find nothing much but necessity, the mother of invention.

—**KATIE ROSE** PEWAUKEE, WISCONSIN

PREP: 15 MINUTES **COOK:** 25 MINUTES
MAKES: 4 SERVINGS

- 1 **pound ground chicken**
- 12 **ounces baby portobello mushrooms, halved**
- 1 **medium onion, chopped**
- 1 **tablespoon olive oil**
- 2 **garlic cloves, minced**
- 3 **tablespoons white wine or chicken broth**
- 2 **cups chicken broth**
- ½ **cup heavy whipping cream**
- 2 **tablespoons lemon juice**
- ¼ **teaspoon salt**
- ⅛ **teaspoon white pepper**
- 1 **cup (8 ounces) sour cream**
  Hot cooked egg noodles or pasta

1. In a large skillet, cook the chicken, mushrooms and onion in oil over medium-high heat until meat is no longer pink. Add garlic; cook 1 minute longer.

2. Stir in wine. Bring to a boil; cook until liquid is almost evaporated. Add the broth, cream, lemon juice, salt and pepper. Bring to a boil; cook until liquid is reduced by half.

3. Reduce heat. Gradually stir in sour cream; heat through (do not boil). Serve with noodles.

Sweet & Sassy Baby Back Ribs

My family loves this recipe and I always have to triple it when the entire gang is home. I usually have to make three to four slabs. Any leftover ribs taste great when reheated.

—TERRI KANDELL ADDISON, MICHIGAN
Teacher, Brooklyn Elementary School, Brooklyn, Michigan

PREP: 2 HOURS 5 MINUTES **GRILL:** 15 MINUTES
MAKES: 8 SERVINGS

- 2 **cups ketchup**
- 2 **cups cider vinegar**
- 1 **cup dark corn syrup**
- ¼ **cup packed brown sugar**
- ¼ **cup root beer**
- ½ **teaspoon salt**
- ½ **teaspoon garlic powder**
- ½ **teaspoon onion powder**
- ½ **teaspoon hot pepper sauce**
- 4 **pounds pork baby back ribs**

1. In a large saucepan, combine the first nine ingredients. Bring to a boil. Reduce heat; simmer, uncovered, for 20-25 minutes or until slightly thickened, stirring occasionally. Set aside 3 cups for basting and serving.

2. Brush remaining sauce over ribs. Place bone side down on a rack in a large shallow roasting pan. Cover tightly with foil and bake at 325° for 1½ to 2 hours or until tender.

3. Moisten a paper towel with cooking oil; using long-handled tongs, lightly coat the grill rack. Grill ribs, covered, over medium heat for 15-25 minutes or until browned, turning and brushing occasionally with some of the reserved sauce. Cut into serving-size pieces; serve with sauce.

Flank Steak with Cilantro & Blue Cheese Butter

PREP: 15 MINUTES + MARINATING **GRILL:** 15 MINUTES
MAKES: 8 SERVINGS

- ½ **cup canola oil**
- ¼ **cup cider vinegar**
- ¼ **cup honey**
- 1 **tablespoon reduced-sodium soy sauce**
- ½ **teaspoon paprika**
- 1 **beef flank steak (2 pounds)**

BUTTER
- 3 **tablespoons butter, softened**
- ¾ **cup crumbled blue cheese**
- 1 **green onion, finely chopped**
- 1 **tablespoon minced fresh cilantro**
- ⅛ **teaspoon salt**
- ⅛ **teaspoon pepper**

1. Combine first five ingredients in a large resealable plastic bag. Add the beef; seal bag and turn to coat. Refrigerate for up to 4 hours.

2. Drain and discard marinade. Moisten a paper towel with cooking oil; using long-handled tongs, lightly coat the grill rack.

3. Grill steak, covered, over medium heat or broil 4 in. from the heat for 6-8 minutes on each side or until meat reaches desired doneness (for medium-rare, a thermometer should read 145°; medium, 160°; well-done, 170°).

4. Meanwhile, combine butter and blue cheese in a small bowl. Stir in the onion, cilantro, salt and pepper.

5. Let steak stand for 5 minutes; thinly slice across the grain. Serve with blue cheese butter.

> ❝I love the combination of the sweet citrus marinade and the strong tang of the blue cheese butter! Also, my kids love flank steak.❞
>
> —**GWEN WEDEL** AUGUSTA, MICHIGAN

Argentine Lasagna

My family is from Argentina, which has a strong Italian heritage and large cattle ranches. This all-in-one lasagna is packed with meat, cheese and veggies.

—**SYLVIA MAENENR** OMAHA, NEBRASKA
Teacher, St. Vincent de Paul Elementary School, Omaha, Nebraska

PREP: 30 MINUTES **BAKE:** 55 MINUTES + STANDING
MAKES: 12 SERVINGS

- 1 **pound ground beef**
- 1 **large sweet onion, chopped**
- ½ **pound sliced fresh mushrooms**
- 1 **garlic clove, minced**
- 1 **can (15 ounces) tomato sauce**
- 1 **can (6 ounces) tomato paste**
- ¼ **teaspoon pepper**
- 4 **cups (16 ounces) shredded part-skim mozzarella cheese, divided**
- 1 **jar (15 ounces) Alfredo sauce**
- 1 **carton (15 ounces) ricotta cheese**
- 3 **cups frozen peas, thawed**
- 1 **package (10 ounces) frozen chopped spinach, thawed and squeezed dry**
- 1 **package (9 ounces) no-cook lasagna noodles**
  Fresh basil leaves and grated Parmesan cheese, optional

1. In a Dutch oven, cook the beef, onion, mushrooms and garlic over medium heat until meat is no longer pink; drain. Stir in the tomato sauce, tomato paste, pepper and 2 cups mozzarella cheese; set aside.

2. In a large bowl, combine the Alfredo sauce, ricotta cheese, peas and spinach.

3. Spread 1 cup meat sauce into a greased 13-in. x 9-in. baking dish. Layer with four noodles, 1¼ cups meat sauce and 1¼ cups spinach mixture. Repeat layers three times. Sprinkle with remaining mozzarella cheese. (Pan will be full.)

4. Cover and bake at 350° for 45 minutes. Uncover; bake 10 minutes longer or until cheese is melted. Let stand for 10 minutes before cutting. Garnish with basil and serve with Parmesan cheese if desired.

> "Combining pineapple, mango and spices makes a sauce for chicken that is so unique and a favorite of so many friends and family. We like to grill the chicken with vegetable kabobs."
> —**KIM WAITES** RUTHERFORDTON, NORTH CAROLINA

Pineapple-Mango Chicken

PREP/TOTAL TIME: 30 MINUTES
MAKES: 4 SERVINGS

- 1½ cups undrained crushed pineapple
- ½ cup golden raisins
- ¼ teaspoon ground cinnamon
- ¼ teaspoon ground cloves
- ⅛ teaspoon ground nutmeg
- 2 medium mangoes, peeled and chopped
- 4 boneless skinless chicken breast halves (5 ounces each)
- ½ teaspoon salt
- ⅛ teaspoon pepper
- Hot cooked wild rice mix

1. In a small saucepan, combine the first five ingredients; bring to a boil over medium heat. Reduce heat; simmer, uncovered, for 4-6 minutes or until sauce is thickened and raisins are plumped, stirring occasionally. Stir in mangoes; heat through. Set aside.

2. Moisten a paper towel with cooking oil; using long-handled tongs, lightly coat the grill rack. Sprinkle chicken with salt and pepper. Grill chicken, covered, over medium heat or broil 4 in. from the heat for 5-8 minutes on each side or until a thermometer reads 170°. Serve with sauce and rice.

Quick Cajun Chicken Penne

I used to work at a restaurant that served a variation of chicken with penne pasta. I didn't know how easy it would be to make until I gave it a shot at home. Now it's always a requested meal around my house.

—RUSTY KOLL ELMWOOD, ILLINOIS
Teacher, Illinois Virtual High School, Elmwood, Illinois

PREP/TOTAL TIME: 30 MINUTES **MAKES:** 6 SERVINGS

- 1 **package (16 ounces) penne pasta**
- 4 **boneless skinless chicken breast halves (5 ounces each)**
- 2 **teaspoons blackened seasoning**
- 2 **containers (10 ounces each) refrigerated Alfredo sauce**
- 2 **plum tomatoes, chopped**
- 3 **green onions, thinly sliced**

1. Cook pasta according to package directions; drain.

2. Moisten a paper towel with cooking oil; using long-handled tongs, lightly coat the grill rack. Sprinkle chicken with blackened seasoning. Grill chicken, covered, over medium heat or broil 4 in. from the heat for 5-8 minutes on each side or until a thermometer reads 170°. Cut into bite-size pieces.

3. In a large skillet, heat Alfredo sauce over medium heat until warm; stir frequently. Add tomatoes, onions, pasta and chicken and toss to coat; heat through.

Chicken Marsala Lasagna

I love chicken Marsala, but most recipes do not serve a crowd. This version is one I invented and makes enough for 12 people.

—**DEBBIE SHANNON** RINGGOLD, GEORGIA

PREP: 50 MINUTES **BAKE:** 55 MINUTES + STANDING
MAKES: 12 SERVINGS

- 4 teaspoons Italian seasoning, divided
- 1 teaspoon salt
- 12 ounces boneless skinless chicken breasts, cubed
- 1 tablespoon olive oil
- ¼ cup finely chopped onion
- ½ cup butter, cubed
- 12 garlic cloves, minced
- ½ pound sliced baby portobello mushrooms
- 1½ cups beef broth
- ¾ cup Marsala wine, divided
- ¼ teaspoon coarsely ground pepper
- 3 tablespoons cornstarch
- ½ cup finely chopped fully cooked ham
- 1 carton (15 ounces) ricotta cheese
- 1 package (10 ounces) frozen chopped spinach, thawed and squeezed dry
- 2 cups (8 ounces) shredded Italian cheese blend
- 1 cup grated Parmesan cheese, divided
- 2 eggs, lightly beaten
- 12 lasagna noodles, cooked, rinsed and drained

1. Combine 2 teaspoons Italian seasoning and salt; sprinkle over chicken. In a large skillet, saute chicken in oil until no longer pink. Remove and keep warm.

2. In the same skillet, cook onion in butter over medium heat for 2 minutes. Add garlic; cook 2 minutes longer. Stir in mushrooms; cook 4-5 minutes longer or until tender.

3. Stir in the broth, ½ cup wine and pepper; bring to a boil. Combine the cornstarch and remaining wine until smooth; stir into the pan. Bring to a boil; cook and stir for 2 minutes or until thickened. Stir in ham and chicken.

4. In a large bowl, combine the ricotta cheese, spinach, Italian cheese blend, ¾ cup Parmesan cheese, eggs and remaining Italian seasoning. Spread 1 cup chicken mixture into a greased 13-in. x 9-in. baking dish. Layer with three noodles, about ¾ cup chicken mixture and about 1 cup ricotta mixture. Repeat layers three times.

5. Cover and bake at 350° for 40 minutes. Sprinkle with remaining Parmesan cheese. Bake, uncovered, for 10-15 minutes or until bubbly and cheese is melted. Let stand for 10 minutes before cutting.

❝I learned about the librarian position at Rossville Elementary when my husband went in for an interview and mentioned that his wife had just received her library science degree. They urged him to have me come in. We were pleasantly surprised when they hired us both. That was 10 years ago, and I still couldn't wish to work for a better school.❞

—**DEBBIE SHANNON** RINGGOLD, GEORGIA
Staff, Rossville Elementary School, Rossville, Georgia

"My mother had a recipe similar to this one but lost it, and no one could find it. After an exhaustive search on the Internet, I decided to re-create the salad from memory. Mom thinks I did a pretty good job!"

—DAPHNE DELANEY LAKE WACCAMAW, NORTH CAROLINA
Teacher, Bladenboro Middle School, Bladenboro, North Carolina

Shrimp Mac & Cheese Salad

PREP: 35 MINUTES **COOK:** 10 MINUTES
MAKES: 16 SERVINGS

- 4 **cups uncooked elbow macaroni**
- ¼ **cup butter, cut up**
- ¼ **cup all-purpose flour**
- 1½ **cups half-and-half cream**
- 4 **ounces Gouda cheese, shredded**
- ½ **cup shredded cheddar cheese**
- ½ **cup shredded part-skim mozzarella cheese**
- 2 **pounds peeled and deveined cooked medium shrimp, cut into pieces**
- 1 **cup chopped onion**
- 1 **cup chopped sweet red pepper**
- 1 **cup mayonnaise**
- ½ **cup chopped celery**
- ½ **cup chopped dill pickle**
- ⅛ **teaspoon salt**
- ⅛ **teaspoon pepper**
- 8 **lettuce leaves**

1. Cook macaroni according to package directions; drain and set aside.

2. Meanwhile, in a large saucepan, melt butter. Stir in flour until smooth; gradually add cream. Bring to a boil; cook and stir for 2 minutes or until thickened. Remove pan from heat; stir in cheeses until melted. Add macaroni; stir to coat. Transfer to a large bowl; cool to room temperature.

3. In another large bowl, combine the shrimp, onion, red pepper, mayonnaise, celery, pickle, salt and pepper. Fold in cooled macaroni mixture; cover and chill. Serve on lettuce.

Cheddar Bacon Chicken

It's tempting to seek out new flavors when baking chicken, but then again, with bacon, barbecue sauce and cheddar cheese so easy to grab from the fridge, why linger in doubt? Pull out this combination the next time you get the "what's for dinner?" text.

—BRENDA COLEMAN JACKSON, ALABAMA

PREP/TOTAL TIME: 30 MINUTES **MAKES:** 4 SERVINGS

- 4 **boneless skinless chicken breast halves (5 ounces each)**
- ¼ **cup reduced-sodium teriyaki sauce**
- ¼ **cup barbecue sauce**
- 4 **slices ready-to-serve fully cooked bacon, cut in half**
- 4 **slices cheddar cheese**

1. Dip both sides of chicken in teriyaki sauce; place on a greased 15-in. x 10-in. x 1-in. baking pan. Bake the chicken, uncovered, at 425° for 13-18 minutes or until a thermometer reads 170°.

2. Spread barbecue sauce over chicken; top with bacon and cheese. Bake for 3-5 minutes longer or until cheese is melted.

> "This is so easy...in just 5 minutes dinner can be in the oven and baking. A few pantry staples are poured over the chicken and before you know it, out comes a sweet, succulent main course. I like to serve it with rice or potatoes and an Asian frozen veggie mix."
>
> —GWYN BRANDT HIBBING, MINNESOTA
> *Staff, Assumption Catholic School, Hibbing, Minnesota*

Honey-Roasted Chicken

PREP/TOTAL TIME: 30 MINUTES **MAKES:** 4 SERVINGS

- 4 boneless skinless chicken breast halves (6 ounces each)
- ½ cup honey
- ¼ cup reduced-sodium teriyaki sauce
- 2 tablespoons orange juice
- 1½ teaspoons prepared mustard
- ½ teaspoon salt
- ¼ teaspoon pepper

1. Place chicken in a greased 13-in. x 9-in. baking dish. Combine remaining ingredients; pour over chicken.

2. Bake, uncovered, at 375° for 22-26 minutes or until a thermometer reads 170°, basting occasionally.

Mushroom-Artichoke Brunch Bake

While the potatoes are baking, take care of the rest of the prep work. The original recipe makes a pretty vegetarian egg bake. However, you can also add a layer of little smoked sausages cut lengthwise in half over the artichokes if you want a more substantial meal.

—SUZANNE FRANCIS MARYSVILLE, WASHINGTON

PREP: 30 MINUTES **BAKE:** 40 MINUTES
MAKES: 12 SERVINGS

- 3 **cups frozen shredded hash brown potatoes, thawed**
- 2 **tablespoons butter, melted, divided**
- ½ **teaspoon salt**
- 2½ **cups sliced fresh mushrooms**
- 1 **can (14 ounces) water-packed artichoke hearts, rinsed, drained and quartered**
- 3 **cups (12 ounces) shredded cheddar cheese**
- 12 **eggs**
- 1¾ **cups 2% milk**
- 1 **can (4 ounces) chopped green chilies, drained**

1. Place potatoes in a greased 13-in. x 9-in. baking dish; drizzle with 1 tablespoon butter and sprinkle with salt. Bake at 350° for 20-25 minutes or until lightly browned.

2. Meanwhile, in a small skillet, saute mushrooms in remaining butter until tender. Place artichokes on paper towels; pat dry. Sprinkle the mushrooms, artichokes and cheese over the potatoes. In a large bowl, whisk the eggs, milk and green chilies; pour over cheese.

3. Bake, uncovered, for 40-45 minutes or until a knife inserted near the center comes out clean. Let stand for 5 minutes before serving.

❝I have been a paraprofessional at Liberty Elementary School since 1990. The staff and students are very caring. The students have donated money to the American Red Cross for Haiti, for leukemia, and more recently for Japan after the tsunami disaster.❞

—SUZANNE FRANCIS MARYSVILLE, WASHINGTON
Staff, Liberty Elementary School, Marysville, Washington

1. Brush tomatoes with 2 teaspoons oil; sprinkle with oregano, basil and ¼ teaspoon salt and pepper. Transfer to an ungreased 15-in. x 10-in. x 1-in. baking pan. Bake at 350° for 20-25 minutes or until tender.

2. Brush the zucchini and yellow squash with 2 tablespoons oil; sprinkle with ¼ teaspoon salt. Place vegetables in a grill wok or basket. Grill, uncovered, over medium heat for 8-12 minutes or until tender, stirring occasionally.

3. Remove and discard stems and gills from the mushrooms. Brush mushrooms and eggplant with 1 tablespoon oil; sprinkle with remaining salt. Grill mushrooms, covered, over medium heat for 12-15 minutes or until tender. Grill eggplant, covered, over medium heat for 4-5 minutes on each side or until tender.

4. In a small bowl, combine the goat cheese, parsley, ½ teaspoon garlic and remaining pepper.

5. Place mushrooms on a greased baking sheet; spread each with 2 teaspoons cheese mixture. Layer with zucchini, squash, 2 teaspoons cheese mixture, eggplant and remaining cheese mixture. Top with mozzarella cheese and tomato. Bake at 350° for 8-10 minutes or until cheese is melted.

6. In a large skillet, saute the remaining garlic in remaining oil for 1 minute. Add spinach; cook for 4-5 minutes or until wilted. Divide among four plates; top each with a mushroom stack. Drizzle with vinaigrette.

Grilled Vegetables & Goat Cheese Napoleons

PREP: 50 MINUTES **BAKE:** 10 MINUTES
MAKES: 4 SERVINGS

- 2 plum tomatoes, halved lengthwise
- ¼ cup olive oil, divided
- ⅛ teaspoon dried oregano
- ⅛ teaspoon dried basil
- ¾ teaspoon salt, divided
- ½ teaspoon pepper, divided
- 1 large zucchini, cut into ½-inch slices
- 1 large yellow summer squash, cut into ½-inch slices
- 4 large portobello mushrooms
- 4 slices eggplant (½ inch thick)
- 1 package (5.3 ounces) fresh goat cheese
- 1 teaspoon minced fresh parsley
- 1 teaspoon minced garlic, divided
- 4 ounces fresh mozzarella cheese, cut into 4 slices
- 1 package (10 ounces) fresh spinach
- ¼ cup balsamic vinaigrette

"My recipe started out as an experiment for vegetarian friends at a small dinner party. It slowly evolved into this savory dish. I find everyone loves it (even nonvegetable enthusiasts) and I frequently receive requests to make it."

—JOAN MEYER NEW YORK, NEW YORK

White Bean Tuna Salad

I love tuna, and this recipe is a great way to use the canned variety. The Mediterranean flavors really pack a punch.

—LAUREEN PITTMAN RIVERSIDE, CALIFORNIA
Volunteer, Hawarden Hills Academy, Riverside, California

PREP/TOTAL TIME: 30 MINUTES
MAKES: 6 SERVINGS

VINAIGRETTE

- ½ cup olive oil
- ¼ cup white wine vinegar
- 2 to 3 tablespoons lemon juice
- 2 tablespoons snipped fresh dill
- 1 tablespoon Dijon mustard
- 1 tablespoon honey
- ½ teaspoon kosher salt
- ¼ teaspoon pepper

SALAD

- 1 can (15 ounces) white kidney or cannellini beans, rinsed and drained
- 2 cans (5 ounces each) albacore white tuna in water
- 1 cup chopped roasted sweet red peppers
- ½ cup chopped red onion
- ½ cup chopped pitted Greek olives
- ½ cup chopped oil-packed sun-dried tomatoes
- ½ cup minced fresh parsley
- 2 teaspoons minced fresh oregano
- 6 leaves red leaf lettuce

1. In a small bowl, whisk the vinaigrette ingredients until well blended.

2. In a large bowl, combine the beans, tuna, red peppers, onion, olives, tomatoes, parsley and oregano. Drizzle with the vinaigrette; gently toss to coat. Serve on lettuce.

Sizzling Chicken Lo Mein

All the students at my high school love this yummy chicken dish. It is the most requested recipe I have.

—**KRIS CAMPION** MARSHALL, MINNESOTA
Teacher, Marshall High School, Marshall, Minnesota

PREP/TOTAL TIME: 30 MINUTES
MAKES: 4 SERVINGS

- 8 **ounces uncooked linguine**
- ¾ **pound boneless skinless chicken breasts, cubed**
- 2 **tablespoons olive oil**
- 5 **tablespoons stir-fry sauce, divided**
- 4 **tablespoons teriyaki sauce, divided**
- 1 **package (12 ounces) frozen stir-fry vegetable blend**

1. Cook linguine according to the package directions. Meanwhile, in a large skillet or wok, stir-fry chicken in oil until no longer pink. Add 2 tablespoons each stir fry sauce and teriyaki sauce. Remove chicken from pan.

2. Stir-fry vegetables and 1 tablespoon each stir-fry sauce and teriyaki sauce in the same pan for 4-6 minutes or until vegetables are crisp-tender. Drain linguine. Add the linguine, chicken and remaining sauces to the pan; stir-fry for 2-3 minutes or until heated through.

Turkey Florentine Sandwiches

PREP/TOTAL TIME: 20 MINUTES **MAKES:** 2 SERVINGS

- ½ cup sliced fresh mushrooms
- 2 teaspoons olive oil
- 1 cup fresh baby spinach
- 2 garlic cloves, minced
- 4 ounces sliced deli turkey breast
- 2 slices part-skim mozzarella cheese
- 4 slices whole wheat bread
  Cooking spray

1. In a nonstick skillet, saute mushrooms in oil until tender. Add spinach and garlic; cook 1 minute longer.

2. Layer the spinach mixture, turkey and cheese on two bread slices; top with remaining bread. Spritz outsides of sandwiches with cooking spray. Cook on a panini maker or indoor grill for 4-5 minutes or until bread is browned and cheese is melted.

Nutrition Facts: 1 sandwich equals 346 calories, 14 g fat (5 g saturated fat), 35 mg cholesterol, 937 mg sodium, 27 g carbohydrate, 4 g fiber, 27 g protein. **Diabetic Exchanges:** *3 lean meat, 2 starch, 1 fat.*

Healthy Entrees

❝Upgrade a lunchtime classic to a dinnertime feast with a few fancy yet simple tweaks.❞

KAREN REYNOLDS RUTHERFORDTON, NORTH CAROLINA
Teacher, Isothermal Community College, Spindale, North Carolina

Barbecued Chicken-Stuffed Potatoes

PREP/TOTAL TIME: 30 MINUTES
MAKES: 8 SERVINGS

4 large potatoes
  Cooking spray
1 teaspoon garlic salt with parsley
1½ cups cubed cooked chicken breast
⅔ cup barbecue sauce
1 can (16 ounces) chili beans, undrained
1 can (2¼ ounces) sliced ripe olives, drained
2 green onions, sliced
1½ cups (6 ounces) shredded reduced-fat
  Colby-Monterey Jack cheese
2 plum tomatoes, chopped
½ cup reduced-fat sour cream

1. Scrub and pierce potatoes. Coat with cooking spray and rub with garlic salt with parsley; place on a microwave-safe plate. Microwave, uncovered, on high for 18-22 minutes or until tender, turning once.

2. Cut each potato in half lengthwise. Scoop out the pulp, leaving ½-in. shells. Discard pulp or save for another use.

3. In a large bowl, combine chicken and barbecue sauce. Spoon into potato shells. Top with beans, olives and green onions; sprinkle with cheese. Place on a baking sheet. Bake, uncovered, at 375° for 10-12 minutes or until heated through. Serve with tomatoes and sour cream.

Editor's Note: *This recipe was tested in a 1,100-watt microwave.*

Nutrition Facts: *1 stuffed potato half equals 237 calories, 8 g fat (4 g saturated fat), 36 mg cholesterol, 737 mg sodium, 25 g carbohydrate, 5 g fiber, 19 g protein.*
Diabetic Exchanges: *2 lean meat, 1½ starch, ½ fat.*

66This tasty dish combines some of my favorite things: the toppings for supreme nachos, tender chicken and the warm comfort of a baked potato. We serve stuffed baked potatoes or a baked potato bar at wintertime potluck lunches in the teachers' lounge.99

—ELLEN FINGER LANCASTER, PENNSYLVANIA
Teacher, Penn Manor School District, Lancaster, Pennsylvania

"My heart-healthy, one-skillet meal is quick and easy to prepare yet elegant enough for company. Vegetarian teachers and students alike appreciate this stew at school potlucks."

—JANE SIEMON VIROQUA, WISCONSIN

Teacher, Youth Initiative High School, Viroqua, Wisconsin

Tuscan Portobello Stew

PREP: 20 MINUTES **COOK:** 20 MINUTES
MAKES: 4 SERVINGS

- 2 large portobello mushrooms, coarsely chopped
- 1 medium onion, chopped
- 3 garlic cloves, minced
- 2 tablespoons olive oil
- ½ cup white wine or vegetable broth
- 1 can (28 ounces) diced tomatoes, undrained
- 2 cups chopped fresh kale
- 1 bay leaf
- 1 teaspoon dried thyme
- ½ teaspoon dried basil
- ½ teaspoon dried rosemary, crushed
- ¼ teaspoon salt
- ¼ teaspoon pepper
- 2 cans (15 ounces each) white kidney or cannellini beans, rinsed and drained

1. In a large skillet, saute the mushrooms, onion and garlic in oil until tender. Add the wine. Bring to a boil; cook until liquid is reduced by half. Stir in the tomatoes, kale and seasonings. Bring to a boil. Reduce heat; cover and simmer for 8-10 minutes.

2. Add beans; heat through. Discard bay leaf.

Nutrition Facts: *1¼ cups stew equals 309 calories, 8 g fat (1 g saturated fat), 0 cholesterol, 672 mg sodium, 46 g carbohydrate, 13 g fiber, 12 g protein.* **Diabetic Exchanges:** *2 starch, 2 vegetable, 1½ fat, 1 lean meat.*

"I'm the media assistant, more commonly known as librarian, and technology instructor at Sam Case Primary. I love my job because I get to work with kids and hopefully make a difference in their education and their lives. The best part of my day is getting to read stories to the kids. Sam Case Primary is more than a school, it's family. I lost my husband a few years ago to cancer, and it was my Sam Case family that helped get me through. I don't know what I would have done without the love and support of the staff, students and families.

—**CATHY RAU** NEWPORT, OREGON
Staff, Sam Case Primary School, Newport, Oregon

Weeknight Pasta Supper

After a long day at school, I want something that is healthy but also quick to prepare; this pasta dish fits my needs.

—**CATHY RAU** NEWPORT, OREGON

PREP: 20 MINUTES **COOK:** 20 MINUTES
MAKES: 4 SERVINGS

- 3 **cups uncooked bow tie pasta**
- 10 **ounces lean ground turkey**
- 8 **ounces sliced baby portobello mushrooms**
- 2 **garlic cloves, minced**
- 2 **teaspoons olive oil**
- 1 **can (14½ ounces) fire-roasted diced tomatoes, undrained**
- ¼ **cup dry red wine or chicken broth**
- 5 **pitted Greek olives, chopped**
- 1 **teaspoon dried basil**
- 1 **teaspoon dried oregano**
- 1 **teaspoon dried parsley flakes**
- ½ **teaspoon salt**
- ⅛ **teaspoon coarsely ground pepper**
- 2 **cups fresh baby spinach, chopped**
- 1 **tablespoon grated Parmesan cheese**

1. Cook pasta according to the package directions.

2. Meanwhile, in a large nonstick skillet, cook turkey until no longer pink; drain. Remove meat; set aside and keep warm.

3. In the same skillet, cook mushrooms and garlic in oil until tender. Stir in the tomatoes, wine, olives, seasonings and turkey. Bring to a boil. Reduce heat; simmer, uncovered, for 10 minutes.

4. Drain pasta. Stir into turkey mixture. Stir in spinach; cook 1-2 minutes longer or until spinach is wilted. Sprinkle with cheese.

Nutrition Facts: *1½ cups equal 411 calories, 11 g fat (3 g saturated fat), 57 mg cholesterol, 751 mg sodium, 52 g carbohydrate, 4 g fiber, 24 g protein.*

Taco Salad Tacos

I was making tacos one night and noticed I was out of spicy taco sauce. Using a combination of spices and fat-free Catalina salad dressing saved our family taco night!

—**CHERYL PLAINTE** PRUDENVILLE, MICHIGAN

PREP/TOTAL TIME: 30 MINUTES
MAKES: 4 SERVINGS

- 1 **pound extra-lean ground beef (95% lean)**
- 1 **medium onion, chopped**
- 1 **tablespoon chili powder**
- 1 **teaspoon garlic powder**
- 1 **teaspoon reduced-sodium beef bouillon granules**
- 1 **teaspoon ground cumin**
- ¼ **teaspoon salt**

SALAD

- 3 **cups torn romaine**
- 1 **large tomato, seeded and chopped**
- 1 **medium sweet orange pepper, chopped**
- 3 **green onions, chopped**
- 8 **taco shells, warmed**
- ½ **cup fat-free Catalina salad dressing**
  Shredded reduced-fat Colby-Monterey Jack cheese and reduced-fat sour cream, optional

1. In a large skillet, cook beef and onion over medium heat until the meat is no longer pink. Stir in the chili powder, garlic powder, bouillon, cumin and salt; remove from the heat.

2. In a large bowl, combine the romaine, tomato, orange pepper and green onions. Spoon beef mixture into taco shells; top with salad mixture. Drizzle with dressing. Serve with cheese and sour cream if desired.

Nutrition Facts: *2 tacos (calculated without cheese and sour cream) equal 334 calories, 11 g fat (4 g saturated fat), 65 mg cholesterol, 722 mg sodium, 33 g carbohydrate, 6 g fiber, 26 g protein.* **Diabetic Exchanges:** *3 lean meat, 2 vegetable, 1½ starch.*

1. In a large nonstick skillet, cook the chicken over medium heat until no longer pink; drain and set aside.

2. In the same skillet, cook the onion, pepper and garlic in oil until tender. Stir in the curry, ginger, pepper and salt; cook 1 minute longer.

3. Stir in the tomatoes, apple and raisins; bring to a boil. Reduce heat; simmer, uncovered, for 6-8 minutes. Stir in the chutney, mayonnaise, mustard and chicken; heat through. Serve on buns.

Nutrition Facts: *1 sandwich equals 288 calories, 10 g fat (2 g saturated fat), 40 mg cholesterol, 486 mg sodium, 39 g carbohydrate, 5 g fiber, 14 g protein.* **Diabetic Exchanges:** *2 starch, 2 lean meat, 1 vegetable, ½ fat.*

❝These delicious sloppy joes pack a burst of unexpected flavors in every bite. They'll surely jazz up your sloppy joe repertoire. For potlucks, keep the chicken mixture warm in a slow cooker and allow everyone to fill their own buns.❞

—**JAMIE MILLER** MAPLE GROVE, MINNESOTA
Volunteer, Heritage Christian Academy, Maple Grove, Minnesota

Curried Chicken Sloppy Joes

PREP: 20 MINUTES **COOK:** 30 MINUTES
MAKES: 10 SERVINGS

- 1¼ pounds ground chicken
- 1 cup chopped sweet onion
- ½ cup chopped sweet orange pepper
- 2 garlic cloves, minced
- 1 tablespoon olive oil
- 2 teaspoons curry powder
- 1 teaspoon minced fresh gingerroot
- ½ teaspoon coarsely ground pepper
- ¼ teaspoon salt
- 1 can (14½ ounces) petite diced tomatoes, undrained
- 1 medium tart apple, peeled and diced
- ½ cup golden raisins
- 3 tablespoons mango chutney
- ¼ cup reduced-fat mayonnaise
- 1 tablespoon Dijon mustard
- 10 whole wheat hamburger buns, split

"As teachers, our summers should be filled with relaxation, but often that is not the case. On the rare occasion that my teacher friends and I get to sit on the deck and enjoy a summer lunch, this is what we always have. We each take a bundle and eat right out of the parchment paper. Makes cleanup very easy!"
—**MELISSA CHILTON** HARLOWTON, MONTANA

Mediterranean Cod

PREP: 25 MINUTES **BAKE:** 15 MINUTES
MAKES: 4 SERVINGS

- 4 **cups shredded cabbage**
- 1 **large sweet onion, thinly sliced**
- 4 **garlic cloves, minced**
- 4 **cod fillets (6 ounces each)**
- ¼ **cup pitted Greek olives, chopped**
- ½ **cup crumbled feta cheese**
- ¼ **teaspoon salt**
- ¼ **teaspoon pepper**
- 4 **teaspoons olive oil**

1. Cut parchment paper or heavy-duty foil into four 18-in. x 12-in. pieces; place 1 cup cabbage on each. Top with onion, garlic, cod, olives, cheese, salt and pepper; drizzle with oil.

2. Fold parchment paper over fish. Bring edges of paper together on all sides and crimp to seal, forming a large packet. Repeat with remaining ingredients. Place on baking sheets.

3. Bake at 450° for 12-15 minutes or until fish flakes easily with a fork. Open packets carefully to allow steam to escape.

Nutrition Facts: *1 packet equals 270 calories, 10 g fat (3 g saturated fat), 72 mg cholesterol, 532 mg sodium, 12 g carbohydrate, 3 g fiber, 31 g protein.* **Diabetic Exchanges:** *5 lean meat, 2 vegetable, 2 fat.*

"All the fruit in this salad gives it a natural sweetness. I use whole wheat pasta for added fiber. Since I purchase cooked chicken breast at the store, I only have to cook the pasta for a healthy, delectable dinner. With its minimal cooking, this entree is great for the summer."

—**REGINA REYNOLDS** STRUTHERS, OHIO
Staff, Canfield Village Middle School, Canfield, Ohio

California Chicken Salad

PREP/TOTAL TIME: 30 MINUTES
MAKES: 14 SERVINGS

- 2 cups uncooked whole wheat spiral pasta
- ¼ cup mayonnaise
- ¼ cup sour cream
- 4½ teaspoons 2% milk
- 1 tablespoon sugar
- 1 tablespoon balsamic vinegar
- 1 teaspoon salt
- ¼ teaspoon pepper
- 2 cups cubed cooked chicken breast
- 1 large tart apple, chopped
- 1 cup green grapes, halved
- ½ cup unsweetened pineapple tidbits
- ⅓ cup mandarin oranges
- 1 celery rib, finely chopped
- 14 Boston or Bibb lettuce leaves

1. Cook pasta according to the package directions. Drain pasta and rinse in cold water.

2. In a large bowl, combine mayonnaise, sour cream, milk, sugar, vinegar, salt and pepper. Stir in chicken, apple, grapes, pineapple, oranges, celery and cooked pasta. Chill until serving.

3. Spoon ½ cup onto each lettuce leaf.

Nutrition Facts: *½ cup chicken salad equals 127 calories, 5 g fat (1 g saturated fat), 20 mg cholesterol, 209 mg sodium, 13 g carbohydrate, 2 g fiber, 8 g protein.*
Diabetic Exchanges: *1 lean meat, ½ starch, ½ fruit, ½ fat.*

Pork Medallions with Squash & Greens

PREP: 35 MINUTES **COOK:** 10 MINUTES
MAKES: 8 SERVINGS

- 2 **quarts water**
- 4 **cups chopped mustard greens**
- 1 **medium butternut squash, peeled and cut into ½-inch cubes**
- 3 **medium leeks (white portion only), halved and sliced**
- 3 **tablespoons olive oil**
- 2 **garlic cloves, minced**
- ⅛ **teaspoon crushed red pepper flakes**
- 1½ **cups reduced-sodium chicken broth**
- ½ **teaspoon salt**

PORK MEDALLIONS

- 2 **pork tenderloins (¾ pound each), cut into eight slices**
- ⅓ **cup all-purpose flour**
- ½ **teaspoon salt**
- ¼ **teaspoon pepper**
- ¼ **teaspoon dried rosemary, crushed**
- 1 **teaspoon cornstarch**
- ½ **cup apple cider or juice**
- ⅓ **cup reduced-sodium chicken broth**
- 1 **tablespoon olive oil**
- 1 **tablespoon butter**
- 1 **medium tart apple, peeled and chopped**

1. In a large saucepan, bring water to a boil. Add mustard greens; cook, uncovered, for 3-5 minutes or until tender.

2. Meanwhile, in a Dutch oven, saute squash and leeks in oil until tender. Add garlic and pepper flakes; saute 1 minute longer. Stir in broth and salt. Bring to a boil. Reduce heat; simmer, uncovered, for 8 minutes or until liquid has almost evaporated. Drain greens and add to squash mixture; set aside and keep warm.

3. Cover the pork with plastic wrap. Flatten to ¼-in. thickness. Remove plastic. In a large resealable plastic bag, combine the flour, salt, pepper and rosemary. Add pork, a few pieces at a time, and shake to coat.

4. In a small bowl, whisk the cornstarch, apple cider and broth until smooth; set aside.

5. In a large skillet, cook pork in oil and butter until meat juices run clear. Remove and keep warm. Add the apple to the pan; cook and stir for 2-4 minutes or until crisp-tender.

6. Stir cornstarch mixture; add to the pan. Bring to a boil; cook and stir for 2 minutes or until thickened. Add the pork; heat through. Top with apple mixture; serve with squash mixture.

Nutrition Facts: *3 ounces cooked pork with ¾ cup squash mixture equals 272 calories, 11 g fat (3 g saturated fat), 51 mg cholesterol, 669 mg sodium, 24 g carbohydrate, 5 g fiber, 20 g protein.* **Diabetic Exchanges:** *2 lean meat, 1½ starch, 1½ fat.*

66 The colors of the dish remind me of autumn, my favorite season. Butternut squash is nutritious as well as colorful. This is an example of cooking it a way other than mashed and sweetened. The pork tenderloin medallions are mildly seasoned with rosemary and are very tender. 99

—LOUISE NOWAK COLUMBIA, CONNECTICUT
Teacher, Horace W. Porter School, Columbia, Connecticut

Tender Salsa Beef

This is my Mexican-style twist on comfort food. To keep it kid-friendly, use mild salsa.

—STACIE STAMPER NORTH WILKESBORO, NORTH CAROLINA

PREP: 15 MINUTES **COOK:** 8 HOURS
MAKES: 8 SERVINGS

1½ **pounds beef stew meat, cut into ¾-inch cubes**
2 **cups salsa**
1 **tablespoon brown sugar**
1 **tablespoon reduced-sodium soy sauce**
1 **garlic clove, minced**
4 **cups hot cooked brown rice**

1. In a 3-qt. slow cooker, combine the beef, salsa, brown sugar, soy sauce and garlic. Cover and cook on low for 8-10 hours or until meat is tender. Using a slotted spoon, serve beef with rice.

Nutrition Facts: *½ cup beef mixture with ½ cup rice equals 259 calories, 7 g fat (2 g saturated fat), 53 mg cholesterol, 356 mg sodium, 28 g carbohydrate, 2 g fiber, 19 g protein.* **Diabetic Exchanges:** *2 starch, 2 lean meat.*

Herbed Salmon Fillets

On a busy day, I turn to this sensational salmon recipe for dinner. It's fast, healthy and tastes great.

—**KAREN ENSIGN** PROVIDENCE, UTAH

PREP/TOTAL TIME: 30 MINUTES **MAKES:** 8 SERVINGS

2½ **pounds salmon fillet**
1 **tablespoon minced fresh parsley**
1 **tablespoon minced fresh thyme**
1 **tablespoon olive oil**
3 **garlic cloves, minced**
2 **teaspoons grated lemon peel**
2 **teaspoons grated lime peel**
½ **teaspoon salt**
½ **teaspoon pepper**

1. Place salmon on a large baking sheet coated with cooking spray. In a small bowl, combine the remaining ingredients; spread over fillet. Bake at 400° for 12-14 minutes or until fish flakes easily with a fork. Cut salmon into eight pieces.

Nutrition Facts: *3 ounces cooked salmon equals 238 calories, 15 g fat (3 g saturated fat), 71 mg cholesterol, 219 mg sodium, 1 g carbohydrate, trace fiber, 24 g protein.* **Diabetic Exchanges:** *4 lean meat, 1 fat.*

"Honey, smoky chipotle pepper and soy sauce help to flavor this no-fuss pork tenderloin. Serve it with veggies or rice for a satisfying meal."

—DIANE COTTON FRANKLIN, NORTH CAROLINA
Teacher, South Macon Elementary School, Franklin, North Carolina

Honey-Glazed Pork Tenderloins

PREP: 15 MINUTES **BAKE:** 20 MINUTES
MAKES: 6 SERVINGS

- ½ teaspoon garlic powder
- ½ teaspoon ground chipotle pepper
- ½ teaspoon pepper
- 2 pork tenderloins (1 pound each)
- 1 tablespoon canola oil
- ½ cup honey
- 2 tablespoons reduced-sodium soy sauce
- 1 tablespoon balsamic vinegar
- 1 teaspoon sesame oil

1. Combine the first three ingredients; rub over pork. In a large ovenproof skillet, brown pork in canola oil on all sides.

2. In a small bowl, combine the honey, soy sauce, vinegar and sesame oil; spoon over pork. Bake, uncovered, at 350° for 20-25 minutes or until a thermometer reads 145°, basting occasionally with pan juices. Let stand for 5 minutes before slicing.

Nutrition Facts: *4 ounces cooked pork equals 288 calories, 8 g fat (2 g saturated fat), 84 mg cholesterol, 265 mg sodium, 24 g carbohydrate, trace fiber, 31 g protein.* **Diabetic Exchanges:** *4 lean meat, 1 starch, ½ fat.*

1. In a stockpot, brown the roast in oil on all sides. Remove and set aside. Add onion and garlic to the pan; cook until tender. Return meat to the pan. Add 2 cups water. Bring to a boil. Reduce heat; cover and simmer for 1½ to 2 hours or until meat is tender.

2. Remove meat to a cutting board. Cut into ¾-in. pieces; return to pan. Stir in the tomatoes, eggplant, potatoes, beans, tomato sauce, cinnamon, salt, pepper and remaining water.

3. Bring to a boil. Reduce heat; cover and simmer for 20-25 minutes or until vegetables are tender, adding the okra and green beans during the last 5 minutes of cooking. Meanwhile, cook the noodles according to package directions. Serve with stew.

Nutrition Facts: *1 cup stew with ⅓ cup noodles equals 248 calories, 7 g fat (2 g saturated fat), 45 mg cholesterol, 315 mg sodium, 32 g carbohydrate, 6 g fiber, 16 g protein.* **Diabetic Exchanges:** *2 lean meat, 1½ starch, 1 vegetable.*

❝This was one of my Lebanese grandmother's original recipes. It is one of my family's favorite winter meals, so we have it often in our home. This enables me to indulge in memories of her and the wonderful aromas and flavors I associated with her kitchen.❞

—**MARY ROBBINS** CLARKSVILLE, ARKANSAS
Teacher, Westside Elementary School, Hartman, Arkansas

Vegetable Beef Stew

PREP: 25 MINUTES **COOK:** 2½ HOURS
MAKES: 14 SERVINGS

- 1½ **pounds boneless beef chuck roast**
- 1 **tablespoon canola oil**
- 1 **large sweet onion, chopped**
- 3 **garlic cloves, peeled and sliced**
- 3 **cups water, divided**
- 1 **can (28 ounces) diced tomatoes, undrained**
- 1 **medium eggplant, peeled and cut into ¾-inch cubes**
- 2 **medium potatoes, peeled and cut into ¾-inch cubes**
- 1 **can (15 ounces) garbanzo beans or chickpeas, rinsed and drained**
- 1 **can (15 ounces) tomato sauce**
- 1 **teaspoon ground cinnamon**
- ⅛ **teaspoon salt**
- ⅛ **teaspoon pepper**
- 1 **package (16 ounces) frozen sliced okra, thawed**
- 1½ **cups frozen cut green beans, thawed**
- 4½ **cups uncooked egg noodles**

Savory Oven-Fried Chicken

PREP: 20 MINUTES + MARINATING **BAKE:** 50 MINUTES
MAKES: 4 SERVINGS

- ½ cup buttermilk
- 1 tablespoon Dijon mustard
- 2 garlic cloves, minced
- 1 teaspoon hot pepper sauce
- 4 bone-in chicken breast halves (12 ounces each), skin removed
- ½ cup whole wheat flour
- 1½ teaspoons paprika
- 1 teaspoon baking powder
- 1 teaspoon dried thyme
- ¼ teaspoon salt
- ¼ teaspoon pepper
  Cooking spray

1. In a large resealable plastic bag, combine the buttermilk, mustard, garlic and pepper sauce. Add chicken; seal bag and turn to coat. Refrigerate for 8 hours or overnight. Drain and discard marinade.

2. In a large resealable plastic bag, combine the flour, paprika, baking powder, thyme, salt and pepper. Add chicken, one piece at a time, and shake to coat.

3. Place chicken bone side down on a rack in a shallow baking pan. Spritz chicken with cooking spray. Bake, uncovered, at 425° for 50-60 minutes or until a thermometer reads 170°.

Nutrition Facts: *1 chicken breast half equals 355 calories, 8 g fat (2 g saturated fat), 153 mg cholesterol, 394 mg sodium, 10 g carbohydrate, 2 g fiber, 58 g protein.*

66You won't believe how moist this chicken is. It has a nicely seasoned crumb crust that bakes up to a golden color. It's tasty, healthy and easy.99

—RANEE BULLARD EVANS, GEORGIA
Teacher, Augusta Christian Schools, Martinez, Georgia

"A delightful and tasty rub makes this quick recipe fantastic. While the fish is sitting to allow the flavors to blend, you can easily assemble the salsa. My family thinks this is marvelous."

—LAURA FISHER WESTFIELD, MASSACHUSETTS
Teacher, Southampton Road Elementary School, Westfield, Massachusetts

Blackened Catfish with Mango Avocado Salsa

PREP: 20 MINUTES + CHILLING **COOK:** 10 MINUTES
MAKES: 4 SERVINGS (2 CUPS SALSA)

- 2 **teaspoons dried oregano**
- 2 **teaspoons ground cumin**
- 2 **teaspoons paprika**
- 2¼ **teaspoons pepper, divided**
- ¾ **teaspoon salt, divided**
- 4 **catfish fillets (6 ounces each)**
- 1 **medium mango, peeled and cubed**
- 1 **medium ripe avocado, peeled and cubed**
- ⅓ **cup finely chopped red onion**
- 2 **tablespoons minced fresh cilantro**
- 2 **tablespoons lime juice**
- 2 **teaspoons olive oil**

1. Combine the oregano, cumin, paprika, 2 teaspoons pepper and ½ teaspoon salt; rub over the fillets. Refrigerate for at least 30 minutes.

2. Meanwhile, in a small bowl, combine the mango, avocado, red onion, cilantro, lime juice and remaining salt and pepper. Chill until serving.

3. In a large cast-iron skillet, cook fillets in oil over medium heat for 5-7 minutes on each side or until fish flakes easily with a fork. Serve with salsa.

Nutrition Facts: *1 fillet with ½ cup salsa equals 376 calories, 22 g fat (4 g saturated fat), 80 mg cholesterol, 541 mg sodium, 17 g carbohydrate, 6 g fiber, 28 g protein.*
Diabetic Exchanges: *5 lean meat, 1 starch, ½ fat.*

"I would describe my roles as instructional coach and wannabe chef. Although this is my first year as an instructional coach, I've been in education for 18 years. I work with both teachers and students grades K-5. As an instructional coach, my role is to develop a partnership with teachers to improve instruction for their students. I love my position as a coach because I get the best of both worlds working with my peers, the teachers, and students."

—KARLA SHEELEY WORDEN, ILLINOIS
Coach, Glasgow Elementary School, St. Louis, Missouri

Chipotle-Black Bean Chili

I love soup weather, and this chili is ideal to warm you up on a chilly or rainy day. The whole can of chipotles in adobo makes this a pretty spicy chili, but you can cut back and adjust to your taste.

—KARLA SHEELEY WORDEN, ILLINOIS

PREP: 20 MINUTES **COOK:** 1¼ HOURS
MAKES: 10 SERVINGS (3 QUARTS)

- 1 tablespoon Creole seasoning
- 1 beef top sirloin steak (2 pounds), cut into ½-inch cubes
- 3 tablespoons olive oil
- 1 large sweet onion, chopped
- 3 chipotle peppers in adobo sauce, seeded and finely chopped
- 2 tablespoons minced garlic
- ⅓ cup masa harina
- 2 tablespoons chili powder
- 2 tablespoons Worcestershire sauce
- 1 tablespoon ground cumin
- 1 teaspoon ground cinnamon
- ¼ teaspoon salt
- ¼ teaspoon cayenne pepper
- 4 cups reduced-sodium beef broth
- 1 can (28 ounces) diced tomatoes, undrained
- 3 cans (15 ounces each) black beans, rinsed and drained
  Shredded cheddar cheese and/or finely chopped red onion, optional

1. Place Creole seasoning in a large resealable plastic bag. Add beef, a few pieces at a time, and shake to coat.

2. In a Dutch oven, saute beef in oil in batches. Stir in the onion, chipotle peppers and garlic. Cook 3 minutes longer or until onion is tender. Drain.

3. Stir in masa harina, chili powder, Worcestershire sauce, cumin, cinnamon, salt and cayenne. Cook and stir for 3-5 minutes. Stir in the broth and tomatoes. Bring to a boil. Reduce heat; simmer, uncovered, for 45 minutes or until beef is tender.

4. Stir in beans; heat through. Garnish with cheddar cheese and/or red onion if desired.

Editor's Note: *Wear disposable gloves when cutting hot peppers; the oils can burn skin. Avoid touching your face.*

Nutrition Facts: *1¼ cups chili (calculated without garnishes) equals 314 calories, 8 g fat (2 g saturated fat), 39 mg cholesterol, 900 mg sodium, 31 g carbohydrate, 8 g fiber, 28 g protein.* **Diabetic Exchanges:** *4 lean meat, 2 starch.*

Spicy Chicken Sausage Lettuce Wraps

PREP: 25 MINUTES **COOK:** 10 MINUTES
MAKES: 6 SERVINGS

- 2 **cups coleslaw mix**
- 2 **cups shredded yellow summer squash**
- 2 **medium Asian or Bosc pears, chopped**
- ¼ **cup canola oil**
- 3 **tablespoons rice vinegar**
- 1 **teaspoon minced fresh gingerroot**
- 1 **teaspoon finely chopped crystallized ginger**
- ½ **teaspoon salt**
- 1½ **cups frozen pepper strips, thawed**
- 1 **small red onion, thinly sliced**
- 1 **package (12 ounces) fully cooked spicy chicken sausage links, cut into ½-inch slices**
- ¼ **cup Asian toasted sesame salad dressing**
- 12 **Bibb or Boston lettuce leaves**
- 2 **tablespoons minced fresh cilantro**

1. In a large bowl, combine the coleslaw mix, squash and pears. Whisk together the oil, vinegar, ginger, crystallized ginger and salt; drizzle over slaw mixture. Toss to coat; set aside.

2. In a large nonstick skillet coated with cooking spray, saute peppers and onion until crisp-tender. Add the sausage; cook 4-5 minutes longer. Stir in the salad dressing; heat through.

3. Spoon the sausage mixture onto lettuce leaves. Top with slaw mixture; sprinkle with cilantro. Fold lettuce over filling.

Nutrition Facts: *2 lettuce wraps equal 273 calories, 16 g fat (2 g saturated fat), 37 mg cholesterol, 656 mg sodium, 19 g carbohydrate, 4 g fiber, 12 g protein.* **Diabetic Exchanges:** *2½ fat, 2 lean meat, 1 starch.*

66I love dishes that you can put together and eat with your hands. I've found that kids really like this fresh-tasting chicken wrap.99

—**VANESSA CAMPBELL** FORD, VIRGINIA
Teacher, Dinwiddie Middle School, Dinwiddie, Virginia

Grilled Tandoori Chicken Kabobs

When I prepare this recipe for tandoori chicken, it brings back memories of my childhood and my rich Indian heritage. This has a nice spice level, but if you like your food on the mild side, then reduce each spice a little.

—RAVINDER AUJLA GRIDLEY, CALIFORNIA
Volunteer, Manzanita Elementary School, Gridley, California

PREP: 30 MINUTES + MARINATING **GRILL:** 10 MINUTES
MAKES: 6 SERVINGS

- 1¼ **cups plain yogurt**
- ⅓ **cup chopped onion**
- 2 **tablespoons lemon juice**
- 2 **garlic cloves, minced**
- 2 **teaspoons garam masala**
- 2 **teaspoons minced fresh gingerroot**
- 1 **teaspoon salt**
- 1 **teaspoon cayenne pepper**
- 3 **drops yellow food coloring, optional**
- 3 **drops red food coloring, optional**
- 2 **pounds boneless skinless chicken breasts, cut into 1-inch cubes**
- 2 **teaspoons minced fresh cilantro**
- 1 **medium lemon, cut into six wedges**

1. In a large resealable plastic bag, combine the first eight ingredients. Add food coloring if desired. Add the chicken; seal bag and turn to coat. Refrigerate for at least 8 hours or overnight.

2. Drain and discard marinade. Thread chicken onto six metal or soaked wooden skewers. Moisten a paper towel with cooking oil; using long-handled tongs, lightly coat the grill rack.

3. Grill chicken, covered, over medium heat or broil 4 in. from the heat for 10-15 minutes or until juices run clear, turning occasionally. Sprinkle with cilantro; garnish with lemon wedges.

Editor's Note: *Look for garam masala in the spice aisle.*

Nutrition Facts: *1 kabob equals 192 calories, 5 g fat (2 g saturated fat), 88 mg cholesterol, 366 mg sodium, 4 g carbohydrate, trace fiber, 32 g protein.* **Diabetic Exchange:** *4 lean meat.*

"My son fishes for salmon on the Kenai River in Alaska and smokes much of what he catches. My mother passed this recipe on to me to help me find new ways to cook with salmon. Regular salmon also works in this quiche, but the smoked flavor can't be beat!"

—ROSE MARIE CHERVEN ANCHORAGE, ALASKA
Teacher, Anchorage School District, Anchorage, Alaska

Smoked Salmon Quiche

PREP: 30 MINUTES **BAKE:** 35 MINUTES + STANDING
MAKES: 8 SERVINGS

- 1 **sheet refrigerated pie pastry**
- 1 **cup (4 ounces) shredded reduced-fat Swiss cheese**
- 1 **tablespoon all-purpose flour**
- 3 **plum tomatoes, seeded and chopped**
- 2 **tablespoons finely chopped onion**
- 2 **teaspoons canola oil**
- 3 **ounces smoked salmon fillets, flaked (about ½ cup)**
- 4 **eggs**
- 1 **cup whole milk**
- ¼ **teaspoon salt**

1. On a lightly floured surface, unroll pastry. Transfer to a 9-in. pie plate. Trim pastry to ½ in. beyond edge of plate; flute edges.

2. In a small bowl, combine cheese and flour. Transfer to pastry.

3. In a large skillet, saute tomatoes and onion in oil just until tender. Remove from the heat; stir in salmon. Spoon over cheese mixture.

4. In a small bowl, whisk the eggs, milk and salt. Pour into pastry. Bake at 350° for 35-40 minutes or until a knife inserted near the center comes out clean. Let stand for 15 minutes before cutting.

Nutrition Facts: *1 piece equals 235 calories, 13 g fat (5 g saturated fat), 122 mg cholesterol, 348 mg sodium, 17 g carbohydrate, trace fiber, 12 g protein.* **Diabetic Exchanges:** *2 medium-fat meat, 1 starch.*

> "This was my mother's recipe and is a nice way to incorporate eggplant into a meal. The thick, chunky sauce is splendid. I like to have it with a glass of red wine, crusty Italian bread and a tossed salad."
> —**JEAN LAWRENCE** ROCHESTER, NEW YORK
> *Staff, Cathedral School at Holy Rosary, Rochester, New York*

Pasta with Eggplant Sauce

PREP: 35 MINUTES **COOK:** 15 MINUTES
MAKES: 6 SERVINGS

- 1 **large eggplant, cut into 1-inch cubes**
- ½ **cup finely chopped onion**
- 2 **tablespoons minced fresh parsley**
- 1 **garlic clove, chopped**
- ¼ **cup olive oil**
- 1 **can (14½ ounces) Italian stewed tomatoes, cut up**
- ½ **cup dry red wine or chicken broth**
- 1 **can (6 ounces) Italian tomato paste**
- 1 **can (4½ ounces) sliced mushrooms, drained**
- 1 **teaspoon sugar**
- 1 **teaspoon dried oregano**
- ½ **teaspoon salt**
- ¾ **pound thin spaghetti**
  Grated Parmesan cheese

1. In a Dutch oven, saute the eggplant, onion, parsley and garlic in oil until tender.

2. Stir in tomatoes, wine, tomato paste, mushrooms, sugar, oregano and salt. Bring to a boil. Reduce heat; simmer, uncovered, for 10-15 minutes or until thickened, stirring occasionally.

3. Meanwhile, cook pasta according to the package directions. Drain pasta. Serve with sauce. Sprinkle with cheese.

Nutrition Facts: *¾ cup pasta with ⅔ cup sauce (calculated without Parmesan cheese) equals 385 calories, 11 g fat (1 g saturated fat), 0 cholesterol, 782 mg sodium, 61 g carbohydrate, 7 g fiber, 11 g protein.*

Chicken & Tortellini Spinach Salad

Not only is this attractive salad easy to make, but it is delicious, light and satisfying.

—**MICHELLE ASHTON** ST. JOHNS, ARIZONA

PREP: 25 MINUTES **COOK:** 15 MINUTES
MAKES: 9 SERVINGS

- 2 **packages (9 ounces each) refrigerated cheese tortellini**
- 2 **packages (6 ounces each) fresh baby spinach**
- 1 **package (22 ounces) frozen grilled chicken breast strips, cut into 1-inch pieces**
- 12 **slices red onion, halved**
- 1 **cup dried cranberries**
- 1 **cup (4 ounces) crumbled feta cheese**

BALSAMIC VINAIGRETTE
- ⅓ **cup olive oil**
- ⅓ **cup balsamic vinegar**
- 1 **tablespoon tomato paste**
- 2 **garlic cloves, minced**
- 1 **teaspoon dried oregano**
- ⅛ **teaspoon salt**
- ⅛ **teaspoon pepper**
- ¼ **cup grated Parmesan cheese**

1. In a large saucepan, cook tortellini according to package directions. Meanwhile, in a large bowl, combine the spinach, chicken, onion, cranberries and feta cheese. Drain pasta. Cool for 5 minutes. Add to spinach mixture.

2. For vinaigrette, in a small bowl, whisk oil, vinegar, tomato paste, garlic, oregano, salt and pepper. Pour over spinach mixture; gently toss to coat. Sprinkle with Parmesan cheese.

Nutrition Facts: *2 cups salad equals 432 calories, 17 g fat (6 g saturated fat), 74 mg cholesterol, 820 mg sodium, 43 g carbohydrate, 4 g fiber, 30 g protein.* **Diabetic Exchanges:** *3 lean meat, 2½ starch, 1½ fat, 1 vegetable.*

> I am a librarian and intervention aide for kindergarten through third grade. I am very proud of the school's reading achievements. We are a 'Reading First' school and have been very successful with the program!

—**MICHELLE ASHTON** ST. JOHNS, ARIZONA
Staff, Coronado Elementary School, St. Johns, Arizona

Lime-Cilantro Marinade for Chicken

This marinade is low-calorie and low-sodium. It is wonderful for chicken, but you can also use it on pork or fish.

—ROZ WALTON AUBURN, MAINE
Staff, Auburn School Department, Auburn, Maine

PREP: 5 MINUTES + MARINATING **GRILL:** 10 MINUTES
MAKES: 6 SERVINGS

- ½ cup minced fresh cilantro
- ¼ cup lime juice
- ¼ cup orange juice
- ¼ cup olive oil
- 1 tablespoon chopped shallot
- 1 teaspoon dried minced garlic
- 1 teaspoon pepper
- ⅛ teaspoon salt
- 6 boneless skinless chicken breast halves (5 ounces each)

1. In a blender, combine the first eight ingredients; cover and process until smooth. Place marinade in a large resealable plastic bag. Add the chicken; seal bag and turn to coat. Refrigerate for at least 2 hours.

2. Drain and discard marinade. Moisten a paper towel with cooking oil; using long-handled tongs, lightly coat the grill rack. Grill chicken, covered, over medium heat or broil 4 in. from the heat for 5-7 minutes on each side or until a thermometer reads 170°.

Nutrition Facts: *1 chicken breast half equals 175 calories, 6 g fat (1 g saturated fat), 78 mg cholesterol, 80 mg sodium, 1 g carbohydrate, trace fiber, 29 g protein.* **Diabetic Exchanges:** *4 lean meat, ½ fat.*

Apple-Spice Angel Food Cake

PREP: 10 MINUTES **BAKE:** 35 MINUTES + COOLING
MAKES: 16 SERVINGS

- 1 package (16 ounces) angel food cake mix
- 1 cup water
- ⅔ cup unsweetened applesauce
- ½ cup finely chopped pecans, toasted
- 1 teaspoon apple pie spice
  Reduced-fat whipped topping and/or apple slices, optional

1. In a large bowl, combine cake mix and water. Beat on low speed for 30 seconds. Beat on medium speed for 1 minute. Fold in the applesauce, pecans and pie spice.

2. Gently spoon into an ungreased 10-in. tube pan. Cut through batter with a knife to remove air pockets. Bake on the lowest oven rack at 350° for 35-45 minutes or until lightly browned and entire top appears dry. Immediately invert pan; cool completely, about 1 hour.

3. Run a knife around side and center tube of pan. Remove cake to a serving plate. Garnish with whipped topping and/or apple slices if desired.

Desserts

❝I dressed up an angel food cake mix with some nuts, spice and applesauce to make an easy and light dessert. I serve it with a dollop of whipped topping mixed with 1/2 cup of sour cream.❞

JOAN BUEHNERKEMPER TEUTOPOLIS, ILLINOIS
Teacher, Altamont Community High School, Altamont, Illinois

Blushing Fruit Tarts with Amaretto Truffle Sauce

PREP: 40 MINUTES + CHILLING
BAKE: 25 MINUTES + COOLING **MAKES:** 4 TARTS

- 2 **cups all-purpose flour**
- 3 **tablespoons sugar**
  Dash salt
- ¾ **cup unsalted butter, cubed**
- 2 **egg yolks, beaten**
- ¼ **cup chopped almonds**
- 3 **tablespoons coarse sugar**

FILLING

- ½ **cup chopped dried apricots**
- ½ **cup dried cranberries**
- ½ **cup dried cherries**
- 1 **tablespoon sugar**
- 1 **cup amaretto, divided**
- 1¼ **cups fresh or frozen blueberries**
- 2 **teaspoons cornstarch**

SAUCE

- 1 **cup white baking chips**
- ½ **cup heavy whipping cream**
- 3 **tablespoons amaretto**

1. Place the flour, sugar and salt in a food processor. Cover and pulse until blended. Add butter; pulse until mixture resembles coarse crumbs. While processing, gradually add egg yolks until dough forms a ball. Divide dough into five portions; wrap each portion in plastic wrap. Refrigerate for 30 minutes or until easy to handle.

2. Roll out four portions into 6-in. circles. Press into 4-in. fluted tart pans with removable bottoms. Trim edges. Line unpricked pastry shells with a double thickness of heavy-duty foil. Fill with dried beans, uncooked rice or pie weights. Place on a baking sheet.

3. Bake at 400° for 8 minutes. Remove foil and weights; bake 4 minutes longer. Cool on a wire rack. Meanwhile, crumble remaining pastry; toss with almonds and sugar. Set aside.

4. In a small saucepan, combine the apricots, cranberries, cherries, sugar and ¾ cup amaretto. Bring to a boil. Add blueberries; cook 10 minutes longer. Combine cornstarch and remaining amaretto until smooth. Gradually stir into pan. Bring to a boil; cook and stir for 2 minutes or until thickened.

5. Pour into crusts; sprinkle with crumbled pastry. Bake at 400° 10-15 minutes longer or until topping is golden brown. Cool on a wire rack.

6. Place baking chips in a small bowl. In a small saucepan, bring cream just to a boil. Pour over chips; whisk until smooth. Stir in amaretto. Cool, stirring occasionally. Drizzle over tarts.

Editor's Note: *Let pie weights cool before storing. Beans and rice may be reused for pie weights, but not for cooking.*

> ❝I love to see my students discover the trials and triumphs of cooking. Some students have misread a recipe and used 1/4 cup of garlic powder instead of 1/4 teaspoon!❞

—**DENISE POUNDS** HUTCHINSON, KANSAS
Educational Aide for Family and Consumer Sciences, Hutchinson Middle School 7, Hutchinson, Kansas

"I took this wonderful tart into school for a potluck we had during homecoming. I work with fourth graders and we typically eat at staggered times starting with kindergarten and working our way up to fourth grade. By the time I got to eat lunch, the tart was gone but there was a note left telling me how good it was."

—**DIANNA WARA** WASHINGTON, ILLINOIS
Staff, Lincoln Grade School, Washington, Illinois

Orange & Blackberry Panther Tart

PREP: 25 MINUTES **BAKE:** 35 MINUTES + COOLING
MAKES: 10 SERVINGS

- 1 **sheet refrigerated pie pastry**
- 1 **package (8 ounces) cream cheese, softened**
- 3 **tablespoons confectioners' sugar**
- 2 **tablespoons orange marmalade**
- 3 **cups fresh blackberries**
- ½ **cup macadamia nuts, finely chopped**
- 3 **tablespoons sugar**
- 1 **tablespoon all-purpose flour**
- 1 **tablespoon butter, melted**
- ½ **cup white baking chips**
- ½ **teaspoon shortening**
- ¼ **teaspoon apple pie spice**

1. On a lightly floured surface, roll dough into a 12-in. circle. Transfer to a parchment paper-lined baking sheet.

2. In a small bowl, combine the cream cheese, confectioners' sugar and marmalade. Spread over the pastry to within 1¼ in. of edges. Top with blackberries to within 1 in. of cream cheese edge. Fold up edges of pastry over filling, leaving center uncovered.

3. In a small bowl, combine the nuts, sugar, flour and butter; sprinkle over blackberries. Bake at 400° for 35-40 minutes or until crust is golden and filling is bubbly. Using the parchment paper, slide tart onto a wire rack to cool.

4. In a microwave, melt the white baking chips and shortening; stir until smooth. Stir in apple pie spice. Drizzle over tart.

"During the school year, I teach third grade. But in the summer, I work as a crew member of a replica privateer schooner. One fall, as my new students and I were getting to know one another, I told the class I worked on a ship, the kind of ship you see in pirate movies. I jokingly told them that I was a pirate. It wasn't until parent-teacher conferences when a parent said, 'So, Ms. Jackson, you're a pirate too? How do you find the time?' that I realized the students had believed me."

—NICHOLE JACKSON BEVERLY, MASSACHUSETTS
Teacher, L.D. Batchelder School, North Reading, Massachusetts

Brandy Pear Pie

I tapped into my French heritage for this recipe by incorporating Calvados, an apple brandy from the Normandy region of France. The sweet filling is balanced out by a buttery crust, making for an indulgent treat.

—NICHOLE JACKSON BEVERLY, MASSACHUSETTS

PREP: 1 HOUR 20 MINUTES
BAKE: 50 MINUTES + COOLING **MAKES:** 8 SERVINGS

2½ cups all-purpose flour
½ teaspoon salt
1 cup cold butter
½ cup ice water

FILLING

1 cup raisins
½ cup apple brandy
½ cup sugar
¼ cup all-purpose flour
½ teaspoon ground cinnamon
¼ teaspoon salt
¼ teaspoon ground nutmeg
4 cups cubed peeled fresh pears
2 tablespoons lemon juice
2 tablespoons butter

1. In a large bowl, combine flour and salt; cut in butter until crumbly. Gradually add water, tossing with a fork until a ball forms. Divide dough in half so that one portion is slightly larger than the other; wrap each in plastic wrap. Refrigerate for at least 1 hour or until easy to handle.

2. Meanwhile, in a small saucepan over low heat, cook raisins in brandy for 13-15 minutes or until raisins are plump. Strain, reserving liquid. Set raisins aside.

3. In a large bowl, combine the sugar, flour, cinnamon, salt and nutmeg. Add the pears, lemon juice, raisins and ½ teaspoon of reserved liquid.

4. On a lightly floured surface, roll out larger portion of dough to fit a 9-in. pie plate. Transfer pastry to pie plate. Trim pastry even with edges. Add pear filling; dot with butter.

5. Roll out remaining pastry to fit top of pie. Place over filling. Trim, seal and flute edges. Cut slits in pastry. Cover edges loosely with foil.

6. Bake at 400° for 45-55 minutes or until bubbly. Cool on a wire rack for at least 30 minutes.

Brownie Waffle Sundaes

PREP/TOTAL TIME: 30 MINUTES
MAKES: 8 WAFFLES

  2 **ounces unsweetened chocolate, chopped**
1¼ **cups all-purpose flour**
  1 **cup packed brown sugar**
½ **teaspoon salt**
½ **teaspoon baking soda**
¼ **teaspoon ground cinnamon**
  2 **eggs**
½ **cup 2% milk**
¼ **cup canola oil**
  1 **teaspoon vanilla extract**
¼ **cup chopped pecans**
  4 **scoops vanilla ice cream**
¼ **cup chopped pecans, toasted**
    Hot caramel and/or fudge ice cream toppings

1. In a microwave, melt chocolate; stir until smooth. Cool slightly.

2. In a large bowl, combine the flour, brown sugar, salt, baking soda and cinnamon. In another bowl, whisk the eggs, milk, oil and vanilla; stir into dry ingredients until smooth. Stir in pecans and melted chocolate (batter will be thick).

3. Bake in a preheated waffle iron according to manufacturer's directions until golden brown. Serve with ice cream, pecans and ice cream toppings.

❝One of my best friends loves chocolate as much as I do, so these waffle sundaes are one of our top picks for a treat. I make the decadent dessert when we get together to play board games or cards. The crisp chocolate waffles have a hint of cinnamon.❞

—VICKI DUBOIS MILLTOWN, INDIANA
Teacher, Marengo Elementary School, Marengo, Indiana

Grapefruit Layer Cake

PREP: 45 MINUTES **BAKE:** 30 MINUTES + COOLING
MAKES: 16 SERVINGS

OVEN-DRIED CITRUS SLICES
- 2 **grapefruit slices**
- 2 **orange slices**
- 1 **teaspoon sugar**

CAKE
- ¾ **cup butter, softened**
- 1½ **cups sugar**
- 2 **eggs**
- 1 **teaspoon vanilla extract**
- ½ **teaspoon grated lemon peel**
- 3 **cups cake flour**
- 3 **teaspoons baking powder**
- ¾ **teaspoon salt**
- ¼ **teaspoon baking soda**
- ¾ **cup 2% milk**
- ½ **cup white grapefruit juice**

FROSTING
- 3 **packages (two 8 ounces, one 3 ounces) cream cheese, softened**
- 2 **tablespoons butter, softened**
- 8 **cups confectioners' sugar**
- 2 **tablespoons plus 2 teaspoons grated grapefruit peel**
- 2 **teaspoons grated lemon peel**
- 2 **teaspoons grated orange peel**
- ½ **teaspoon vanilla extract**

1. Place grapefruit and orange slices on a greased and foil-lined baking sheet. Sprinkle with sugar. Bake at 170° for about 2 hours or until dried (fruit will be slightly tacky). Remove to wire racks. Let stand for 2-3 days or until completely dried.

2. In a large bowl, cream butter and sugar until light and fluffy, about 5 minutes. Add eggs, one at a time, beating well after each addition. Stir in vanilla and lemon peel; mix well. Combine the flour, baking powder, salt and baking soda; add to creamed mixture alternately with milk and grapefruit juice. Beat just until combined.

3. Transfer to two greased and floured 9-in. round baking pans. Bake at 350° for 21-24 minutes or until a toothpick inserted near the center comes out clean. Cool for 10 minutes before removing to wire racks to cool completely.

4. In a large bowl, beat cream cheese and butter until fluffy. Add the confectioners' sugar, citrus peels and vanilla; beat until smooth.

5. Cut each cake horizontally into two layers. Spread frosting between layers and over top and sides of cake. Garnish with citrus slices.

"I grew up in Florida where we were constantly trying to use citrus fruit in different ways. This luscious cake was one of my 'grapefruit experiments.' A nice, bright citrus taste shines through in every moist bite."

—**SARA PLESO** SPARTA, TENNESSEE

> "Both my boys, who have food allergies, really love these cupcakes! Because it is budget-friendly, I make my own oat flour by grinding whole oats in my blender."
> —**DESIREE GLANZER** CARPENTER, SOUTH DAKOTA

Gluten-Free Chocolate Cupcakes

PREP: 15 MINUTES **BAKE:** 20 MINUTES + COOLING
MAKES: 1 DOZEN

- 2 **cups gluten-free oat flour**
- 1 **cup sugar**
- ¼ **cup baking cocoa**
- 1 **teaspoon baking soda**
- ½ **teaspoon salt**
- 1 **cup water**
- ⅓ **cup canola oil**
- 1 **teaspoon cider vinegar**
- ½ **teaspoon vanilla extract**
- 2 **teaspoons confectioners' sugar**

1. In a large bowl, combine the flour, sugar, cocoa, baking soda and salt. In another bowl, combine the water, oil, vinegar and vanilla. Stir into dry ingredients just until moistened.

2. Fill paper-lined muffin cups three-fourths full. Bake at 350° for 20-25 minutes or until a toothpick inserted near the center comes out clean. Cool for 10 minutes before removing from pan to a wire rack to cool completely. Dust with confectioners' sugar.

Editor's Note: *Read all ingredient labels for possible gluten content prior to use. Ingredient formulas can change, and production facilities vary among brands. If you're concerned that your brand may contain gluten, contact the company.*

"This splurge dessert is the kind you just have to linger over. There is nothing better than a chocolate cake with a warm melted center."

—DEB CARPENTER HASTINGS, MICHIGAN
Staff, Hastings Area School System, Hastings, Michigan

Spiced Chocolate Molten Cakes

PREP/TOTAL TIME: 30 MINUTES **MAKES:** 2 SERVINGS

¼ cup butter, cubed
2 ounces semisweet chocolate, chopped
1½ teaspoons dry red wine
½ teaspoon vanilla extract
1 egg
2 teaspoons egg yolk
½ cup confectioners' sugar
3 tablespoons all-purpose flour
⅛ teaspoon ground ginger
⅛ teaspoon ground cinnamon
Additional confectioners' sugar

1. In a microwave, melt butter and chocolate; stir until smooth. Stir in wine and vanilla.

2. In a small bowl, beat the egg, egg yolk and confectioners' sugar until thick and lemon-colored. Beat in the flour, ginger and cinnamon until well blended. Gradually beat in butter mixture.

3. Transfer to two greased 6-oz. ramekins or custard cups. Place ramekins on a baking sheet. Bake at 425° for 10-12 minutes or until a thermometer inserted near the center reads 160° and sides of cakes are set.

4. Remove from the oven and let stand for 1 minute. Run a knife around edges of ramekins; invert onto dessert plates. Dust with additional confectioners' sugar. Serve immediately.

2. In a food processor, cover and pulse pineapple until almost smooth. Stir into batter. Transfer to three greased and floured 9-in. round baking pans. Bake at 350° for 20-25 minutes or until a toothpick inserted near the center comes out clean.

3. Cool for 10 minutes before removing from pans to wire racks to cool completely.

4. For frosting, in a large bowl, beat butter until fluffy. Beat in the confectioners' sugar, extract and enough water to achieve a spreading consistency.

5. To assemble, place one cake layer on a serving plate; spread with half of the preserves. Repeat layers. Top with remaining cake layer. Frost top and sides. Garnish with pineapple slices and coconut if desired.

Pina Colada Cake

As an avid baker, I wanted to create something that was mine and from the heart—a cake that tasted just like the perfect pina colada drink. I feel like I accomplished just that with this recipe.

—**STEPHANIE MCSHAN** APOPKA, FLORIDA

PREP: 35 MINUTES **BAKE:** 20 MINUTES + COOLING
MAKES: 12 SERVINGS

- 1 **cup butter, softened**
- 2 **cups sugar**
- 6 **eggs**
- 1 **teaspoon coconut extract**
- 3 **cups all-purpose flour**
- 1 **teaspoon baking powder**
- ½ **teaspoon baking soda**
- 1 **cup (8 ounces) sour cream**
- 1 **can (8 ounces) crushed pineapple, undrained**

FROSTING
- 1 **cup butter, softened**
- 4 **cups confectioners' sugar**
- 2 **teaspoons coconut extract**
- 3 **to 4 tablespoons water**

FILLING
- 1 **jar (18 ounces) pineapple preserves**
  Dried pineapple slices and toasted coconut, optional

1. In a large bowl, cream butter and sugar until light and fluffy. Add eggs, one at a time, beating well after each addition. Beat in extract. Combine the flour, baking powder and baking soda; add to the creamed mixture alternately with sour cream, beating well after each addition.

> ❝The best part of being a family intervention specialist at Hiawassee Elementary is the opportunity to positively influence the lives of the entire school body. I also use my love of baking to make a difference in the lives of those closest to me. Cooking is a passion that I have always held deep in my heart. I love representing my school with something I love as much as I love working with the kids.❞

—**STEPHANIE MCSHAN** APOPKA, FLORIDA
Teacher, Hiawassee Elementary School, Orlando, Florida

¼ teaspoon cream of tartar
1 teaspoon vanilla extract
2 cups unsalted butter, softened
⅓ cup creamy peanut butter

1. In a large bowl, combine the first six ingredients. Whisk the buttermilk, coffee, oil, eggs and vanilla until blended; add to dry ingredients. (Batter will be very thin.) Fill paper-lined muffin cups two-thirds full.

2. Bake at 350° for 18-20 minutes or until a toothpick comes out clean. Cool 10 minutes; remove from pans. Cool completely.

3. In a bowl, cream the peanut butter, butter, confectioners' sugar and enough milk to achieve piping consistency. Cut a small hole in the corner of a pastry or plastic bag; insert a small round tip and fill with peanut butter mix. Insert tip into top center of each cupcake; pipe about 1 tablespoon filling into each.

4. Place chocolate chips in a small bowl. Heat cream just to a boil. Pour over chips. Whisk until smooth. Dip top of each cupcake into ganache; place on wire racks to set.

5. In a large heavy saucepan, combine the brown sugar, egg whites, salt and cream of tartar over low heat. With a hand mixer, beat on low speed for 1 minute. Continue beating on low over low heat until frosting reaches 160°, about 8-10 minutes. Pour into a large bowl; add vanilla. Beat on high until stiff peaks form, about 5 minutes.

6. Add butter, 1 tablespoon at a time; beat well after each addition. If mixture begins to look curdled, place frosting bowl in another bowl filled with hot water for a few seconds. Continue adding butter and beating until smooth. Beat in peanut butter until smooth.

7. Place frosting in a pastry or plastic bag with large star tip; pipe onto each cupcake. Store in an airtight container in the refrigerator. Let stand at room temperature before serving.

GRAND PRIZE

Chocolate Ganache Peanut Butter Cupcakes

I've been baking cakes for years and enjoy trying new combinations of flavors. One day I decided to blend peanut butter and chocolate. As soon as I took the first bite, I knew I had created something divine!

—RONDA SCHABES VICKSBURG, MICHIGAN

PREP: 55 MINUTES **BAKE:** 20 MINUTES + COOLING
MAKES: 2 DOZEN

2 cups sugar
1¾ cups all-purpose flour
¾ cup baking cocoa
½ teaspoon salt
½ teaspoon baking soda
½ teaspoon baking powder
1 cup buttermilk
1 cup strong brewed coffee, room temperature
½ cup canola oil
2 eggs
1 teaspoon vanilla extract

FILLING
½ cup creamy peanut butter
3 tablespoons unsalted butter, softened
1 cup confectioners' sugar
2 to 4 tablespoons 2% milk

GANACHE
2 cups (12 ounces) semisweet chocolate chips
½ cup heavy whipping cream

PEANUT BUTTER FROSTING
1 cup packed brown sugar
4 egg whites
¼ teaspoon salt

> 66Working as the office aide at Sunset Lake Elementary School is special because my daughters and I were once students there.99

—RONDA SCHABES VICKSBURG, MICHIGAN
Staff, Sunset Lake Elementary School, Vicksburg, Michigan

Mocha Chocolate Chip Cheesecake

My mom was known for outstanding desserts, which she served often. One bite of this chocolaty cheesecake brings me back to those special times.

—**CARA LANGER** OVERLAND PARK, KANSAS

PREP: 1 HOUR **BAKE:** 1 HOUR + CHILLING
MAKES: 16 SERVINGS

- 1½ cups chocolate wafer crumbs
- ⅓ cup sugar
- 6 tablespoons butter, melted

FILLING

- ½ cup heavy whipping cream
- 1 tablespoon instant coffee granules
- 3 packages (8 ounces each) cream cheese, softened
- 1 cup sugar
- 1 teaspoon vanilla extract
- 3 eggs, lightly beaten
- 1 cup (6 ounces) miniature semisweet chocolate chips, divided

1. Place a greased 9-in. springform pan on a double thickness of heavy-duty foil (about 18 in. square). Securely wrap foil around pan.

2. In a large bowl, combine the wafer crumbs, sugar and butter. Press onto the bottom of prepared pan.

3. In a small saucepan, combine cream and coffee granules. Cook and stir until granules are dissolved; set aside to cool.

4. In a large bowl, beat cream cheese and sugar until smooth. Beat in coffee mixture and vanilla. Add eggs; beat on low speed just until combined. Fold in ¾ cup chocolate chips; pour into crust. Sprinkle with remaining chips. Place springform pan in a large baking pan; add 1 in. of hot water to larger pan.

5. Bake at 325° for 60-70 minutes or until center is just set and top appears dull. Remove springform pan from water bath. Cool on a wire rack for 10 minutes. Carefully run a knife around edge of pan to loosen; cool 1 hour longer. Refrigerate overnight. Remove sides of pan.

"The combination of tart canned cherries and dried cherries makes this pie so yummy. It just might be the best cherry pie I have ever tasted!"

—JERRI GRADERT LINCOLN, NEBRASKA
Teacher, Kahoa Elementary School, Lincoln, Nebraska

Double Cherry Pie

PREP: 25 MINUTES **BAKE:** 45 MINUTES + COOLING
MAKES: 8 SERVINGS

- **3** cans (14½ ounces each) pitted tart cherries, undrained
- **1** cup dried cherries
- **½** teaspoon almond extract
- **1** cup sugar
- **¼** cup cornstarch
- **¼** teaspoon salt
- **¼** teaspoon ground nutmeg
  Pastry for double-crust pie (9 inches)
- **1** tablespoon butter

1. Drain cherries, reserving 1 cup juice. Set cherries aside. In a small saucepan, combine dried cherries and reserved juice. Bring to a boil; let stand for 5 minutes. Drain and set aside to cool.

2. In a large bowl, combine the tart cherries, dried cherries and extract. In a small bowl, combine the sugar, cornstarch, salt and nutmeg. Add to cherry mixture; toss to coat.

3. Divide dough in half so that one portion is slightly larger than the other. Roll out larger portion to fit a 9-in. pie plate. Transfer pastry to pie plate. Trim pastry even with edges. Pour filling into crust. Dot with butter.

4. Roll out remaining pastry to fit top of pie. Place over filling. Trim, seal and flute edges. Cut slits in pastry. Bake at 375° for 40-45 minutes or until crust is golden brown and filling is bubbly. Cover edges with foil during the last 30 minutes to prevent overbrowning if necessary. Cool on a wire rack.

Orange Sandwich Cookies

PREP: 30 MINUTES **BAKE:** 10 MINUTES/BATCH + COOLING
MAKES: 28 COOKIES

- 1   cup butter, softened
- 4   ounces cream cheese, softened
- 1¾ cups confectioners' sugar
- ½   cup thawed orange juice concentrate
- 4   teaspoons grated orange peel
- ½   teaspoon vanilla extract
- 2½ cups all-purpose flour
- ½   teaspoon baking soda
- ¼   teaspoon salt
- 10 drops yellow plus 2 drops red food coloring
     Additional confectioners' sugar

FILLING

- ½   cup butter, softened
- 4   ounces cream cheese, softened
- ¼   teaspoon vanilla extract
- 2   cups confectioners' sugar
- 1   tablespoon orange juice concentrate
- ⅛   teaspoon grated orange peel

1. In a large bowl, cream butter and cream cheese until light and fluffy. Gradually beat in confectioners' sugar. Beat in the orange juice concentrate, peel and vanilla. Combine the flour, baking soda and salt; gradually add to creamed mixture and mix well. Stir in food coloring. (Dough will be soft.)

2. Drop by rounded tablespoonfuls 3 in. apart onto ungreased baking sheets. Flatten slightly with a glass dipped in confectioners' sugar.

3. Bake at 400° for 6-9 minutes or until edges begin to brown. Remove to wire racks to cool completely.

4. For filling, in a small bowl, cream the butter, cream cheese and vanilla until light and fluffy. Gradually beat in confectioners' sugar. Add orange juice concentrate and peel.

5. Spread filling over half of the cookies; top with remaining cookies. Store in the refrigerator.

❝These cookies taste just like the orange Creamsicle treats you remember as a kid. Soft orange cookies are filled with a buttery smooth filling.❞

—**BENITA VILLINES** SPRING HILL, TENNESSEE
Teacher, Lewisburg Middle School, Lewisburg, Tennessee

Devil's Food Cake

PREP: 50 MINUTES **BAKE:** 30 MINUTES + COOLING
MAKES: 12 SERVINGS

- 4 **egg whites**
- ½ **cup butter, softened**
- 1¾ **cups sugar**
- 1 **teaspoon vanilla extract**
- 2 **cups all-purpose flour**
- ½ **cup baking cocoa**
- ½ **teaspoon baking soda**
- ¼ **teaspoon salt**
- 1 **cup water**

PUDDING

- 1 **cup sugar**
- ¼ **cup all-purpose flour**
- ½ **teaspoon salt**
- 2 **cups 2% milk**
- 2 **egg yolks, beaten**
- 3 **ounces unsweetened chocolate, chopped**
- 1 **tablespoon butter**
- 1 **teaspoon vanilla extract**

FROSTING

- 1 **cup sugar**
- 3 **egg whites**
- 3 **tablespoons cold water**
- 2 **tablespoons light corn syrup**
- ½ **teaspoon cream of tartar**
- ⅛ **teaspoon salt**
- 1 **teaspoon vanilla extract**

1. Place egg whites in a large bowl; let stand at room temperature for 30 minutes. Meanwhile, in a large bowl, cream butter and sugar until light and fluffy. Beat in vanilla. Combine the flour, cocoa, baking soda and salt; add to the creamed mixture alternately with water, beating well after each addition.

2. Beat egg whites with clean beaters until stiff peaks form; fold into batter. Transfer to a greased 13-in. x 9-in. baking pan. Bake at 350° for 30-35 minutes or until a toothpick inserted near the center comes out clean. Cool on a wire rack.

3. For pudding, in a large heavy saucepan, combine the sugar, flour and salt. Stir in milk until smooth. Cook and stir over medium-high heat until thickened and bubbly. Reduce heat to low; cook and stir 2 minutes longer. Remove from the heat.

4. Stir a small amount of hot mixture into egg yolks; return all to the pan, stirring constantly. Bring to a gentle boil; cook and stir 2 minutes longer. Remove from the heat. Stir in chocolate until smooth. Stir in butter and vanilla. Cool to room temperature, stirring occasionally. Spread over cake.

5. In a large heavy saucepan, combine the sugar, egg whites, water, corn syrup, cream of tartar and salt over low heat. With a hand mixer, beat on low speed for 1 minute. Continue beating on low over low heat until frosting reaches 160°, about 8-10 minutes.

6. Pour into a large bowl; add vanilla. Beat on high until stiff peaks form, about 7 minutes. Spread over cake. Store in the refrigerator.

❝This is my grandmother's homemade chocolate cake. I remember enjoying it with her whenever she came for a visit. The creamy chocolate custard filling makes it so good.❞

—**BONNIE CAPPER-ECKSTEIN** MAPLE GROVE, MINNESOTA
Teacher, Palmer Lake Elementary, Brooklyn Park, Minnesota

"Cake rolls make a lovely presentation for a party, and they are simple to cut into even slices. My father taught me how to make them, and sometimes we get together and make them for family and friends."
—**MALENA COLEMAN** ROCKFIELD, INDIANA
Staff, Southwest Parke Community Schools, Montezuma, Indiana

Peaches & Cream Jelly Roll

PREP: 20 MINUTES **BAKE:** 10 MINUTES + CHILLING
MAKES: 12 SERVINGS

- **3 eggs**
- **¼ teaspoon vanilla extract**
- **⅛ teaspoon salt**
- **¾ cup sugar**
- **¾ cup biscuit/baking mix**
- **1 cup heavy whipping cream**
- **¼ cup confectioners' sugar, divided**
- **3 cups chopped peeled fresh peaches**

1. Line a greased 15-in. x 10-in. x 1-in. baking pan with waxed paper and grease the paper; sprinkle with flour and set aside.

2. In a bowl, beat eggs on high speed for 3 minutes. Beat in vanilla and salt. Gradually add sugar, beating until mixture becomes thick and lemon-colored. Fold in biscuit mix. Spread in prepared pan.

3. Bake at 375° for 8-10 minutes or until cake springs back when lightly touched. Cool for 5 minutes. Invert onto a kitchen towel dusted with confectioners' sugar. Gently peel off waxed paper. Roll up cake in the towel jelly-roll style, starting with a short side. Cool completely on a wire rack.

4. For filling, in a small bowl, beat cream until it begins to thicken. Add 3 tablespoons confectioners' sugar; beat until stiff peaks form.

5. Unroll cake; spread half of whipped cream over cake to within ½ in. of edges. Top with peaches and remaining whipped cream. Roll up again. Place seam side down on a serving platter. Dust with remaining confectioners' sugar. Refrigerate for 2 hours.

Almond Cake with Raspberry Sauce

For such a simple cake, the taste is surprisingly delectable and the appearance very elegant. The drizzle of raspberry sauce not only adds to the enjoyment of the dessert, but makes it look beautiful on the plate.

—**JOAN SULLIVAN** GAMBRILLS, MARYLAND

PREP: 30 MINUTES **BAKE:** 40 MINUTES + COOLING
MAKES: 12 SERVINGS (¼ CUP SAUCE)

- 1   **can (8 ounces) almond paste**
- ¾   **cup plus 1 tablespoon sugar, divided**
- ½   **cup butter, softened**
- 3   **eggs, lightly beaten**
- 1   **tablespoon orange liqueur**
- ¼   **teaspoon almond extract**
- ¼   **cup all-purpose flour**
- ¼   **teaspoon plus ⅛ teaspoon baking powder**
- ¼   **cup confectioners' sugar**
- 1   **package (10 ounces) frozen sweetened raspberries, thawed**

1. Line an 8-in. round baking pan with parchment paper; coat paper with cooking spray and set aside.

2. In a large bowl, combine the almond paste, ¾ cup sugar and butter; beat for 2 minutes until blended. Beat in the eggs, liqueur and extract. Combine flour and baking powder; add to creamed mixture just until combined.

3. Spread into prepared pan. Bake at 350° for 40-45 minutes or until a toothpick inserted near center comes out clean. Cool completely on a wire rack.

4. Invert cake onto cake plate; remove parchment paper. Sprinkle with confectioners' sugar.

5. Place raspberries in a food processor; cover and process until pureed. Strain, reserving juice; discard the seeds.

6. In a small saucepan over medium heat, cook raspberry juice and remaining sugar for 15-18 minutes or until mixture is reduced to ¼ cup. Serve with cake.

Peanut Butter-Chocolate Cheesecake

PREP: 1 HOUR **BAKE:** 1 HOUR + CHILLING
MAKES: 12 SERVINGS

- 32 **Nutter Butter cookies**
- ⅓ **cup butter, melted**
- 4 **packages (8 ounces each) cream cheese, softened**
- 1 **cup sugar**
- 3 **ounces semisweet chocolate, melted**
- 3 **ounces bittersweet chocolate, melted**
- 1 **teaspoon vanilla extract**
- 4 **eggs, lightly beaten**

PEANUT BUTTER MOUSSE

- 1½ **teaspoons unflavored gelatin**
- 2 **tablespoons cold water**
- 1 **cup heavy whipping cream**
- 3 **tablespoons creamy peanut butter**
- 2 **tablespoons sugar**
- 2 **egg yolks**

GARNISH

- 3 **ounces semisweet chocolate, chopped**
  Chocolate curls and sweetened whipped cream, optional

1. Place a greased 9-in. springform pan on a double thickness of heavy-duty foil (about 18 in. square). Securely wrap foil around pan.

2. Place cookies in a food processor; cover and process until fine crumbs. Stir in butter. Press onto the bottom and 2 in. up the sides of prepared pan; set aside.

3. In a large bowl, beat cream cheese and sugar until smooth. Beat in the melted chocolates and vanilla. Add eggs; beat on low speed just until combined. Pour into crust. Place springform pan in a large baking pan; add 1 in. of hot water to larger pan.

4. Bake at 325° for 60-65 minutes or until center is just set and top appears dull. Remove springform pan from water bath. Cool on a wire rack for 10 minutes. Carefully run a knife around edge of pan to loosen; cool 1 hour longer.

5. For peanut butter mousse, sprinkle gelatin over cold water; let stand for 1 minute. Microwave on high for 20-30 seconds. Stir and let stand for 1 minute or until gelatin is dissolved.

6. Meanwhile, in a saucepan, heat the cream, peanut butter and sugar until bubbles form around sides of pan. Whisk a small amount of hot mixture into the egg yolks. Return all to the pan, whisking constantly.

7. Cook and stir over low heat until mixture is thickened and coats the back of a spoon. Stir in gelatin mixture. Quickly transfer to a bowl; place in ice water and stir for 15 minutes or until cold and thickened. Pour over cheesecake. Refrigerate overnight. Remove sides of pan.

8. For garnish, in a microwave, melt chocolate. Drizzle over cheesecake. Garnish with chocolate curls and whipped cream if desired.

> **When I think of this specialty cheesecake, three words come to mind: 'decadent,' 'fun' and 'delicious.' One bite and you'll agree this dessert is pure bliss.**
>
> —**JULIE RUBLE** CHARLOTTE, NORTH CAROLINA
> *Teacher, Woodlawn School, Mooresville, North Carolina*

Lime Muffins with Coconut Streusel

PREP: 30 MINUTES **BAKE:** 20 MINUTES
MAKES: 1 DOZEN

- 2 **cups all-purpose flour**
- ¾ **cup sugar**
- 1 **teaspoon baking powder**
- ¾ **teaspoon baking soda**
- ½ **teaspoon salt**
- ¾ **cup buttermilk**
- ¾ **cup (6 ounces) key lime yogurt**
- 1 **egg**
- ¼ **cup butter, melted**
- 2 **teaspoons key lime juice**
- 1 **teaspoon grated lime peel**
- 1 **teaspoon vanilla extract**

TOPPING

- 3 **tablespoons sugar**
- 2 **tablespoons all-purpose flour**
- 2 **tablespoons flaked coconut**
- 2 **tablespoons finely chopped macadamia nuts**
- 2 **tablespoons butter, melted**

1. In a large bowl, combine the first five ingredients. In another bowl, combine the buttermilk, yogurt, egg, butter, lime juice, lime peel and vanilla. Stir into dry ingredients just until moistened. Fill greased muffin cups three-fourths full.

2. In a small bowl, combine topping ingredients; sprinkle over muffins. Bake at 375° for 18-22 minutes or until a toothpick inserted into muffin comes out clean. Cool for 5 minutes before removing from pan to a wire rack. Serve warm.

❝Looking for a way to dazzle brunch guests? A dozen of these tempting gems should do the trick. The coconut-macadamia nut streusel is the perfect complement to the fresh lime flavor.❞

—**TERESA GRISSOM** ZIONSVILLE, INDIANA
Staff, Union Elementary School, Zionsville, Indiana

"My family loves the flavor of pumpkin pie, but this is a delicious, creamy, healthier alternative, and we don't miss the crust at all. It firms up as it cools."
—**ABBY BOOTH** COWETA, OKLAHOMA

Pumpkin Pecan Custard

PREP: 20 MINUTES **BAKE:** 35 MINUTES + CHILLING
MAKES: 8 SERVINGS

- 1 **can (15 ounces) solid-pack pumpkin**
- 1 **can (12 ounces) reduced-fat evaporated milk**
- ¾ **cup egg substitute**
- ⅓ **cup packed brown sugar**
- 1½ **teaspoons vanilla extract**
- 1 **teaspoon ground cinnamon**
- ½ **teaspoon ground ginger**
- ¼ **teaspoon ground cloves**
- ⅛ **teaspoon salt**

TOPPING

- 3 **tablespoons all-purpose flour**
- 3 **tablespoons brown sugar**
- ½ **teaspoon ground cinnamon**
- 2 **tablespoons cold butter**
- ½ **cup chopped pecans**

1. In a large bowl, combine the first nine ingredients. Transfer to eight 6-oz. ramekins or custard cups. Place in a baking pan; add 1 in. of boiling water to pan. Bake, uncovered, at 325° for 20 minutes.

2. Meanwhile, for topping, in a small bowl, combine the flour, brown sugar and cinnamon. Cut in butter until crumbly. Stir in pecans. Sprinkle over custard. Bake 15-20 minutes longer or until a knife inserted near the center comes out clean.

3. Remove ramekins from water bath; cool for 10 minutes. Cover and refrigerate for at least 4 hours.

"When I place a pan of these bars in the teachers' lounge and come back after the last bell, the pan is always empty. You'll have the same results at potlucks and other gatherings. The white chips and cranberries make the bars seem extra special."

—**MIRELLA HACKETT** CHANDLER, ARIZONA
Teacher, San Marcos Elementary School, Chandler, Arizona

Cranberry Bars with Cream Cheese Frosting

PREP: 30 MINUTES **BAKE:** 25 MINUTES + COOLING
MAKES: 4 DOZEN

- ¾ **cup butter, softened**
- 1 **cup sugar**
- ¾ **cup sour cream**
- 2 **eggs**
- ½ **teaspoon almond extract**
- ½ **teaspoon vanilla extract**
- 1½ **cups all-purpose flour**
- 1 **teaspoon baking powder**
- ⅛ **teaspoon salt**
- 1 **cup white baking chips**
- 1 **cup dried cranberries**
- ½ **cup chopped walnuts**

FROSTING
- 2 **packages (8 ounces each) cream cheese, softened**
- ¼ **cup butter, softened**
- 2 **cups confectioners' sugar**
- 1 **teaspoon vanilla extract**
- ½ **cup dried cranberries, chopped**

1. In a large bowl, cream butter and sugar until light and fluffy. Beat in the sour cream, eggs and extracts. Combine the flour, baking powder and salt; gradually add to creamed mixture and mix well. Fold in the chips, cranberries and walnuts. Spread into a greased 15-in. x 10-in. x 1-in. baking pan.

2. Bake at 350° for 25-30 minutes or until a toothpick inserted near the center comes out clean. Cool completely on a wire rack.

3. For frosting, in a small bowl, beat cream cheese and butter until fluffy. Add confectioners' sugar and vanilla; beat until smooth. Fold in cranberries. Spread over the top. Cut into bars. Refrigerate leftovers.

Lemon Curd Chiffon Pie

PREP: 30 MINUTES **BAKE:** 10 MINUTES + CHILLING
MAKES: 8 SERVINGS

- 9 whole graham crackers, broken into large pieces
- ½ cup chopped pecans
- 3 tablespoons sugar
- ¼ teaspoon vanilla extract
- ⅛ teaspoon salt
- 5 tablespoons butter, melted

FILLING

- 1½ cups heavy whipping cream
- 3 tablespoons sugar
- 3 teaspoons vanilla extract
- 1 jar (11 ounces) lemon curd
- 1 package (8 ounces) cream cheese, softened
- 1 tablespoon grated lemon peel
- 1½ teaspoons unflavored gelatin
- ⅓ cup lemon juice
- 1 tablespoon limoncello

BERRY SAUCE

- ½ pint fresh raspberries
- ½ pint fresh blueberries
- ½ pint fresh strawberries
- ¼ cup sugar
- 1 tablespoon seedless raspberry jam
- 1 tablespoon lemon juice
- 1 tablespoon raspberry liqueur

1. Place the graham crackers, pecans, sugar, vanilla and salt in a food processor; cover and pulse until mixture resembles fine crumbs. Add the butter; process until blended.

2. Press crumb mixture onto the bottom and up the sides of a greased 9-in. deep-dish pie plate. Bake at 350° for 10-12 minutes or until light golden brown. Cool completely on a wire rack.

3. In a small bowl, combine the cream, sugar and vanilla. Beat until stiff peaks form; set aside. In a large bowl, beat the lemon curd, cream cheese and lemon peel until blended; set aside.

4. Sprinkle gelatin over lemon juice; let stand for 1 minute. Microwave on high for 20 seconds. Stir and let stand for 1 minute or until gelatin is dissolved. Stir in limoncello. Gradually beat into lemon curd mixture until well blended. Fold in whipped cream mixture; pour into the crust. Refrigerate for 3 hours or until set.

5. In a small saucepan over medium heat, combine the berries, sugar and jam. Cook and stir for 3-5 minutes or until fruit is softened. In a blender, cover and process berry mixture for 1-2 minutes or until blended. Strain, reserving juice. Discard seeds.

6. Return juice to the saucepan; cook for 15-18 minutes or until reduced to desired consistency, stirring occasionally. Stir in lemon juice and raspberry liqueur. Chill for 1 hour. Garnish servings with sauce.

❝Although I volunteer in the classroom, I have a special interest in helping in the kitchen, lunchroom and school garden as a way to promote healthy living. My refreshing Lemon Curd Chiffon Pie is deceptively light and incredibly luscious.❞

—CALLIE PALEN-LOWRIE LOUISVILLE, KENTUCKY
Volunteer, Fireside Elementary School, Louisville, Kentucky

Gluten-Free Rhubarb Bars

PREP: 20 MINUTES **BAKE:** 35 MINUTES + COOLING
MAKES: 3 DOZEN

- 2 **cups gluten-free all-purpose baking flour**
- 1 **teaspoon baking powder**
- ½ **cup cold butter**
- 2 **eggs, beaten**
- 3 **tablespoons 2% milk**
- 5 **cups sliced fresh or frozen rhubarb, thawed**
- 1 **package (3 ounces) strawberry gelatin**

TOPPING
- 1 **cup sugar**
- 1 **cup gluten-free all-purpose baking flour**
- ½ **cup cold butter**

1. In a large bowl, combine flour and baking powder. Cut in butter until mixture resembles coarse crumbs. Stir in eggs and milk just until moistened. Press onto the bottom of a 15-in. x 10-in. x 1-in. baking pan coated with cooking spray. Top with rhubarb; sprinkle with gelatin.

2. For topping, in a small bowl, combine sugar and flour. Cut in butter until mixture resembles coarse crumbs. Sprinkle over top. Bake at 375° for 35-40 minutes or until lightly browned. Cool on a wire rack. Cut into bars.

Editor's Note: *Read all ingredient labels for possible gluten content prior to use. Ingredient formulas can change, and production facilities vary among brands. If you're concerned that your brand may contain gluten, contact the company.*

If using frozen rhubarb, measure rhubarb while still frozen, then thaw completely. Drain in a colander, but do not press liquid out.

❝Nothing tastes like spring more than rhubarb and strawberry. The crust and crumb topping on these bars are so tasty, nobody will know they're eating gluten-free.❞

—**LAURA WILSON** VIRGINIA, MINNESOTA

Black Forest Fudge Sauce

PREP/TOTAL TIME: 15 MINUTES
MAKES: 24 SERVINGS (2 TABLESPOONS EACH)

- 2 **cups (16 ounces) sour cream**
- 1 **cup sugar**
- 1 **cup baking cocoa**
- 1 **jar (6 ounces) maraschino cherries, drained and chopped**
- 3 **teaspoons vanilla extract**
- ¼ **teaspoon almond extract**
  Ice cream

1. In a small heavy saucepan, combine the sour cream, sugar and cocoa. Cook and stir over medium-low heat until sugar is dissolved and mixture is smooth. Stir in cherries and extracts. Serve warm over ice cream. Refrigerate leftovers.

"As a fourth-grade teacher at Pendergast Elementary School, I find fulfillment in knowing I'm helping my students reach their greatest potential. I also enjoy baking for my fellow colleagues. If I wasn't a teacher, I would like to own my own bakery."

—**JENNY WEAVER** GLENDALE, ARIZONA
Teacher, Pendergast Elementary School, Phoenix, Arizona

French Toast Cupcakes

PREP: 25 MINUTES **BAKE:** 20 MINUTES + COOLING
MAKES: 1½ DOZEN

- ½ cup butter, softened
- 1½ cups sugar
- 2 eggs
- 2 teaspoons vanilla extract
- 2 cups all-purpose flour
- 2 teaspoons ground cinnamon
- ½ teaspoon baking powder
- ½ teaspoon baking soda
- ¼ teaspoon salt
- ¼ teaspoon ground nutmeg
- 1⅓ cups buttermilk

MAPLE BUTTERCREAM FROSTING

- ½ cup butter, softened
- ¼ cup shortening
- ½ cup maple syrup
- Dash salt
- 2½ cups confectioners' sugar
- 6 bacon strips, cooked and crumbled, optional

1. In a large bowl, cream butter and sugar until light and fluffy. Add eggs, one at a time, beating well after each addition. Beat in vanilla. Combine the flour, cinnamon, baking powder, baking soda, salt and nutmeg; add to the creamed mixture alternately with buttermilk, beating well after each addition.

2. Fill paper-lined muffin cups two-thirds full. Bake at 350° for 17-22 minutes or until a toothpick inserted near the center comes out clean. Cool for 10 minutes before removing from pans to wire racks to cool completely.

3. For frosting, in a small bowl, beat butter and shortening until fluffy. Beat in maple syrup and salt. Add confectioners' sugar; beat until smooth. Frost cupcakes. Sprinkle with bacon if desired.

Chocolate-Filled Cream Puffs

PREP: 40 MINUTES + FREEZING
BAKE: 25 MINUTES/BATCH **MAKES:** 3 DOZEN

- 1 **cup water**
- ½ **cup butter, cubed**
- 1 **cup all-purpose flour**
- 4 **eggs**

CHOCOLATE CREAM FILLING

- ¾ **cup sugar**
- 5 **tablespoons baking cocoa**
- 3 **tablespoons cornstarch**
- ½ **teaspoon salt**
- 2 **cups 2% milk**
- 2 **egg yolks, lightly beaten**
- 1 **tablespoon butter**
- 1 **teaspoon vanilla extract**
  Hot fudge ice cream topping and citrus sugar, white chocolate shavings or confectioners' sugar, optional

1. In a large saucepan, bring water and butter to a boil. Add flour all at once and stir until a smooth ball forms. Remove from the heat; let stand for 5 minutes. Add eggs, one at a time, beating well after each addition. Continue beating until mixture is smooth and shiny.

2. Drop by rounded tablespoonfuls 3 in. apart onto greased baking sheets. Bake at 400° for 20-25 minutes or until golden brown. Remove to wire racks. Immediately split puffs open; remove tops and set aside. Discard soft dough from inside. Cool puffs. Freeze in airtight containers for up to 2 months.

To use frozen cream puffs: Thaw at room temperature for 10 minutes. Place cream puffs on a baking sheet. Bake at 375° for 3-4 minutes or until crisp.

3. For filling, in a large heavy saucepan, combine the sugar, cocoa, cornstarch and salt. Stir in milk until smooth. Cook and stir over medium-high heat until thickened and bubbly. Reduce heat to low; cook and stir 2 minutes longer.

4. Remove from the heat. Stir a small amount of hot mixture into egg yolks; return all to the pan, stirring constantly. Bring to a gentle boil; cook and stir 2 minutes longer. Remove from the heat. Gently stir in butter and vanilla. Cover with waxed paper or plastic wrap. Cool for 15 minutes without stirring.

5. To serve, spoon chocolate cream filling into cream puffs; replace tops. Top with warmed hot fudge sauce and citrus sugar, white chocolate shavings or confectioners' sugar if desired.

Editor's Note: *Citrus sugar can be made by pressing grated citrus peels into sugar to release their oils. Store citrus sugar in an airtight container at room temperature for 2-3 weeks or until the flavor diminishes.*

“I make my cream puffs every year for the birthday of one of our counselors. He adores them, as does everyone else. In fact, I have to triple the batch when I take them to school.”

—DIANA VOLAND MARTINSVILLE, INDIANA
Staff, Martinsville Middle School, Martinsville, Indiana

Chocolate-Coffee Bean Ice Cream Cake

PREP: 15 MINUTES + FREEZING **MAKES:** 12 SERVINGS

1¾ cups chocolate wafer crumbs (about 28 wafers)
¼ cup butter, melted
2 quarts coffee ice cream, softened
⅓ cup chocolate-covered coffee beans, finely chopped
2¼ cups heavy whipping cream
1 cup plus 2 tablespoons confectioners' sugar
½ cup plus 1 tablespoon baking cocoa
½ teaspoon vanilla extract
Chocolate curls and additional chocolate-covered coffee beans

1. In a small bowl, combine wafer crumbs and butter; press onto the bottom and up the sides of a greased 9-in. springform pan. Freeze for 10 minutes.

2. In a large bowl, combine ice cream and coffee beans; spoon over crust. Cover and freeze for 2 hours or until firm.

3. In a large bowl, beat cream until it begins to thicken. Add confectioners' sugar, cocoa and vanilla; beat until stiff peaks form. Spread over ice cream. (Pan will be full.)

4. Cover and freeze for 4 hours or overnight. Remove from the freezer 10 minutes before serving. Garnish with chocolate curls and coffee beans.

66At our school, we celebrate faculty birthdays. I needed a quick recipe that would be appealing to everyone. This tall, impressive dessert certainly fit my needs and was a huge hit with the group.99

—**KAREN BECK** ALEXANDRIA, PENNSYLVANIA

"My grandmother and aunts made this for family gatherings to go along with fresh homemade ice cream. I now share it with my family and friends during special gatherings."

—**KEITH GABLE** GODDARD, KANSAS

Teacher, Oak Street Elementary School, Goddard, Kansas

Family-Favorite Peanut Butter Cake

PREP: 20 MINUTES **BAKE:** 15 MINUTES + COOLING
MAKES: 24 SERVINGS

- ½ cup creamy peanut butter
- 6 tablespoons butter, cubed
- 1 cup water
- 2 cups all-purpose flour
- 1½ cups sugar
- ½ cup buttermilk
- ¼ cup unsweetened applesauce
- 2 eggs, lightly beaten
- 1¼ teaspoons baking powder
- 1 teaspoon vanilla extract
- ½ teaspoon salt
- ¼ teaspoon baking soda

FROSTING

- ¼ cup butter, cubed
- ¼ cup creamy peanut butter
- 2 tablespoons fat-free milk
- 1¾ cups confectioners' sugar
- 1 teaspoon vanilla extract

1. In a large saucepan, bring peanut butter, butter and water just to a boil. Immediately remove from the heat; stir in the flour, sugar, buttermilk, applesauce, eggs, baking powder, vanilla, salt and baking soda until smooth.

2. Pour into a 15-in. x 10-in. x 1-in. baking pan coated with cooking spray. Bake at 375° for 15-20 minutes or until golden brown and a toothpick inserted near the center comes out clean. Cool on a wire rack for 20 minutes.

3. In a small saucepan, melt butter and peanut butter over medium heat; add milk. Bring to a boil. Remove from the heat. Gradually whisk in confectioners' sugar and vanilla until smooth. Spread over warm cake. Cool completely on a wire rack. Refrigerate leftovers.

"Strawberry shortcake is one of my favorite desserts, so I thought it would be great to capture all that wonderful flavor in a cookie. The pastry-like treat is topped with pink strawberry frosting."

—**ALLISON ANDERSON** AVONDALE, ARIZONA

Strawberry Shortcake Cookies

PREP: 35 MINUTES + CHILLING
BAKE: 15 MINUTES/BATCH + COOLING **MAKES:** 2 DOZEN

- 2 **cups all-purpose flour**
- ½ **cup sugar**
  Dash salt
- ⅔ **cup cold butter**
- 2 **tablespoons water**
- 1 **teaspoon vanilla extract**

FROSTING

- ½ **cup butter, softened**
- ¾ **cup fresh strawberries, sliced**
- 2 **tablespoons 2% milk**
- 5 **cups confectioners' sugar**
  Additional sliced fresh strawberries, optional

1. In a large bowl, combine the flour, sugar and salt. Cut in butter until mixture resembles coarse crumbs. Combine water and vanilla; stir into crumb mixture just until moistened. Cover and refrigerate for 1-2 hours or until firm.

2. On a lightly floured surface, roll out to ¼-in. thickness; cut with a floured 3-in. round cookie cutter. Place 1 in. apart on greased baking sheets.

3. Bake at 325° for 15-18 minutes or until lightly browned. Cool for 2 minutes before removing to wire racks to cool completely.

4. In a large bowl, beat the butter, strawberries and milk until combined. Gradually add confectioners' sugar; beat until blended. Spread over cookies; garnish with additional sliced strawberries if desired.

Chocolate Ganache Cake with Raspberry Sauce

"Divine" and "heavenly" are the words that come to mind when I take a bite of this fudgy, luscious cake. Nothing soothes the soul like chocolate.

—LAURA MOORE PRESCOTT, ARIZONA

PREP: 1 HOUR **BAKE:** 25 MINUTES + COOLING
MAKES: 16 SERVINGS

- 2 pounds semisweet chocolate, chopped
- 1¼ cups butter, cubed
- 8 eggs
- ¼ cup all-purpose flour

GANACHE
- 2 cups (12 ounces) semisweet chocolate chips
- ¾ cup heavy whipping cream

SAUCE
- 2 packages (12 ounces each) frozen unsweetened raspberries, thawed
- 1 cup sugar
- 2 tablespoons cornstarch
- 2 tablespoons cold water
- 1 teaspoon orange extract

CHOCOLATE WHIPPED CREAM
- 1 cup heavy whipping cream
- 3 tablespoons sugar
- 2 tablespoons baking cocoa
- ½ teaspoon vanilla extract

1. Grease a 10-in. springform pan and dust with baking cocoa; set aside.

2. In a large saucepan, melt chocolate and butter over medium heat; stir until smooth. Set aside to cool. In a large bowl, beat eggs on medium-high speed for 5 minutes. Using low speed, add the flour, 1 tablespoon at a time. Gradually add chocolate mixture; beat on medium for 2 minutes. Pour into prepared pan.

3. Bake at 350° for 25-28 minutes or just until set. Cool on a wire rack to room temperature. Remove sides of pan and invert onto a serving plate; invert again, so top side is up.

4. For ganache, in a small saucepan over low heat, melt chocolate chips with cream; stir until smooth. Cool until slightly thickened, stirring occasionally. Spread ganache over top of cake, allowing some to drape over the sides.

5. For sauce, in a large saucepan, heat raspberries. Transfer raspberries to a fine mesh strainer over a large bowl. Mash and strain raspberries, reserving juice. Discard seeds.

6. In another saucepan, combine the sugar, cornstarch, water and reserved raspberry juice until smooth. Bring to a boil. Reduce heat to medium; cook and stir for 2-3 minutes or until mixture reaches desired consistency. Stir in orange extract.

7. For whipped cream, in a small bowl, beat cream until it begins to thicken. Add sugar, cocoa and vanilla; beat until soft peaks form. Garnish cake with chocolate whipped cream and sauce.

❝On my first day as the office clerk at WTS, I learned that my best childhood friend taught one of the school's fifth-grade classes. We had lost contact over 35 years ago! It's one reason this school is special to me.❞

—LAURA MOORE PRESCOTT, ARIZONA
Staff, Washington Traditional School, Prescott, Arizona

1. Line three 8-in. round baking pans with parchment paper; coat paper with cooking spray and set aside.

2. In a small bowl, melt chocolate; set aside.

3. In a large bowl, cream butter, sugar and salt until light and fluffy. Add eggs, one at a time, beating well after each addition. Beat in extract. In a small bowl, sift flour and baking powder; add to the creamed mixture alternately with milk, beating well after each addition.

4. Pat peaches dry with paper towels. Fold in the peaches, chocolate and macadamia nuts. Divide among prepared pans.

5. Bake at 350° for 35-40 minutes or until a toothpick inserted near the center comes out clean. Cool for 15 minutes before removing from pans to wire racks to cool completely.

6. For frosting, in a microwave, melt chocolate with cream; cool to room temperature. In a large bowl, cream butter and extract until light and fluffy; add cooled chocolate mixture. Gradually beat in confectioners' sugar.

7. Spread between layers and over top and sides of cake. Sprinkle with coconut and macadamia nuts.

White Chocolate-Coconut Layer Cake

PREP: 25 MINUTES **BAKE:** 35 MINUTES + COOLING
MAKES: 12 SERVINGS

- 8 ounces white baking chocolate, chopped
- ¾ cup butter, softened
- 1½ cups sugar
- ⅛ teaspoon salt
- 4 eggs
- 1 teaspoon coconut extract
- 2½ cups cake flour
- 6 teaspoons baking powder
- 1¼ cups 2% milk
- 1 cup frozen unsweetened sliced peaches, thawed and finely chopped
- ½ cup macadamia nuts, chopped, toasted

FROSTING

- 6 ounces white baking chocolate, chopped
- ¼ cup heavy whipping cream
- 1 cup butter, softened
- ½ teaspoon coconut extract
- 4 cups confectioners' sugar
- 1 cup flaked coconut, toasted
- ¼ cup macadamia nuts, chopped, toasted

"To create this heavenly dessert, I took a recipe I had been making for years and added my own touches. I added fresh peaches and macadamia nuts to the batter and substituted white chocolate for dark. My family gives the results 'thumbs up.'"

—**DARL COLLINS** MARKLEVILLE, INDIANA
Teacher, Blackford High School, Hartford City, Indiana

"This recipe is so special to me because it was passed down from my grandmother to my mother and now to me. This family classic is now often requested for any type of work function."
—LEANN SCHMID COVINGTON, KENTUCKY
Teacher, Camp Ernst Middle School, Burlington, Kentucky

Carrot Cake Cupcakes

PREP: 25 MINUTES **BAKE:** 20 MINUTES + COOLING
MAKES: 28 CUPCAKES

- 2 **cups sugar**
- 1¼ **cups canola oil**
- 3 **eggs**
- 1 **teaspoon vanilla extract**
- 2½ **cups all-purpose flour, divided**
- 2 **teaspoons ground cinnamon**
- 1 **teaspoon baking soda**
- ½ **teaspoon salt**
- 2 **cups grated carrots**
- 1 **can (8 ounces) unsweetened crushed pineapple, undrained**
- 1 **cup raisins**

FROSTING
- 4 **ounces cream cheese, softened**
- ¼ **cup butter, softened**
- 2½ **cups confectioners' sugar**
- 1 **tablespoon 2% milk**

1. In a large bowl, beat the sugar, oil, eggs and vanilla until well blended. Combine 2 cups flour, cinnamon, baking soda and salt; gradually beat into sugar mixture until blended. Stir in carrots and pineapple. Toss the raisins with the remaining flour until coated; fold into batter.

2. Fill paper-lined muffin cups two-thirds full. Bake at 350° for 20-25 minutes or until a toothpick inserted near the center comes out clean. Cool for 10 minutes before removing from pans to wire racks to cool completely.

3. For frosting, in a small bowl, beat cream cheese and butter until fluffy. Add confectioners' sugar and milk; beat until smooth. Frost cupcakes. Refrigerate leftovers.

"This recipe began as a writing assignment between my fifth-grade student, Joey Johnson, and myself. Joey likes to cook, and he and I enjoy talking about recipes. When I got the email about the opportunity to submit a recipe for a *Taste of Home* contest, I challenged Joey to write up a recipe."
—**SHARON BALESTRA** BLOOMFIELD, NEW YORK
Staff, Bloomfield Elementary School, Bloomfield, New York

Full-of-Goodness Oatmeal Cookies

I love to bake, and bring in extra treats to leave in the faculty lounge. To avoid being blamed for ruining their diets, I came up with this healthier version of oatmeal cookies. Snacking on these is a good choice instead of a guilty indulgence.

—**SHARON BALESTRA** BLOOMFIELD, NEW YORK

PREP: 35 MINUTES **BAKE:** 10 MINUTES/BATCH
MAKES: 6 DOZEN

- 2 **tablespoons hot water**
- 1 **tablespoon ground flaxseed**
- 1 **cup pitted dried plums, chopped**
- 1 **cup chopped dates**
- ½ **cup raisins**
- ⅓ **cup butter, softened**
- ¾ **cup packed brown sugar**
- 1 **egg**
- 2 **teaspoons vanilla extract**
- ½ **cup unsweetened applesauce**
- ¼ **cup maple syrup**
- 1 **tablespoon grated orange peel**

- 3 **cups quick-cooking oats**
- 1 **cup all-purpose flour**
- ½ **cup whole wheat flour**
- 1 **teaspoon baking soda**
- 1 **teaspoon ground cinnamon**
- ½ **teaspoon salt**
- ¼ **teaspoon ground nutmeg**
- ¼ **teaspoon ground cloves**

1. In a small bowl, combine water and flaxseed. In a large bowl, combine the plums, dates and raisins. Cover with boiling water. Let flaxseed and plum mixtures stand for 10 minutes.

2. Meanwhile, in a large bowl, cream butter and brown sugar until light and fluffy. Beat in egg and vanilla. Beat in the applesauce, maple syrup and orange peel. Combine the oats, flours, baking soda, cinnamon, salt, nutmeg and cloves; gradually add to creamed mixture and mix well. Drain plum mixture; stir plum mixture and flaxseed into dough.

3. Drop by rounded teaspoonfuls 2 in. apart onto lightly greased baking sheets. Bake at 350° for 8-11 minutes or until set. Cool for 2 minutes before removing from pans to wire racks.

Chocolate-Hazelnut Cream Pie

PREP: 20 MINUTES **BAKE:** 15 MINUTES + CHILLING
MAKES: 8 SERVINGS

- 16 **Oreo cookies**
- ¼ **cup butter, melted**
- 1 **package (8 ounces) cream cheese, softened**
- ¾ **cup Nutella**
- ½ **cup confectioners' sugar**
- 1 **teaspoon vanilla extract**
- 1 **cup heavy whipping cream**

TOPPING
- ¼ **cup heavy whipping cream**
- 1 **tablespoon light corn syrup**
- 2 **teaspoons butter**
- ⅛ **teaspoon salt**
- 2 **ounces semisweet chocolate, finely chopped**
- 2 **tablespoons chopped hazelnuts, toasted**

1. Place cookies in a food processor; cover and pulse for 1-2 minutes or until mixture resembles fine crumbs. Add butter; process until blended. Press crumb mixture onto the bottom and up the sides of a greased 9-in. pie plate.

2. Bake at 350° for 13-15 minutes. Cool on a wire rack for 30 minutes.

3. Meanwhile, in a large bowl, beat the cream cheese, Nutella, confectioners' sugar and vanilla until smooth.

4. In a small bowl, beat whipping cream until stiff peaks form; fold into cream cheese mixture. Pour into pie crust. Refrigerate for 30 minutes.

5. In a small saucepan over medium heat, bring the cream, corn syrup, butter and salt to a boil. Remove from the heat; add chocolate. Cover and let stand for 5 minutes; stir until smooth. Set aside to cool to room temperature. Spread over pie. Garnish with hazelnuts. Chill for 1 hour.

> "We've all seen peanut butter pies, so why not kick it up a notch and try a Nutella pie? This rich dessert is just fabulous. I sometimes add sliced bananas on top of the crust and then spoon the Nutella mixture over them for a banana hazelnut cream pie."

—**ANNA SMITH** NORTH SALT LAKE, UTAH
Teacher, Central Davis Junior High, Layton, Utah

Ricotta Pie with Chocolate and Raspberry

PREP: 1 HOUR **BAKE:** 30 MINUTES + COOLING
MAKES: 6 MINI PIES

- 3 **cups all-purpose flour**
- 1 **cup plus 2 tablespoons butter**
- 3 **egg yolks**
- 3 **tablespoons cold water**

RASPBERRY LAYER

- 1½ **cups fresh or frozen raspberries, thawed**
- ¼ **cup sugar**
- 2 **tablespoons cornstarch**
- 1 **cup semisweet chocolate chips**

FILLING

- 1½ **cups ricotta cheese**
- 2 **tablespoons all-purpose flour**
- 1½ **teaspoons vanilla extract**
- 2 **eggs**
- ½ **cup sugar**

FINISHING

- 1 **egg white**
- 2 **tablespoons coarse sugar**

1. Place the flour in a large bowl; cut in the butter until crumbly. In a small bowl, whisk egg yolks and water; gradually add to flour mixture, tossing with a fork until dough forms a ball. Divide dough in half so that one portion is slightly larger than the other. Wrap smaller portion in plastic and refrigerate.

2. Divide the remaining dough into six portions. Roll out each portion to fit a 5-in. pie plate; transfer pastry to pie plates. Set aside.

3. Press raspberries through a sieve; discard seeds. In a small saucepan, combine sugar and cornstarch. Stir in raspberry puree. Bring to a boil; cook and stir for 2 minutes or until thickened. Remove from heat. Spread over the bottom of each crust. Sprinkle with chocolate chips.

4. In a large bowl, beat the ricotta cheese, flour and vanilla until blended. In a small bowl, beat eggs on high speed for 3 minutes. Gradually add sugar, beating until mixture becomes thick and lemon-colored. Fold into ricotta mixture. Spread into pastry shells.

5. Roll out remaining pastry; make lattice crusts. Trim, seal and flute edges. Whisk egg white; brush over lattice tops. Sprinkle with coarse sugar.

6. Transfer pies to a baking sheet. Bake at 350° for 30-35 minutes or until crust is golden and filling is set. Cool on a wire rack. Refrigerate until serving.

"My grandmother recalls that each generation has added and perfected a new little twist on this family favorite. My mother upped the chocolate factor, and I added the thin layer of raspberry to give it a tangy twist."

—**STEPHEN DEBENEDICTIS** WAKEFIELD, MASSACHUSETTS
Teacher, Lynch Elementary School, Winchester, Massachusetts

Almond-Chocolate Crescents

PREP/TOTAL TIME: 30 MINUTES **MAKES:** 8 ROLLS

- ¼ **cup almond paste**
- ¾ **cup semisweet chocolate chips**
- 1 **tablespoon shortening**
- 1 **tube (8 ounces) refrigerated crescent rolls**

1. Divide almond paste into eight portions; shape each into a small log. Set aside. In a microwave, melt chocolate chips and shortening; stir until smooth.

2. Unroll crescent dough; separate into triangles. Spread each with 1 tablespoon chocolate mixture; set aside remaining mixture for drizzling. Place one portion almond paste at wide end of each triangle. Roll up and place point side down 2 in. apart on an ungreased baking sheet; curve ends to form a crescent.

3. Bake at 375° for 11-13 minutes or until golden brown. Remove to wire rack to cool completely. Drizzle with reserved chocolate mixture.

"I teach music and chorus at Gorham Middle School. The best part of my position is the subject I teach. It is ever changing, always interesting and fun. Helping students understand and create music, whether it is through singing harmonies in chorus, playing a riff on the guitar or creating a soundtrack for a movie on their laptops, is truly rewarding."

—**TRACY WHEELER** BRIDGTON, MAINE

Teacher, Gorham Middle School, Gorham, Maine

Toffee Cheesecake Tiramisu

PREP: 30 MINUTES + CHILLING **MAKES:** 12 SERVINGS

- 1¼ **cups brewed espresso**
- 4 **tablespoons rum, divided**
- 4 **tablespoons coffee liqueur, divided**
- 1 **package (7 ounces) crisp ladyfinger cookies, divided**
- 1 **carton (8 ounces) whipped cream cheese**
- 1 **carton (8 ounces) mascarpone cheese**
- ½ **cup sugar**
- 1 **cup heavy whipping cream, whipped**
- 2 **teaspoons baking cocoa, divided**
- ¾ **cup toffee bits**

1. Cool espresso to room temperature. In a shallow bowl, combine the espresso, 2 tablespoons rum and 2 tablespoons liqueur. Quickly dip 12 cookies in half of the espresso mixture. Arrange in an ungreased 11-in. x 7-in. dish.

2. In a large bowl, combine the cream cheese, mascarpone cheese, sugar, remaining rum and liqueur. Fold a fourth of the whipped cream into the cream cheese mixture, then fold in remaining whipped cream.

3. Spoon half of cream cheese mixture over ladyfingers; spread evenly. Dust with 1 teaspoon cocoa. Repeat layers. Sprinkle with toffee bits. Cover and refrigerate for at least 4 hours or overnight.

Editor's Note: *This recipe was prepared with Alessi brand ladyfinger cookies.*

Sweet Chipotle Pretzels

PREP: 10 MINUTES **BAKE:** 10 MINUTES + COOLING
MAKES: 4 CUPS

- 4 **cups miniature pretzels**
- 1 **egg white**
- 1 **tablespoon water**
- ½ **cup packed brown sugar**
- 1½ **teaspoons ground cinnamon**
- ¼ **teaspoon ground allspice**
- ⅛ **teaspoon ground chipotle pepper**

1. Place pretzels in a large bowl. Whisk the egg white and water until frothy; stir in the brown sugar, cinnamon, allspice and chipotle pepper. Pour over pretzels; toss to coat.

2. Arrange in single layer on parchment paper-lined baking sheets. Bake at 350° for 10-12 minutes or until dry. Cool completely on a wire rack. Store pretzels in an airtight container.

Bake Sale Treats

66 Pretzels are a great snack food. I love this recipe because it is sweet as well as spicy, but not too spicy. It's a great combination for munching. 99

—GERALDINE SAUCIER ALBUQUERQUE, NEW MEXICO

"This is a favorite of mine, my husband's, my classes' and my colleagues'. These cookies are just plain yummy! The recipe also makes about 11 dozen... bake sale, here we come."

—DANA CHEW OKEMAH, OKLAHOMA
Teacher, Bearden Elementary, Okemah, Oklahoma

Peanut Butter Oatmeal-Chip Cookies

PREP: 25 MINUTES **BAKE:** 10 MINUTES/BATCH
MAKES: 11 DOZEN

- 2½ cups butter, softened
- 2 cups sugar
- 2 cups packed brown sugar
- ½ cup creamy peanut butter
- 4 eggs
- 2 teaspoons vanilla extract
- 6 cups all-purpose flour
- 2 teaspoons salt
- 2 teaspoons baking soda
- ½ teaspoon baking powder
- 1 package (12 ounces) semisweet chocolate chips
- 1 package (11 ounces) peanut butter and milk chocolate chips
- 1 cup quick-cooking oats

1. In a large bowl, cream the butter, sugars and peanut butter until light and fluffy. Beat in eggs and vanilla. Combine the flour, salt, baking soda and baking powder; gradually add to the creamed mixture and mix well.

2. Stir in the chips and oats. Drop by rounded tablespoonfuls 2 in. apart onto ungreased baking sheets. Bake at 375° for 9-12 minutes or until cookies are golden brown.

3. Cool for 2 minutes before removing from pans to wire racks. Store in an airtight container.

Chocolate Raspberry Cupcakes

These cupcake are so amazing that people have been known to inhale them in two bites. But most prefer to savor each decadent morsel. They can be kept in the fridge for about a week and in the freezer for a month.

—KIM BEJOT AINSWORTH, NEBRASKA

PREP: 30 MINUTES + CHILLING
BAKE: 20 MINUTES + COOLING **MAKES:** 2½ DOZEN

- 1 **cup baking cocoa**
- 2 **cups boiling water**
- 1 **cup butter, softened**
- 2½ **cups sugar**
- 4 **eggs**
- 2 **tablespoons cold strong brewed coffee**
- 2 **teaspoons vanilla extract**
- 2¾ **cups all-purpose flour**
- 2 **teaspoons baking soda**
- ½ **teaspoon baking powder**
- ½ **teaspoon salt**
- 1 **cup seedless raspberry jam**

FROSTING
- 1 **can (13.66 ounces) coconut milk**
- 1 **package (12 ounces) dark chocolate chips**
- ½ **cup butter, cubed**
- ⅓ **cup confectioners' sugar**
- 2 **tablespoons coffee liqueur**
  Toasted coconut

1. In a small bowl, combine cocoa and water; cool.

2. In a large bowl, cream butter and sugar until light and fluffy. Add eggs, one at a time, beating well after each addition. Beat in coffee and vanilla. Combine the flour, baking soda, baking powder and salt; add to creamed mixture alternately with cocoa mixture, beating well after each addition.

3. Fill paper-lined muffin cups two-thirds full. Drop jam by teaspoonfuls into center of each cupcake. Bake at 350° for 18-23 minutes or until a toothpick inserted in the cake portion comes out clean.

4. Cool for 10 minutes before removing from pans to wire racks to cool completely. Spread ½ teaspoon jam over each cupcake.

5. For frosting, spoon 1 cup cream from top of coconut milk; place in a saucepan. Bring just to a boil; remove from heat. Add chocolate chips; whisk until smooth. Stir in butter, confectioners' sugar and coffee liqueur. Refrigerate mixture for 1½ hours or until chilled.

6. In a small bowl, beat chocolate mixture until soft peaks form, about 15 seconds. Frost cupcakes. Garnish with coconut.

> "Helping students think beyond themselves, bring beauty to the world and foster teamwork skills through music is my goal as a music educator. I currently teach instrumental music, music appreciation and African drumming. When I'm not teaching, playing music or baking, I volunteer for Destination ImagiNation, a worldwide creative problem solving organization."

—KIM BEJOT AINSWORTH, NEBRASKA
Teacher, Ainsworth Community Schools, Ainsworth, Nebraska

Sweet & Salty Candy

I've been making this candy for the past few years and serving it at Teacher Appreciation lunches and bake sales. It's special because it never fails to win praise from everyone who tries it. For bake sales, I break the candy up and package it in pretty little cellophane bags from the craft store.

—ANNA GINSBERG AUSTIN, TEXAS

PREP: 15 MINUTES **BAKE:** 10 MINUTES + COOLING
MAKES: ABOUT 1½ POUNDS

- 2 **cups miniature pretzels, coarsely crushed**
- ½ **cup corn chips, coarsely crushed**
- ½ **cup salted peanuts**
- ½ **cup butter, cubed**
- ½ **cup packed brown sugar**
- 1½ **cups semisweet chocolate chips**

1. Line a 13-in. x 9-in. baking pan with foil and grease the foil; set aside. In a large bowl, combine the pretzels, corn chips and peanuts.

2. In a small saucepan, melt butter. Stir in brown sugar until melted. Bring to a boil, stirring frequently. Boil for 1 minute, stirring twice. Pour over pretzel mixture; toss to coat. Transfer to prepared pan.

3. Bake at 350° for 7 minutes. Sprinkle with chocolate chips. Bake 1-2 minutes longer or until the chips are softened. Spread over the top. Cool on a wire rack for 1 hour. Break into pieces. Store in an airtight container.

"As someone who loves to bake, I like to volunteer to bake treats for the staff during Teacher Appreciation Week at my daughter's elementary school. I also got to show off my baking skills for my daughter's class celebration of 'Culture Day' where the kids shared foods from different countries. I brought in homemade scones and talked about Wales. The fourth graders loved them!"

ANNA GINSBERG AUSTIN, TEXAS
Volunteer, Clayton Elementary School, Austin, Texas

"Over the years, I've adapted my most-requested biscotti recipe to add some of my favorite ingredients: cranberries, white chocolate and pistachios. This biscotti keeps and freezes well."

—**SUSAN NELSON** NEWBURY PARK, CALIFORNIA

Teacher, Elmhurst Elementary School, Ventura, California

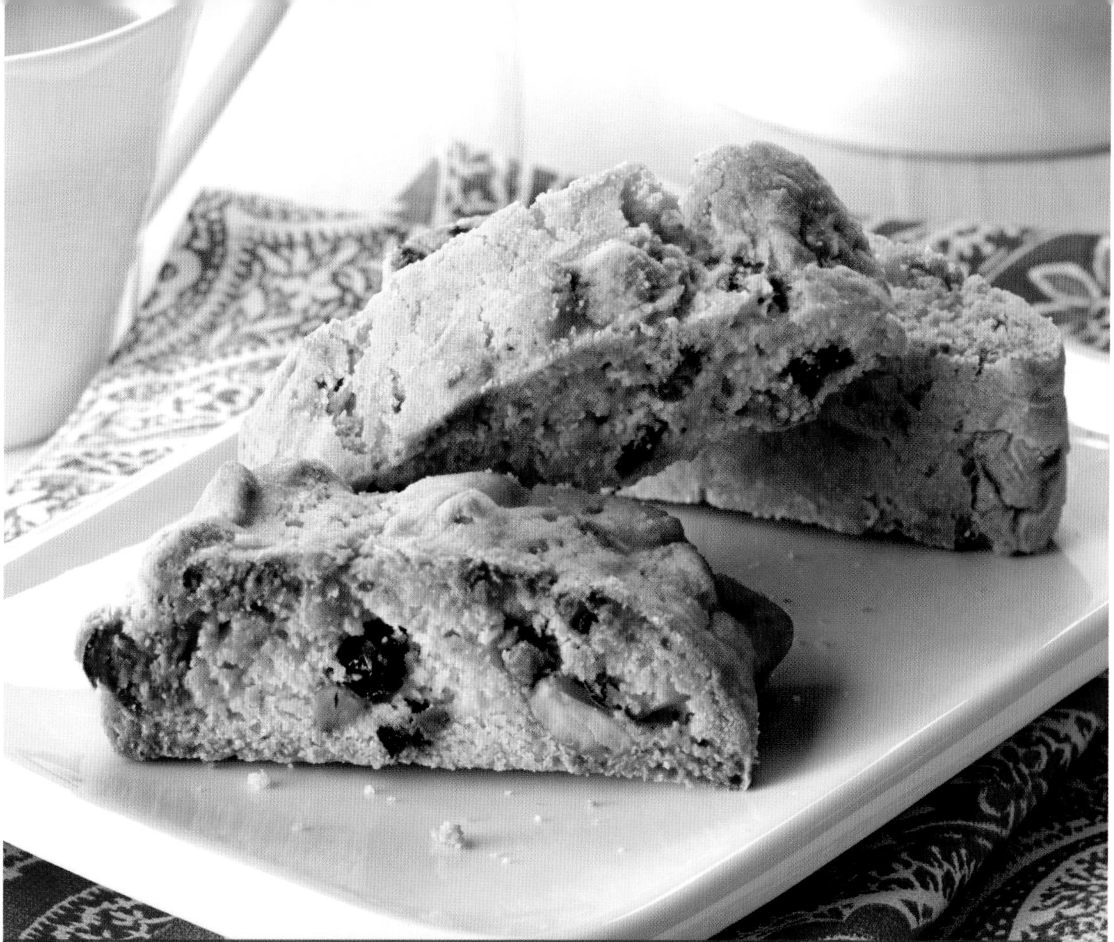

White Chocolate Cranberry Biscotti

PREP: 25 MINUTES **BAKE:** 35 MINUTES
MAKES: 2½ DOZEN

- **¾ cup sugar**
- **½ cup canola oil**
- **2 eggs**
- **1 teaspoon vanilla extract**
- **1¾ cups all-purpose flour**
- **1½ teaspoons baking powder**
- **½ teaspoon salt**
- **¾ cup white baking chips**
- **¾ cup dried cranberries**
- **¾ cup pistachios**

1. In a small bowl, beat sugar and oil until blended. Beat in eggs and vanilla. Combine the flour, baking powder and salt; gradually add to sugar mixture and mix well. Stir in the chips, cranberries and pistachios.

2. Divide dough in half. On a parchment paper-lined baking sheet, shape each half into a 10-in. x 1½-in. rectangle with lightly floured hands. Bake at 325° for 30-35 minutes or until lightly browned.

3. Place pans on wire racks. When cool enough to handle, transfer to a cutting board; cut diagonally with a serrated knife into ½-in. slices. Place cut side down on baking sheets. Bake for 6-7 minutes on each side or until golden brown. Remove to wire racks to cool completely. Store in an airtight container.

Trick-or-Treat Pizza

Don't let your leftover Halloween candy go to waste. Pile ooey-gooey candy onto a big baked cookie kids will go crazy for! We first had this when a friend made it for our family, and we loved it, and now make it ourselves. We like the colorful look of M&M's on top.

—KENDRA BOWEN LOUISVILLE, ILLINOIS

PREP: 10 MINUTES **BAKE:** 20 MINUTES + CHILLING
MAKES: 16 SLICES

- 1 **tube (16½ ounces) refrigerated sugar cookie dough**
  Assorted Halloween candies, unwrapped
- 2 **cups semisweet chocolate chips**
- 3 **tablespoons creamy peanut butter**

1. Let cookie dough stand at room temperature for 5-10 minutes to soften. Press onto an ungreased 14-in. pizza pan. Bake at 350° for 18-22 minutes or until deep golden brown. Cool on pan on a wire rack.

2. Coarsely chop large candies and set aside. In a microwave, melt chocolate chips and peanut butter; stir until smooth. Spread over crust; top with candies. Refrigerate, covered, until chocolate mixture is set. Cut into wedges.

Carrot & Raisin Spice Cupcakes

PREP: 30 MINUTES **BAKE:** 20 MINUTES + COOLING
MAKES: 2 DOZEN

- 4 **eggs**
- 1 **cup canola oil**
- 1 **cup sugar**
- 1 **cup packed brown sugar**
- 1 **teaspoon vanilla extract**
- 2 **cups all-purpose flour**
- 2 **teaspoons baking powder**
- 2 **teaspoons ground cinnamon**
- 1 **teaspoon baking soda**
- 1 **teaspoon salt**
- ½ **teaspoon ground cloves**
- ½ **teaspoon ground nutmeg**
- 3 **cups finely shredded carrots**
- 1 **cup raisins**

FILLING
- 1 **cup sugar**
- 2 **tablespoons plus 1½ teaspoons cornstarch**
- 1 **can (20 ounces) crushed pineapple, drained and chopped**

FROSTING
- 1 **package (8 ounces) reduced-fat cream cheese**
- ½ **cup butter, softened**
- 3½ **cups confectioners' sugar**
- 1 **teaspoon vanilla extract**
  Additional ground cinnamon

1. In a large bowl, beat the eggs, oil, sugars and vanilla until well blended. Combine the flour, baking powder, cinnamon, baking soda, salt, cloves and nutmeg; gradually beat into egg mixture until blended. Stir in carrots and raisins.

2. Fill paper-lined muffin cups three-fourths full. Bake at 350° for 20-25 minutes or until a toothpick inserted near the center comes out clean. Cool for 10 minutes; remove from pans to wire racks to cool completely.

3. Meanwhile, in a small saucepan, combine sugar and cornstarch. Stir in pineapple until blended. Bring to a boil over medium heat. Cook and stir for 2-3 minutes or until thickened. Remove from the heat; set aside to cool.

4. In a large bowl, beat the cream cheese and butter until fluffy. Add confectioners' sugar and vanilla; beat until smooth.

5. Cut a large hole in the corner of a pastry or plastic bag; insert a round tip. Fill with pineapple filling. Push the tip through the top of the cupcake to fill each cupcake. Frost tops and sprinkle with cinnamon. Store in the refrigerator.

"When I was growing up, carrot cake was my favorite dessert, and my dad's carrot cake was the best! After I started cooking for myself, I began using his recipe, but a whole cake is too cumbersome to take to school. I've found carrot cupcakes are the ideal way to share this treat with colleagues."

—BRE ENGLAND INDIANAPOLIS, INDIANA
Staff, Warren Central High School, Indianapolis, Indiana

Sugar Plum Sweet Rolls

My sweet rolls are a cross between cinnamon buns and kolaches. Package some in decorative cellophane bags for homemade gifts or bake sales.

—JANELLE BOOK MILES, TEXAS

PREP: 1 HOUR + RISING **BAKE:** 20 MINUTES
MAKES: 2½ DOZEN

- 2 envelopes (¼ ounce each) active dry yeast
- ½ cup warm water (110° to 115°)
- 2 cups warm whole milk (110° to 115°)
- 1 cup butter, melted
- 3 egg yolks, lightly beaten
- ½ cup sugar
- 2 teaspoons salt
- 6 to 7 cups all-purpose flour

FILLING
- 1⅓ cups pitted dried plums
- 1 cup packed brown sugar
- 1 cup flaked coconut
- 1 cup chopped pecans, toasted
- ½ cup butter, melted
- 2 tablespoons grated orange peel

ICING
- 1 cup confectioners' sugar
- ½ cup chopped pecans, toasted
- 4 teaspoons orange juice
- 2 teaspoons grated orange peel

1. In a large bowl, dissolve yeast in warm water. Add the warm milk, butter, egg yolks, sugar, salt and 5 cups flour. Beat until smooth. Stir in enough remaining flour to form a soft dough (dough will be sticky).

2. Turn onto a floured surface; knead until smooth and elastic, about 6-8 minutes. Place in a greased bowl, turning once to grease the top. Cover and let rise in a warm place until doubled, about 1 hour.

3. Punch dough down. Divide dough in half. On a lightly floured surface, roll each half into a 15-in. x 12-in. rectangle. In a small bowl, combine filling ingredients; spread over each rectangle to within ½ in. of edges. Roll up jelly-roll style, starting with a long side; pinch seams to seal. Cut into 1-in. slices.

4. Place rolls, cut side down, in two greased 13-in. x 9-in. baking pans. Cover and let rise in a warm place until doubled, about 30 minutes. Bake at 375° for 18-22 minutes or until golden brown. Cool in pans for 5 minutes before inverting onto serving plates.

5. Combine the confectioner's sugar, pecans, orange juice and peel until blended. Spoon over warm rolls.

Honey & Oat Yeast Bread

This recipe meets the three most important requirements I have for a recipe: easy, healthy, and kid approved! A woman my husband knows shared the directions for this moist, multi-grain bread with us.

—**LISA BEDORD** POWER, MONTANA

PREP: 30 MINUTES + RISING **BAKE:** 25 MINUTES + COOLING
MAKES: 1 LOAF (12 WEDGES)

- ½ cup water
- 6½ teaspoons butter, divided
- ½ cup old-fashioned oats
- ½ cup unsweetened applesauce
- ¼ cup honey
- 1 teaspoon salt
- 2 teaspoons active dry yeast
- 2 tablespoons warm water (110° to 115°)
- 1 egg
- 1½ cups whole wheat flour
- 1¼ to 1¾ cups all-purpose flour

1. In a small saucepan, bring water and 4½ teaspoons butter just to a boil. In a small bowl, pour boiling liquid over oats. Add applesauce, honey and salt. Let stand until mixture cools to 110°-115°, stirring occasionally.

2. In a large bowl, dissolve yeast in warm water. Add the oatmeal mixture, egg, whole wheat flour and 1 cup all-purpose flour. Beat until smooth. Stir in enough remaining all-purpose flour to form a soft dough (dough will be sticky).

3. Turn onto a floured surface; knead until smooth and elastic, about 6-8 minutes. Place in a greased bowl, turning once to grease the top. Cover and let rise in a warm place until doubled, about 1 hour.

4. Punch dough down. Shape into an 8-in. round loaf on a greased baking sheet. Cover and let rise in a warm place until doubled, about 30 minutes.

5. Melt remaining butter; brush over loaf. Bake at 375° for 25-30 minutes or until golden brown. Cool on wire rack.

Schoolhouse Peanut Brittle

I've made it for years, refined it, and everyone who eats it raves! My specialty is crisp and yummy. I prefer the brittle to be thin, which means spreading it quickly. If you want thicker brittle, you can add a few seconds to your spreading window!

—**BESS KUZMA** DENVER, COLORADO
Administration, Flagstaff Academy Elementary School, Longmont, Colorado

PREP: 5 MINUTES **COOK:** 50 MINUTES + COOLING
MAKES: 2¾ POUNDS

- **3 cups sugar**
- **2 cups water**
- **¾ cup light corn syrup**
- **¾ cup dark corn syrup**
- **2 cups Spanish or cocktail peanuts**
- **2 tablespoons butter, cubed**
- **1 tablespoon baking soda**
- **1 teaspoon vanilla extract**

1. Line three 15-in. x 10-in. x 1-in. pans with parchment paper. (Do not spray or grease.)

2. In a large heavy saucepan, combine the sugar, water and corn syrups. Bring to a boil, stirring constantly to dissolve sugar. Using a pastry brush dipped in water, wash down the sides of the pan to eliminate sugar crystals. Cook, without stirring, over medium heat until a candy thermometer reads 260° (hard-ball stage).

3. Stir in peanuts and butter; cook to 300° (hard-crack stage), about 9 minutes longer, stirring mixture frequently.

4. Remove from the heat; stir in baking soda and vanilla. (Mixture will foam.) Immediately pour into prepared pans, spreading as thin as possible. Cool completely. Break into pieces. Store between layers of waxed paper in airtight containers.

Editor's Note: *We recommend that you test your candy thermometer before each use by bringing water to a boil; the thermometer should read 212°. Adjust your recipe temperature up or down based on your test.*

Apricot-Filled Sandwich Cookies

I bake these delightful cookies every year for Christmas and when I share a tray of my homemade treats with the faculty at school, these are always the first goodies to disappear! I've even had requests to make them for wedding receptions.

—DEB LYON BANGOR, PENNSYLVANIA

PREP: 40 MINUTES **BAKE:** 10 MINUTES/BATCH +COOLING
MAKES: 4 DOZEN

- 1 **cup butter, softened**
- 1 **cup sugar**
- 2 **eggs**
- 3 **cups all-purpose flour**
- ⅔ **cup finely chopped walnuts**

FILLING

- 2 **cups dried apricots**
- ¾ **cup water**
- ¼ **cup sugar**
- ½ **teaspoon ground cinnamon**

TOPPING

- ½ **cup semisweet chocolate chips**
- ½ **teaspoon shortening**
- 4 **teaspoons confectioners' sugar**

1. In a large bowl, cream butter and sugar until light and fluffy. Beat in eggs. Combine flour and walnuts; gradually add to creamed mixture and mix well.

2. Shape into 1½-in.-thick logs. Cut into ¼-in. slices. Place 2 in. apart on ungreased baking sheets.

3. Bake at 350° for 10-12 minutes or until bottoms begin to brown. Cool completely on pans on wire racks.

4. Meanwhile, in a large saucepan, combine apricots and water. Bring to a boil. Cook and stir for 10 minutes or until apricots are tender. Drain apricots and cool to room temperature.

5. In a blender or food processor, combine the sugar, cinnamon and apricots. Cover and process until smooth. Spread over bottoms of half of the cookies; top with remaining cookies.

6. For topping, melt chocolate chips and shortening; stir until smooth. Drizzle over cookies. Sprinkle with confectioners' sugar.

“I'm a reading intervention teacher for fifth- and sixth-grade students at DeFranco Elementary School. The best part of my position is working with small groups, so I am able to see the incredible progress my students make over the year. I often bake for them. Once a student told me, 'Mrs. Lyon, these cupcakes are way better than my mom's—but please don't tell her I said that!'”

—DEB LYON BANGOR, PENNSYLVANIA
Teacher, DeFranco Elementary School, Bangor, Pennsylvania

"I am an artist and photographer, but still make time to volunteer at my 7-year-old granddaughter Amiera's school, Southside Elementary. Amiera and I often bake goodies like Marshmallow Monkey Business and donate them to school functions. I love to develop new recipes, and the awesome office staff at Southside Elementary is always willing to do their part by acting as my taste testers!"

—SUSAN SCARBOROUGH FERNANDINA BEACH, FLORIDA
Volunteer, Southside Elementary School, Fernandina Beach, Florida

Marshmallow Monkey Business

Just like kids, I love fun treats, and these really fit the bill. Plus, they are so easy to make and package! I wrapped these in cello bags with twist ties. As a variation, make the crispy treat with 3 tablespoons of peanut butter and reduce the butter to 2 tablespoons plus 1½ teaspoons.

—SUSAN SCARBOROUGH FERNANDINA BEACH, FLORIDA

PREP: 30 MINUTES **COOK:** 10 MINUTES
MAKES: 20 SERVINGS

- 1   package (10 ounces) large marshmallows
- 3   tablespoons butter
- 6   cups Rice Krispies
- ½   cup chopped dried banana chips
- 20   Popsicle sticks

TOPPING
- 2   cups (12 ounces) semisweet chocolate chips
- 2   tablespoons shortening
- ½   cup chopped salted peanuts
- ½   cup chopped dried banana chips

1. In a large saucepan, heat marshmallows and butter until melted. Remove from the heat. Stir in cereal and banana chips; mix well. Cool for 3 minutes.

2. Transfer mixture to waxed paper; divide into 20 portions. With buttered hands, shape each portion around a Popsicle stick to resemble a small banana.

3. In a microwave, melt chocolate chips and shortening; stir until smooth. Dip ends of "bananas" in chocolate; allow excess to drip off. Sprinkle with peanuts and banana chips. Place on waxed paper; let stand until set. Store in an airtight container.

Chocolate Malt Ball Cookies

I like malt ball candies, so I decided to create a cookie that others would like, too. These chewy cookies have fantastic flavor, but you can vary the amount of malt powder to make the taste stronger or milder.

—LYNNE WEDDELL VACAVILLE, CALIFORNIA
Teacher, Country High School, Vacaville, California

PREP: 30 MINUTES **BAKE:** 10 MINUTES/BATCH + COOLING
MAKES: 2½ DOZEN

- 1 **cup butter, softened**
- 1 **cup packed brown sugar**
- 1 **egg**
- 1¼ **cups old-fashioned oats**
- 1 **cup all-purpose flour**
- ½ **cup whole wheat flour**
- ¼ **cup malted milk powder**
- 1½ **teaspoons baking powder**
- ¼ **teaspoon salt**
- 2 **cups coarsely chopped malted milk balls**

1. In a large bowl, cream butter and brown sugar until light and fluffy. Beat in egg. Combine the oats, flours, milk powder, baking powder and salt; gradually add to the creamed mixture and mix well. Stir in the malted milk balls.

2. Drop by heaping tablespoonfuls 3 in. apart onto ungreased baking sheets. Bake at 350° for 10-14 minutes or until set and edges begin to brown. Cool for 2 minutes before removing from pans to wire racks.

Grandma's Divinity

The snowy white puffs of divinity are special to me. They bring back lovely memories of the times I spent in the kitchen with my grandmother, as well as cooking with my son when he was small.

—ANNE CLAYBORNE WALLAND, TENNESSEE
Staff, Friendsville Elementary School, Friendsville, Tennessee

PREP: 5 MINUTES **COOK:** 40 MINUTES + STANDING
MAKES: 1½ POUNDS (60 PIECES)

    2   egg whites
    3   cups sugar
    ⅔   cup water
    ½   cup light corn syrup
    1   teaspoon vanilla extract
    1   cup chopped pecans

1. Place the egg whites in the bowl of a stand mixer; let stand at room temperature for 30 minutes. Meanwhile, line three 15-in. x 10-in. x 1-in. pans with waxed paper.

2. In a large heavy saucepan, combine the sugar, water and corn syrup; bring to a boil, stirring constantly to dissolve sugar. Cook, without stirring, over medium heat until a candy thermometer reads 252° (hard-ball stage). Just before the temperature is reached, beat egg whites on medium speed until stiff peaks form.

3. Slowly add hot sugar mixture in a thin stream over egg whites, beating constantly and scraping sides of bowl occasionally. Add vanilla. Beat until candy holds its shape, about 5-6 minutes. (Do not overmix or candy will get stiff and crumbly.) Immediately fold in pecans.

4. Quickly drop by heaping teaspoonfuls onto prepared pans. Let stand at room temperature until dry to the touch. Store between waxed paper in an airtight container at room temperature.

Editor's Note: *We recommend that you test your candy thermometer before each use by bringing water to a boil; the thermometer should read 212°. Adjust your recipe temperature up or down based on your test.*

"My biscotti won a blue ribbon at our county fair. It even changed my best friend's mind about biscotti, which she thought was nothing more than stale bread. These cookies have a great gingerbread flavor and are crunchy on the outside and chewy in the center."

—KAREN PAVLOV CANFIELD, OHIO
Teacher, Campbell Elementary School, Campbell, Ohio

Gingerbread Hazelnut Biscotti

PREP: 20 MINUTES **COOK:** 35 MINUTES
MAKES: 2½ DOZEN

- 1¾ **cups all-purpose flour**
- ¾ **cup packed dark brown sugar**
- 1 **teaspoon baking powder**
- ¾ **teaspoon ground cinnamon**
- ½ **teaspoon ground ginger**
- ½ **teaspoon baking soda**
- ½ **teaspoon kosher salt**
- ⅛ **teaspoon ground cloves**
- 1 **cup old-fashioned oats, divided**
- 2 **eggs**
- ¼ **cup molasses**
- 2 **tablespoons canola oil**
- ½ **teaspoon vanilla extract**
- ¾ **cup coarsely chopped hazelnuts, toasted**
- ¾ **cup raisins**
- ¼ **cup white baking chips**
- ½ **teaspoon shortening**

1. In a large bowl, mix the first eight ingredients. Place ½ cup oats in a small food processor; cover and process until ground. Stir remaining oats and ground oats into flour mixture. In a small bowl, whisk the eggs, molasses, oil and vanilla; gradually beat into flour mixture. Stir in the hazelnuts and raisins. (Dough will be thick.)

2. Divide dough in half. Using lightly floured hands, shape each into a 12-in. x 2- in. rectangle on parchment paper-lined baking sheets. Bake at 350° for 25-30 minutes or until a toothpick inserted in center comes out clean. Cool on pans on wire racks about 10 minutes or until firm.

3. Transfer baked rectangles to a cutting board. Using a serrated knife, cut diagonally into ¾-in. slices. Return to baking sheets, cut side down.

4. Bake for 5-6 minutes on each side or until firm. Remove from pans to wire racks to cool completely.

5. In a microwave, melt chips and shortening; stir until smooth. Drizzle over biscotti; let stand until set. Store biscotti between pieces of waxed paper in airtight containers.

Editor's Note: *To toast nuts, spread in a 15-in. x 10-in. x 1-in. baking pan. Bake at 350° for 5-10 minutes or until lightly browned, stirring occasionally. Or, spread in a dry nonstick skillet and heat over low heat until lightly browned, stirring occasionally.*

1. In a small bowl, cream butter and sugar until light and fluffy. Beat in the egg, lemon juice and vanilla. Combine the flour, salt and baking soda; gradually add to creamed mixture and mix well. Beat in coconut.

2. Shape into two 6-in. logs; roll each in colored sugar and wrap in plastic wrap. Refrigerate for 3 hours or until firm.

3. Unwrap and cut into ¼-in. slices. Place 1 in. apart on ungreased baking sheets. Bake at 375° for 10-12 minutes or until set. Cool for 2 minutes before removing from pans to wire racks.

Any Holiday Sprinkle Cookies

You can roll this cookie dough in any colored sugar to suit any holiday. I use red and green for Christmas, pastel colors for Easter and green for St. Patrick's Day. I always include these on cookie trays for school. After rolling dough in sugar, the logs can be frozen for up to 2 months. Let logs thaw out slightly before slicing. They're easier to slice if very firm.

—**LYNN MERENDINO** MARYSVILLE, PENNSYLVANIA

PREP: 25 MINUTES **BAKE:** 10 MINUTES/BATCH
MAKES: 3 DOZEN

- ½ cup butter, softened
- 1 cup sugar
- 1 egg
- 1 tablespoon lemon juice
- 2 teaspoons vanilla extract
- 1¾ cups all-purpose flour
- ¾ teaspoon salt
- ½ teaspoon baking soda
- 1 cup flaked coconut, finely chopped
- 6 tablespoons colored sugar

❝I am an instructional aide working for the Susquenita School District in Duncannon, Pennsylvania. Our school gets its name from the area's two neighboring rivers, the Susquehanna and the Juniata. Working with the students here is so rewarding, and the staff makes me feel like I have a second family here. I thoroughly enjoy bringing baked goods to share with all my friends at school. ❞

—**LYNN MERENDINO** MARYSVILLE, PENNSYLVANIA
Staff, Susquenita High School, Duncannon, Pennsylvania

"This recipe was passed down to me from my aunt who was born in the 1920s. That was a time when things were made from scratch from start to finish. The penuche frosting nicely complements the cake."
—**BETH VORST** COLUMBUS GROVE, OHIO
Teacher, Cory-Rawson Local School District, Rawson, Ohio

Old-Fashioned Butterscotch Cake with Penuche Frosting

PREP: 25 MINUTES + COOLING
BAKE: 25 MINUTES+ COOLING **MAKES:** 18 SERVINGS

- 1½ cups packed brown sugar
- ½ cup shortening
- 2 eggs
- 1 teaspoon vanilla extract
- 2¼ cups all-purpose flour
- 2½ teaspoons baking powder
- 1 teaspoon salt
- 1 cup 2% milk
- 1 cup chopped pecans

PENUCHE FROSTING
- ½ cup butter, cubed
- 2 cups packed brown sugar
- ½ cup 2% milk
- ½ teaspoon salt
- 1 teaspoon vanilla extract
- 3 cups confectioners' sugar

1. In a large bowl, cream brown sugar and shortening until light and fluffy. Add eggs, one at a time, beating well after each addition. Beat in vanilla. Combine the flour, baking powder and salt; add to the creamed mixture alternately with milk, beating well after each addition. Stir in pecans.

2. Transfer to a greased 13-in. x 9-in. baking pan. Bake at 350° for 25-30 minutes or until a toothpick inserted near the center comes out clean. Cool completely on a wire rack.

3. For frosting, in a small saucepan, melt butter. Stir in the brown sugar, milk and salt. Bring to a boil; cook and stir for 3 minutes. Remove from heat and stir in vanilla. Cool to room temperature, about 20 minutes. Gradually beat in confectioners' sugar. Frost cake.

Cherry Oat Bars

Dried cherries and cherry preserves make these from-scratch granola bars a hit at my school's morning staff meetings. Each bar provides a sweet pick-me-up and lasting energy.

—KEVIN JOHNSON GLENDORA, CALIFORNIA

PREP: 30 MINUTES **BAKE:** 25 MINUTES + COOLING
MAKES: 2 DOZEN

2 cups all-purpose flour
2 cups old-fashioned oats
1 cup chopped pecans
½ cup toasted wheat germ
½ cup packed brown sugar
1 teaspoon salt
1 teaspoon baking soda
1 teaspoon ground cinnamon
½ teaspoon ground allspice
1 cup butter, melted
½ cup honey
2 eggs, beaten
1 teaspoon vanilla extract
1 jar (12 ounces) cherry preserves
⅓ cup dried cherries, chopped
½ cup flaked coconut

1. In a large bowl, combine the first nine ingredients. In another bowl, combine the butter, honey, eggs and vanilla. Stir into oat mixture until combined. Set aside 1⅓ cups for topping.

2. Press remaining oat mixture into a greased 13-in. x 9-in. baking pan. Combine preserves and the dried cherries; spread over crust. Sprinkle with coconut and reserved oat mixture; press down lightly.

3. Bake at 350° for 25-30 minutes or until golden brown. Cool on a wire rack. Cut into bars.

Caramel Nut-Chocolate Popcorn Cones

These treats were inspired by the chocolate-covered ice cream cones I used to eat when I was little. These cones are even better since there is no melting or dripping!

—**JULIE BECKWITH** CRETE, ILLINOIS

PREP: 1 HOUR + COOLING **MAKES:** 1 DOZEN

ICE CREAM CONES
- 1 **cup (6 ounces) semisweet chocolate chips**
- ¼ **cup heavy whipping cream**
- 12 **ice cream sugar cones**

CARAMEL CORN
- 7 **cups air-popped popcorn**
- ½ **cup semisweet chocolate chips**
- ¼ **cup chopped pecans**
- 25 **caramels**
- 2 **tablespoons heavy whipping cream**
- ⅛ **teaspoon salt**

TOPPING
- 5 **caramels**
- 2 **teaspoons heavy whipping cream, divided**
- ¼ **cup semisweet chocolate chips**
- ¼ **cup chopped pecans**

1. Tightly cover a large, 3-in.-deep roasting pan with two layers of heavy-duty foil. Poke 12 holes, about 2 in. apart, in the foil to hold ice cream cones; set aside.

2. In a microwave-safe bowl, melt chocolate chips and cream; stir until smooth. Spoon about 2 teaspoons inside each cone, turning to coat. Dip rims of cones into chocolate, allowing excess chocolate to drip into bowl. Place cones in prepared pan. Let stand until chocolate is set.

3. Meanwhile, place the popcorn, chocolate chips and pecans in a large bowl; set aside.

4. In a microwave, melt the caramels, cream and salt on high for 2 minutes, stirring occasionally until smooth. Pour over popcorn mixture and toss to coat.

5. Using lightly greased hands, fill cones with popcorn mixture. Shape popcorn into a 2-in.-diameter ball on top of cones, pressing down until popcorn mixture is firmly attached to cones.

6. For topping, place caramels and 1 teaspoon cream in a small microwave-safe bowl. Microwave on high at 20-second intervals until caramels are melted; stir until smooth. Drizzle over cones.

7. Microwave chocolate chips and remaining cream until smooth. Drizzle over cones. Immediately sprinkle with pecans. Let stand until set. Place in bags and fasten with twist ties or ribbon if desired.

66 I've been a speech-language pathologist for 15 years and love working with the students at Talala Elementary School. They have a clear thirst for learning. It is wonderful to see them take pride in their accomplishments. The school's 'claim to fame' came in the 1960s when it was used by Coronet Films as a movie set for the film *Courtesy for Beginners.* 99

—**JULIE BECKWITH** CRETE, ILLINOIS
Staff, Talala Elementary School, Park Forest, Illinois

"I've been the secretary at St. Mary's Catholic School for seven years. Before that, I worked in my family's restaurant business for nearly 30 years, so you know I love cooking! I also love music and share that enthusiasm with the children during the school week and the annual Christmas program. There are so many moments I'll never forget—like the time a child gave me a card and thanked me for being the best 'principal' ever."

—THERESA MILLER SAULT STE. MARIE, MICHIGAN
Staff, St. Mary's Catholic School, Sault Ste. Marie, Michigan

Lemon Cornmeal Cookies

Anything lemon makes my day brighter, and these soft cookies have a fabulous lemon aroma and flavor.

—THERESA MILLER SAULT STE. MARIE, MICHIGAN

PREP: 30 MINUTES **BAKE:** 15 MINUTES/BATCH
MAKES: 3 DOZEN

- ¾ **cup butter, softened**
- 1 **package (8 ounces) cream cheese, softened**
- 1 **cup sugar**
- 1 **cup packed brown sugar**
- 1 **egg**
- 3 **tablespoons lemon juice**
- 4 **teaspoons grated lemon peel**
- 1 **tablespoon poppy seeds**
- 3⅓ **cups all-purpose flour**
- ¾ **cup cornmeal**
- 1 **teaspoon baking soda**
- 1 **teaspoon ground ginger**
- ¾ **teaspoon salt**
- 1 **package (10 to 12 ounces) white baking chips**

1. In a large bowl, cream the butter, cream cheese and sugars until light and fluffy. Beat in the egg, lemon juice, peel and poppy seeds. Combine the flour, cornmeal, baking soda, ginger and salt; gradually add to creamed mixture and mix well. Stir in chips.

2. Drop by heaping tablespoonfuls 2 in. apart onto parchment paper-lined baking sheets; flatten slightly with a glass. Bake at 350° for 12-15 minutes or until golden brown. Remove to wire racks. Store in an airtight container.

Nutter Butter Truffles

PREP: 1 HOUR + CHILLING **MAKES:** 4 DOZEN

- 1 **package (1 pound) Nutter Butter sandwich cookies**
- 1 **package (8 ounces) cream cheese, softened**
- 8 **ounces milk chocolate candy coating, melted**
- 8 **ounces white candy coating, melted**
- 3 **ounces bittersweet chocolate, melted**

1. Place cookies in a food processor; cover and process until finely crushed. Add cream cheese; process until blended. Roll into 1-in. balls.

2. Dip half of the balls in milk chocolate, allowing excess to drip off. Place on waxed paper. Repeat with remaining balls and white coating. Drizzle bittersweet chocolate over truffles. Let stand until set. Store in an airtight container in the refrigerator.

❝Send guests home with sweet memories of the day! Prepare these truffles five to seven days in advance and store in the fridge for ease.❞

—**KATHY CARLAN** CANTON, GEORGIA
Teacher, Cherokee High School, Canton, Georgia

Raspberry Pecan Squares

The combination of shortbread and raspberry is one of my favorites—especially topped with pecan pie-like filling.

—DONNA LINDECAMP MORGANTON, NORTH CAROLINA
Teacher, Walter Johnson Middle School,
Morganton, North Carolina

PREP: 15 MINUTES **BAKE:** 40 MINUTES + COOLING
MAKES: 16 SQUARES

1¼ cups all-purpose flour
½ cup sugar
½ cup cold butter
⅓ cup seedless raspberry jam

TOPPING
2 eggs
½ cup packed brown sugar
2 tablespoons all-purpose flour
1 teaspoon vanilla extract
⅛ teaspoon salt
⅛ teaspoon baking soda
1 cup chopped pecans

1. In a small bowl, combine flour and sugar; cut in butter until crumbly. Press into a greased 9-in. square baking pan. Bake at 350° for 15-20 minutes or until lightly browned. Spread with jam.

2. In a small bowl, whisk the eggs, brown sugar, flour, vanilla, salt and baking soda; stir in pecans. Pour over jam. Bake 20-25 minutes longer or until set. Cool on a wire rack. Cut into squares.

"As a teacher and chair of the Family & Consumer Sciences Department at Taylorville High School, I love sharing my passion for cooking with students. I enjoy teaching them hands-on skills they can use in real life, whether in a professional or personal setting. Taylorville High School has a lengthy list of notable graduates, including Pat Perry (class of 1977), who became a Major League Baseball pitcher and pitched in the World Series."

—MELISSA WILLIAMS TAYLORVILLE, ILLINOIS
Teacher, Taylorville High School, Taylorville, Illinois

Banana Mocha-Chip Muffins

These moist muffins combine my two favorite things—chocolate and coffee. The added banana flavor is just the icing on the cake.

—MELISSA WILLIAMS TAYLORVILLE, ILLINOIS

PREP: 20 MINUTES **BAKE:** 20 MINUTES **MAKES:** 2 DOZEN

- 5 **teaspoons instant coffee granules**
- 5 **teaspoons hot water**
- ¾ **cup butter, softened**
- 1¼ **cups sugar**
- 1 **egg**
- 1⅓ **cups mashed ripe bananas**
- 1 **teaspoon vanilla extract**
- 2¼ **cups all-purpose flour**
- 1½ **teaspoons baking powder**
- ½ **teaspoon baking soda**
- ½ **teaspoon salt**
- 1½ **cups semisweet chocolate chips**

1. In a small bowl, dissolve coffee granules in hot water. In a large bowl, cream butter and sugar until light and fluffy. Add egg; beat well. Beat in the bananas, vanilla and coffee mixture. Combine the flour, baking powder, baking soda and salt; add to creamed mixture just until moistened. Fold in chocolate chips.

2. Fill paper-lined muffin cups two-thirds full. Bake at 350° for 18-20 minutes or until a toothpick inserted in muffin comes out clean. Cool for 5 minutes before removing from pans to wire racks. Serve warm.

"I'm a substitute teacher, primarily at High Point Elementary School in Orland Park, Illinois. For me, substitute teaching is the perfect job because I get to enjoy teaching a variety of students at all the different learning stages. I especially love working at High Point School because the staff makes me feel like a valued member of their team, and they are always so helpful. To thank them, I often bake a batch of these cookies for everyone at the end of the year."

—CINDY BEBERMAN ORLAND PARK, ILLINOIS
Substitute Teacher, High Point School, Orland Park, Illinois

Hazelnut Espresso Fingers in Chocolate

I make these cookies for the teachers and staff at Christmas and at the end of the school year. Plus they are very popular at school bake sales. They sell for $6 a dozen, and oftentimes, someone asks that I set some aside for later purchase in case we sell out!

—CINDY BEBERMAN ORLAND PARK, ILLINOIS

PREP: 35 MINUTES **BAKE:** 10 MINUTES/BATCH + COOLING
MAKES: 5 DOZEN

- 1½ cups hazelnuts, toasted
- 1 cup butter, softened
- ⅔ cup sugar
- 1 tablespoon instant espresso powder
- 2 teaspoons vanilla extract
- 2 cups all-purpose flour
- ½ teaspoon salt
- ¾ cup milk chocolate chips
- ¾ cup semisweet chocolate chips
- 2 teaspoons shortening

1. Place hazelnuts in a food processor; cover and process until ground. Set aside. In a large bowl, cream butter and sugar until light and fluffy. Beat in espresso powder and vanilla. Combine flour and salt; gradually add to creamed mixture and mix well.

2. Shape scant tablespoonfuls of dough into 2-in. logs. Place 2 in. apart on ungreased baking sheets. Bake at 350° for 9-11 minutes or until edges are lightly browned. Remove to wire racks to cool completely.

3. In a microwave, melt the chocolate chips and shortening; stir until smooth. Dip each cookie halfway into chocolate mixture, allowing excess to drip off. Place on waxed paper; let stand until set.

Party Sugar Cookies

Amp up the glam factor at any event with these lemony treats. Display them in a vase and hand out wrapped ones as favors. They're so popular that I've been asked to make them for other people's parties.

—KARA EDSTROM MAPLE GROVE, MINNESOTA

PREP: 1 HOUR **BAKE:** 10 MINUTES/BATCH + COOLING
MAKES: 26 COOKIE POPS

- 1 **cup butter, softened**
- 1 **package (3 ounces) cream cheese, softened**
- 1 **cup sugar**
- 1 **egg yolk**
- 1 **teaspoon lemon extract**
- 1 **teaspoon vanilla extract**
- 2¼ **cups all-purpose flour**
- ½ **teaspoon salt**
- ¼ **teaspoon baking soda**
- 26 **lollipop sticks**

FROSTING

- 3¾ **cups confectioners' sugar**
- 2 **teaspoons lemon extract**
- 5 **to 6 tablespoons 2% milk**
  Edible glitter and colored sugar

1. In a large bowl, cream the butter, cream cheese and sugar until fluffy. Beat in the egg yolk and extracts until smooth. Combine the flour, salt and baking soda; gradually add to creamed mixture and mix well. Cover and refrigerate for 3 hours.

2. On a lightly floured surface, roll out dough to ¼-in. thickness. Using a 3½-in. star-shaped cookie cutter, cut out 26 stars. Using a 1-in. star-shaped cookie cutter, cut out 26 small stars. Place 2 in. apart on ungreased baking sheets. Press a lollipop stick into each large star.

3. Bake 350° for 9-11 minutes until lightly browned. Carefully remove to wire racks to cool.

4. In a bowl, combine the confectioners' sugar, extract and enough milk to achieve desired consistency. Spread over cookies; immediately attach a small cookie to each large cookie. Decorate as desired with glitter and sugar. Let stand until set.

Editor's Note: *Edible glitter is available from Wilton Industries. Call 800-794-5866 or visit* wilton.com.

Yummy Cookie Bars

I received this recipe from a special coworker at school. These cookies are always a huge success when I make them. I like to make them a day in advance. This allows the bars to set, so they are easier to cut.

—TERESA HAMMAN SLAYTON, MINNESOTA

PREP: 20 MINUTES **BAKE:** 25 MINUTES + COOLING
MAKES: 2 DOZEN

- 1 **package (18¼ ounces) white cake mix**
- ½ **cup canola oil**
- 2 **eggs**
- ½ **cup butter, cubed**
- ½ **cup milk chocolate chips**
- ½ **cup peanut butter chips**
- 1 **can (14 ounces) sweetened condensed milk**

1. In a large bowl, combine the cake mix, oil and eggs. Press half of the dough into a greased 13-in. x 9-in. baking pan.

2. In a small microwave-safe bowl, melt butter and chips; stir until smooth. Stir in milk. Pour over crust. Drop remaining dough by teaspoonfuls over the top.

3. Bake at 350° for 25-30 minutes or until edges are golden brown. Cool completely on a wire rack before cutting into bars.

Raspberry Cheese Danish

PREP/TOTAL TIME: 25 MINUTES **MAKES:** 8 SERVINGS

- 4 **ounces cream cheese, softened**
- ¼ **cup plus ½ cup confectioners' sugar, divided**
- ½ **cup seedless raspberry jam**
- 1 **can (8 ounces) refrigerated crescent rolls**
- 2 **teaspoons 2% milk**

1. In a small bowl, beat cream cheese and ¼ cup confectioners' sugar until smooth. Unroll crescent dough and separate into four rectangles; seal perforations. Cut each rectangle in half, making eight squares.

2. Transfer squares to a parchment paper-lined baking sheet. Spread 1 tablespoon cream cheese mixture diagonally across each square. Top with 1 tablespoon jam. Bring two opposite corners of dough over filling; pinch together firmly to seal.

3. Bake danish at 375° for 10-12 minutes or until golden brown. Combine the milk and remaining confectioners' sugar; drizzle over pastries. Serve warm. Refrigerate leftovers.

general index

Appetizers & Snacks (also see Dips & Spreads)

Artichoke and Sun-Dried Tomato Bruschetta, 25
Artichoke-Spinach Pinwheels, 32
Backwoods Bonfire Bark, 42
Bacon and Fontina Stuffed Mushrooms, 18
Bacon-Sausage Quiche Tarts, 14
BBQ Chicken Pizza Roll-Up, 8
Canadian Meatballs, 38
Family-Favorite Turkey Egg Rolls, 12
Huevos Diablos, 45
Islander Nachos, 23
Marinated Antipasto Medley, 40
Mediterranean Artichoke and Red Pepper Roll-Ups, 48
Mozzarella Appetizer Tartlets, 17
Pear-Blue Cheese Tartlets, 22
Phyllo-Wrapped Brie with Sun-Dried Tomatoes, 26
Pork Canapes, 16
Shrimp Salad Cocktails, 19
Shrimp Spring Rolls, 28
Spanakopita Pinwheels, 6
Spicy Cheese Crackers, 39
Sweet Chipotle Pretzels, 223
Turtle Chips, 15

Apples

Apple-Spice Angel Food Cake, 187
California Chicken Salad, 172
Caramel-Toffee Apple Dip, 41
Crunchy Apple Salad, 74
Crunchy Cool Coleslaw, 90
Curried Chicken Rice Salad, 145
Fruit Salsa with Cinnamon Tortilla Chips, 9

Artichokes

Artichoke & Spinach Enchiladas, 133
Artichoke and Sun-Dried Tomato Bruschetta, 25
Artichoke-Spinach Pinwheels, 32
Cheese-Trio Artichoke & Spinach Dip, 35
Mediterranean Artichoke and Red Pepper Roll-Ups, 48
Mediterranean Turkey Panini, 147

Avocado

Blackened Catfish with Mango Avocado Salsa, 179
Shrimp Salsa, 36

Bacon & Canadian Bacon

Andouille-Stuffed Pork Loin, 146
Bacon and Fontina Stuffed Mushrooms, 18
Bacon Kale Salad with Honey-Horseradish Vinaigrette, 68
Bacon-Sausage Quiche Tarts, 14
Cheddar & Bacon Burgers, 144
Cheddar Bacon Chicken, 159
Eggs Benedict Brunch Braid, 117
French Toast Cupcakes, 210
Hot Bacon Cheddar Spread, 11
Pasta Arrabbiata (Angry Pasta), 127
Sicilian Brussels Sprouts, 107
Turkey Cordon Bleu with Alfredo Sauce, 130

Bananas

Banana Mocha-Chip Muffins, 245
I'm Stuffed French Toast, 140
Islander Nachos, 23
Marshmallow Monkey Business, 234

Beans & Lentils

Black-Eyed Pea Spinach Salad, 69
Chipotle-Black Bean Chili, 180
Jalapeno Hummus, 10
N'Orleans Shrimp with Beans & Rice, 150
Pumpkin Turkey Chili, 123
Quinoa and Black Bean Salad, 59
Sausage & Bean Soup, 83
Southwest Vegetarian Lentil Soup, 75
Tangy Beef Chili, 84
Teacher's Caviar, 47
Tuscan Portobello Stew, 167
White Bean Tuna Salad, 163
White Chicken Chili, 113

Beef (also see Ground Beef)

Baked Reuben Dip, 24
Balsamic Braised Pot Roast, 138
Beef & Barley Soup, 85
Beef Stew with Sesame Seed Biscuits, 118
Chipotle-Black Bean Chili, 180
Coffee Roast Beef, 141
Flank Steak with Cilantro & Blue Cheese Butter, 153
Maple-Glazed Corned Beef, 110
Reuben Pasta Salad, 64
Roast Beef Potpie, 136
Sizzle & Smoke Flat Iron Steaks, 131
Special Sauerbraten, 126
Tender Salsa Beef, 174
Vegetable Beef Stew, 177

Beverages

Champagne Fruit Punch, 31
Chocolate Eggnog, 33
Hot Apple Pie Sipper, 46
Sparkling Fruit Punch, 43
Sparkling Party Punch, 50

Breads

Almond-Chocolate Crescents, 221
Banana Mocha-Chip Muffins, 245
Beef Stew with Sesame Seed Biscuits, 118
Breakfast Biscuit Cups, 102
Dill and Chive Bread, 77
Ham and Cheddar Scones, 71
Honey & Oat Yeast Bread, 231
Jazzed-Up French Bread, 80
Lime Muffins with Coconut Streusel, 204
Raspberry Cheese Danish, 249
Sausage Stuffing Muffins, 55
Sugar Plum Sweet Rolls, 230

Breakfast & Brunch

Almond-Chocolate Crescents, 221
Bacon-Sausage Quiche Tarts, 14
Baked Cranberry Peach Sauce, 95
Banana Mocha-Chip Muffins, 245
Breakfast Biscuit Cups, 102
Broccoli Quiche, 121
Brownie Waffle Sundaes, 191
Caramel-Pecan French Toast Bake, 122
Eggs Benedict Brunch Braid, 117
French Toast Cupcakes, 210
Ham and Cheddar Scones, 71
Huevos Diablos, 45
I'm Stuffed French Toast, 140
Lime Muffins with Coconut Streusel, 204
Mushroom-Artichoke Brunch Bake, 161
Raspberry Cheese Danish, 249
Smoked Salmon Quiche, 183
Sugar Plum Sweet Rolls, 230

Broccoli

Broccoli Quiche, 121
Cranberry Broccoli Slaw, 61

Cabbage

Baked Reuben Dip, 24
Cranberry Broccoli Slaw, 61
Crunchy Cool Coleslaw, 90
Easy Colcannon, 97
Family-Favorite Turkey Egg Rolls, 12
Mediterranean Cod, 171
Reuben Pasta Salad, 64
Sausage & Bean Soup, 83
Shrimp Spring Rolls, 28

Cakes & Cupcakes

Almond Cake with Raspberry Sauce, 202
Apple-Spice Angel Food Cake, 187
Carrot & Raisin Spice Cupcakes, 229
Carrot Cake Cupcakes, 217
Chocolate Ganache Cake with Raspberry Sauce, 215
Chocolate Ganache Peanut Butter Cupcakes, 196
Chocolate Raspberry Cupcakes, 225
Devil's Food Cake, 200
Family-Favorite Peanut Butter Cake, 213
French Toast Cupcakes, 210
Gluten-Free Chocolate Cupcakes, 193
Grapefruit Layer Cake, 192
Old-Fashioned Butterscotch Cake with Penuche Frosting, 239
Peaches & Cream Jelly Roll, 201
Pina Colada Cake, 195
Spiced Chocolate Molten Cakes, 194
White Chocolate-Coconut Layer Cake, 216

Candy

Backwoods Bonfire Bark, 42
Caramel Nut-Chocolate Popcorn Cones, 241
Grandma's Divinity, 236
Marshmallow Monkey Business, 234
Nutter Butter Truffles, 243
Schoolhouse Peanut Brittle, 232
Sweet & Salty Candy, 226
Trick-or-Treat Pizza, 228
Turtle Chips, 15

Caramel

Caramel Nut-Chocolate Popcorn Cones, 241
Caramel-Pecan French Toast Bake, 122
Caramel-Toffee Apple Dip, 41
Turtle Chips, 15

Carrots

Beef Stew with Sesame Seed Biscuits, 118
Carrot & Raisin Spice Cupcakes, 229
Carrot Cake Cupcakes, 217

Cheese

Argentine Lasagna, 154
Artichoke & Spinach Enchiladas, 133
Bacon and Fontina Stuffed Mushrooms, 18
Bacon-Sausage Quiche Tarts, 14
Baked Reuben Dip, 24
Barbecued Chicken-Stuffed Potatoes, 166
BBQ Chicken Pizza Roll-Up, 8
Breakfast Biscuit Cups, 102
Broccoli Quiche, 121
Cheddar & Bacon Burgers, 144
Cheddar Bacon Chicken, 159
Cheese-Trio Artichoke & Spinach Dip, 35
Cheesy Mac & Cheese, 143
Chesapeake Crab Dip, 27
Chicken & Tortellini Spinach Salad, 185
Chicken Marsala Lasagna, 157
Chicken Tortellini in Cream Sauce, 148
Creamy Basil-Feta Spread, 5
Crunchy Apple Salad, 74
Feta Cheese Balls, 34
Fiesta Corn Chip Salad, 60
Flank Steak with Cilantro & Blue Cheese
    Butter, 153
French Onion Soup, 63
Grilled Vegetables & Goat Cheese Napoleons, 162
Ham and Cheddar Scones, 71
Hot Bacon Cheddar Spread, 11
Italian Grilled Cheese Sandwiches, 124
Jazzed-Up French Bread, 80
Layered Curried Cheese Spread, 21
Marinated Antipasto Medley, 40
Mediterranean Artichoke and Red Pepper
    Roll-Ups, 48
Mediterranean Pasta Salad, 87
Mediterranean Turkey Panini, 147
Mozzarella Appetizer Tartlets, 17
Mushroom-Artichoke Brunch Bake, 161
Pear-Blue Cheese Tartlets, 22
Pepperoni Lasagna Roll-ups, 111
Pesto Grilled Cheese Sandwiches, 119
Phyllo-Wrapped Brie with Sun-Dried
    Tomatoes, 26
Portobello Risotto with Mascarpone, 96
Red Pepper & Feta Dip, 29
Ricotta Gnocchi with Spinach & Gorgonzola, 137
Ricotta Pie with Chocolate and Raspberry, 220
Shallot-Blue Cheese Dip, 49
Shrimp Mac & Cheese Salad, 158
Shrimp-Stuffed Poblano Peppers, 114
Smoked Salmon Quiche, 183
Spanakopita Pinwheels, 6

Spicy Cheese Crackers, 39
Swiss Sweet Onion Casserole, 72
Tangy Beef Chili, 84
Thai Chicken Pizza, 132
Turkey Cordon Bleu with Alfredo Sauce, 130
Turkey Florentine Sandwiches, 165

Cheesecakes (See Desserts)

Cherries

Black Forest Fudge Sauce, 209
Blushing Fruit Tarts with Amaretto Truffle
    Sauce, 188
Cherry Oat Bars, 240
Double Cherry Pie, 198
Pork Tenderloin with Dried Cherries, 134

Chicken

Barbecued Chicken-Stuffed Potatoes, 166
BBQ Chicken Pizza Roll-Up, 8
California Chicken Salad, 172
Cheddar Bacon Chicken, 159
Chicken & Tortellini Spinach Salad, 185
Chicken Marsala Lasagna, 157
Chicken Portobello Stroganoff, 151
Chicken Tortellini in Cream Sauce, 148
Curried Chicken Rice Salad, 145
Curried Chicken Sloppy Joes, 170
Grilled Tandoori Chicken Kabobs, 182
Herbed Lemon Chicken, 142
Honey-Roasted Chicken, 160
Lime-Cilantro Marinade for Chicken, 186
Pineapple-Mango Chicken, 155
Quick Cajun Chicken Penne, 156
Savory Oven-Fried Chicken, 178
Sizzling Chicken Lo Mein, 164
Skillet-Roasted Lemon Chicken with
    Potatoes, 128
Spicy Chicken Sausage Lettuce Wraps, 181
Spicy Coconut Chicken Strips, 125
Sunday Paella, 129
Thai Chicken Pizza, 132
White Chicken Chili, 113

Chocolate (also see White Chocolate)

Almond-Chocolate Crescents, 221
Backwoods Bonfire Bark, 42
Banana Mocha-Chip Muffins, 245
Black Forest Fudge Sauce, 209
Brownie Waffle Sundaes, 191
Caramel Nut-Chocolate Popcorn Cones, 241
Chocolate-Coffee Bean Ice Cream Cake, 212
Chocolate Eggnog, 33
Chocolate-Filled Cream Puffs, 211
Chocolate Ganache Cake with Raspberry
    Sauce, 215
Chocolate Ganache Peanut Butter Cupcakes, 196
Chocolate-Hazelnut Cream Pie, 219
Chocolate Malt Ball Cookies, 235
Chocolate Raspberry Cupcakes, 225
Devil's Food Cake, 200
Gluten-Free Chocolate Cupcakes, 193
Hazelnut Espresso Fingers in Chocolate, 246
Marshmallow Monkey Business, 234

Mocha Chocolate Chip Cheesecake, 197
Nutter Butter Truffles, 243
Peanut Butter-Chocolate Cheesecake, 203
Peanut Butter Oatmeal-Chip Cookies, 224
Ricotta Pie with Chocolate and Raspberry, 220
Spiced Chocolate Molten Cakes, 194
Sweet & Salty Candy, 226
Trick-or-Treat Pizza, 228
Turtle Chips, 15

Coconut

Any Holiday Sprinkle Cookies, 238
Baked Cranberry Peach Sauce, 95
Islander Nachos, 23
Pina Colada Cake, 195
Spicy Coconut Chicken Strips, 125
White Chocolate-Coconut Layer Cake, 216

Coffee

Banana Mocha-Chip Muffins, 245
Chocolate-Coffee Bean Ice Cream Cake, 212
Coffee Roast Beef, 141
Hazelnut Espresso Fingers in Chocolate, 246
Mocha Chocolate Chip Cheesecake, 197
Toffee Cheesecake Tiramisu, 222

Cookies & Bars

Any Holiday Sprinkle Cookies, 238
Apricot-Filled Sandwich Cookies, 233
Cherry Oat Bars, 240
Chocolate Malt Ball Cookies, 235
Cranberry Bars with Cream Cheese Frosting, 206
Full-of-Goodness Oatmeal Cookies, 218
Gingerbread Hazelnut Biscotti, 237
Gluten-Free Rhubarb Bars, 208
Hazelnut Espresso Fingers in Chocolate, 246
Lemon Cornmeal Cookies, 242
Orange Sandwich Cookies, 199
Party Sugar Cookies, 247
Peanut Butter Oatmeal-Chip Cookies, 224
Raspberry Pecan Squares, 244
Strawberry Shortcake Cookies, 214
Trick-or-Treat Pizza, 228
White Chocolate Cranberry Biscotti, 227
Yummy Cookie Bars, 248

Corn

Fiesta Corn Chip Salad, 60
Fiesta Corn Salad, 53
Sweet Corn and Potato Gratin, 104
Turkey-Sweet Potato Soup, 108

Cranberries

Baked Cranberry Peach Sauce, 95
Blushing Fruit Tarts with Amaretto Truffle
    Sauce, 188
Cranberry Ambrosia Salad, 57
Cranberry Bars with Cream Cheese Frosting, 206
Cranberry BBQ Pulled Pork, 112
Cranberry Broccoli Slaw, 61
Curried Chicken Rice Salad, 145
Gingered Cran-Orange Salsa over Cream
    Cheese, 37
White Chocolate Cranberry Biscotti, 227

Desserts (also see Cakes & Cupcakes; Cookies & Bars; Pies & Tarts)

Almond-Chocolate Crescents, 221
Black Forest Fudge Sauce, 209
Brownie Waffle Sundaes, 191
Chocolate-Coffee Bean Ice Cream Cake, 212
Chocolate-Filled Cream Puffs, 211
Lime Muffins with Coconut Streusel, 204
Mocha Chocolate Chip Cheesecake, 197
Peanut Butter-Chocolate Cheesecake, 203
Pumpkin Pecan Custard, 205
Toffee Cheesecake Tiramisu, 222

Dips & Spreads

Baked Reuben Dip, 24
Caramel-Toffee Apple Dip, 41
Caramelized Onion Dip, 7
Cheese-Trio Artichoke & Spinach Dip, 35
Chesapeake Crab Dip, 27
Creamy Basil-Feta Spread, 5
Feta Cheese Balls, 34
Fruit Salsa with Cinnamon Tortilla Chips, 9
Gingered Cran-Orange Salsa over Cream Cheese, 37
Hot Bacon Cheddar Spread, 11
Jalapeno Hummus, 10
Layered Curried Cheese Spread, 21
Mango Salsa, 20
Pineapple Shrimp Spread, 44
Pumpkin Mousse Dip, 13
Red Pepper & Feta Dip, 29
Shallot-Blue Cheese Dip, 49
Shrimp Salsa, 36
Smoky Chipotle Orange Dip, 30
Teacher's Caviar, 47

Eggs

Bacon-Sausage Quiche Tarts, 14
Broccoli Quiche, 121
Eggs Benedict Brunch Braid, 117
Huevos Diablos, 45
Mushroom-Artichoke Brunch Bake, 161
Smoked Salmon Quiche, 183

Entrees (also see Sandwiches)

Andouille-Stuffed Pork Loin, 146
Argentine Lasagna, 154
Artichoke & Spinach Enchiladas, 133
Balsamic Braised Pot Roast, 138
Barbecued Chicken-Stuffed Potatoes, 166
Bayou Okra Sausage Stew, 116
Beef Stew with Sesame Seed Biscuits, 118
Blackened Catfish with Mango Avocado Salsa, 179
Broccoli Quiche, 121
Cajun Shrimp, 109
California Chicken Salad, 172
Caramel-Pecan French Toast Bake, 122
Cheddar Bacon Chicken, 159
Cheesy Mac & Cheese, 143
Chicken & Tortellini Spinach Salad, 185
Chicken Marsala Lasagna, 157
Chicken Portobello Stroganoff, 151
Chicken Tortellini in Cream Sauce, 148

Coffee Roast Beef, 141
Creamy Clam Linguini, 149
Curried Chicken Rice Salad, 145
Eggs Benedict Brunch Braid, 117
Flank Steak with Cilantro & Blue Cheese Butter, 153
Grilled Salmon Kyoto, 115
Grilled Tandoori Chicken Kabobs, 182
Grilled Vegetables & Goat Cheese Napoleons, 162
Herbed Lemon Chicken, 142
Herbed Salmon Fillets, 175
Honey-Glazed Pork Tenderloins, 176
Honey-Roasted Chicken, 160
I'm Stuffed French Toast, 140
Lime-Cilantro Marinade for Chicken, 186
Maple-Glazed Corned Beef, 110
Mediterranean Cod, 171
Mushroom-Artichoke Brunch Bake, 161
N'Orleans Shrimp with Beans & Rice, 150
Pasta Arrabbiata (Angry Pasta), 127
Pasta with Eggplant Sauce, 184
Pepperoni Lasagna Roll-ups, 111
Pineapple-Mango Chicken, 155
Pork Chops with Honey-Mustard Sauce, 120
Pork Medallions with Squash & Greens, 173
Pork Tenderloin with Dried Cherries, 134
Quick Cajun Chicken Penne, 156
Ricotta Gnocchi with Spinach & Gorgonzola, 137
Roast Beef Potpie, 136
Savory Oven-Fried Chicken, 178
Shrimp Mac & Cheese Salad, 158
Shrimp-Stuffed Poblano Peppers, 114
Sizzle & Smoke Flat Iron Steaks, 131
Sizzling Chicken Lo Mein, 164
Skillet-Roasted Lemon Chicken with Potatoes, 128
Smoked Salmon Quiche, 183
Special Sauerbraten, 126
Spicy Chicken Sausage Lettuce Wraps, 181
Spicy Coconut Chicken Strips, 125
Spinach Penne Salad, 139
Sunday Paella, 129
Sweet & Sassy Baby Back Ribs, 152
Taco Salad Tacos, 169
Tender Salsa Beef, 174
Thai Chicken Pizza, 132
Turkey Cordon Bleu with Alfredo Sauce, 130
Turkey Potpie Cups, 135
Tuscan Portobello Stew, 167
Vegetable Beef Stew, 177
Weeknight Pasta Supper, 168
White Bean Tuna Salad, 163

Fruit (also see specific kinds)

Apricot-Filled Sandwich Cookies, 233
Blushing Fruit Tarts with Amaretto Truffle Sauce, 188
California Chicken Salad, 172
Champagne Fruit Punch, 31
Cornucopia Salad, 105
Fruit Salsa with Cinnamon Tortilla Chips, 9
Full-of-Goodness Oatmeal Cookies, 218
Gluten-Free Rhubarb Bars, 208
Grapefruit Layer Cake, 192

Lemon Curd Chiffon Pie, 207
Orange & Blackberry Panther Tart, 189
Sausage Stuffing Muffins, 55
Sparkling Fruit Punch, 43
Sparkling Party Punch, 50
Sugar Plum Sweet Rolls, 230

Grapes

California Chicken Salad, 172
Greek Salad with Green Grapes, 62
Shrimp Salad Cocktails, 19

Grilled Recipes

Cheddar & Bacon Burgers, 144
Flank Steak with Cilantro & Blue Cheese Butter, 153
Grilled Salmon Kyoto, 115
Grilled Sweet Potato Wedges, 56
Grilled Tandoori Chicken Kabobs, 182
Grilled Vegetables & Goat Cheese Napoleons, 162
Grilled Zucchini with Onions, 79
Herbed Lemon Chicken, 142
Jazzed-Up French Bread, 80
Lime-Cilantro Marinade for Chicken, 186
Pineapple-Mango Chicken, 155
Quick Cajun Chicken Penne, 156
Sweet & Sassy Baby Back Ribs, 152

Ground Beef

Argentine Lasagna, 154
Cheddar & Bacon Burgers, 144
Italian Wedding Soup, 76
Taco Salad Tacos, 169
Tangy Beef Chili, 84

Ham

Ham and Cheddar Scones, 71
Turkey Cordon Bleu with Alfredo Sauce, 130

Herbs

Chive Horseradish Sauce, 98
Creamy Basil-Feta Spread, 5
Dill and Chive Bread, 77
Gingered Cran-Orange Salsa over Cream Cheese, 37
Herbed Tomato Bisque, 88
Lime-Cilantro Marinade for Chicken, 186
Tossed Salad with Cilantro Vinaigrette, 65
White Bean Tuna Salad, 163

Ice Cream

Black Forest Fudge Sauce, 209
Brownie Waffle Sundaes, 191
Chocolate-Coffee Bean Ice Cream Cake, 212
Chocolate Eggnog, 33
Hot Apple Pie Sipper, 46

Lemon

Herbed Lemon Chicken, 142
Lemon Cornmeal Cookies, 242
Lemon Curd Chiffon Pie, 207
Skillet-Roasted Lemon Chicken with Potatoes, 128

Lime

Lime-Cilantro Marinade for Chicken, 186
Lime Muffins with Coconut Streusel, 204

Mango

Blackened Catfish with Mango Avocado Salsa, 179
Layered Curried Cheese Spread, 21
Mango Salsa, 20
Pineapple-Mango Chicken, 155

Mushrooms

Bacon and Fontina Stuffed Mushrooms, 18
Beef & Barley Soup, 85
Chicken Portobello Stroganoff, 151
Grilled Vegetables & Goat Cheese Napoleons, 162
Portobello Risotto with Mascarpone, 96
Tuscan Portobello Stew, 167
Weeknight Pasta Supper, 168

Nuts

Almond Cake with Raspberry Sauce, 202
Almond-Chocolate Crescents, 221
Blushing Fruit Tarts with Amaretto Truffle
   Sauce, 188
Caramel Nut-Chocolate Popcorn Cones, 241
Caramel-Pecan French Toast Bake, 122
Cherry Oat Bars, 240
Chocolate-Hazelnut Cream Pie, 219
Cornucopia Salad, 105
Cranberry Ambrosia Salad, 57
Curried Chicken Rice Salad, 145
Gingerbread Hazelnut Biscotti, 237
Grandma's Divinity, 236
Greek Salad with Green Grapes, 62
Hazelnut Espresso Fingers in Chocolate, 246
Pecan Rice Pilaf, 81
Pumpkin Pecan Custard, 205
Raspberry Pecan Squares, 244
Sausage Stuffing Muffins, 55
Schoolhouse Peanut Brittle, 232
Sesame Spaghetti Salad with Peanuts, 70
Sweet & Salty Candy, 226
White Chocolate-Coconut Layer Cake, 216
White Chocolate Cranberry Biscotti, 227

Onions

Caramelized Onion Dip, 7
French Onion Soup, 63
Shallot-Blue Cheese Dip, 49
Swiss Sweet Onion Casserole, 72

Orange

Orange Sandwich Cookies, 199
Smoky Chipotle Orange Dip, 30

Pasta & Noodles

Argentine Lasagna, 154
Cheesy Mac & Cheese, 143
Chicken & Tortellini Spinach Salad, 185
Chicken Marsala Lasagna, 157
Chicken Portobello Stroganoff, 151
Chicken Tortellini in Cream Sauce, 148
Creamy Clam Linguini, 149
Italian Wedding Soup, 76
Mediterranean Pasta Salad, 87
Pasta & Sun-Dried Tomato Salad, 89
Pasta Arrabbiata (Angry Pasta), 127
Pasta with Eggplant Sauce, 184

Pepperoni Lasagna Roll-ups, 111
Quick Cajun Chicken Penne, 156
Reuben Pasta Salad, 64
Roasted Vegetable Pasta Salad, 82
Sesame Spaghetti Salad with Peanuts, 70
Shrimp Mac & Cheese Salad, 158
Sizzling Chicken Lo Mein, 164
Spicy Couscous & Tomato Soup, 92
Spinach Penne Salad, 139
Weeknight Pasta Supper, 168

Peaches

Baked Cranberry Peach Sauce, 95
Peaches & Cream Jelly Roll, 201

Peanut Butter

Chocolate Ganache Peanut Butter Cupcakes, 196
Family-Favorite Peanut Butter Cake, 213
Nutter Butter Truffles, 243
Peanut Butter-Chocolate Cheesecake, 203
Peanut Butter Oatmeal-Chip Cookies, 224
Spicy Coconut Chicken Strips, 125
Trick-or-Treat Pizza, 228

Pears

Brandy Pear Pie, 190
Pear-Blue Cheese Tartlets, 22

Peppers

Confetti Jicama Salad, 67
Jalapeno Hummus, 10
Mediterranean Artichoke and Red Pepper
   Roll-Ups, 48
Red Pepper & Feta Dip, 29
Shrimp-Stuffed Poblano Peppers, 114

Pies & Tarts

Blushing Fruit Tarts with Amaretto Truffle
   Sauce, 188
Brandy Pear Pie, 190
Chocolate-Hazelnut Cream Pie, 219
Double Cherry Pie, 198
Lemon Curd Chiffon Pie, 207
Orange & Blackberry Panther Tart, 189
Ricotta Pie with Chocolate and Raspberry, 220

Pineapple

Cranberry Ambrosia Salad, 57
Pina Colada Cake, 195
Pineapple-Mango Chicken, 155
Pineapple Shrimp Spread, 44

Pork (also see Bacon & Canadian Bacon; Ham; Sausage)

Andouille-Stuffed Pork Loin, 146
Cranberry BBQ Pulled Pork, 112
Honey-Glazed Pork Tenderloins, 176
Hot and Sour Soup, 52
Pork Canapes, 16
Pork Chops with Honey-Mustard Sauce, 120
Pork Medallions with Squash & Greens, 173
Pork Tenderloin with Dried Cherries, 134
Sweet & Sassy Baby Back Ribs, 152

Potatoes

Barbecued Chicken-Stuffed Potatoes, 166

Beef Stew with Sesame Seed Biscuits, 118
Easy Colcannon, 97
Mushroom-Artichoke Brunch Bake, 161
Ricotta Gnocchi with Spinach & Gorgonzola, 137
Roast Beef Potpie, 136
Skillet-Roasted Lemon Chicken with Potatoes, 128
Sue's Cream of Baked Potato Soup, 101
Sweet Corn and Potato Gratin, 104
Tarragon Mashed Potato Casserole, 99
Three Potato Salad, 100

Pumpkin

Harvest Pumpkin Soup, 106
Pumpkin Mousse Dip, 13
Pumpkin Pecan Custard, 205
Pumpkin Turkey Chili, 123

Raisins

Carrot & Raisin Spice Cupcakes, 229
Curried Chicken Rice Salad, 145
Gingerbread Hazelnut Biscotti, 237

Raspberries

Almond Cake with Raspberry Sauce, 202
Champagne Fruit Punch, 31
Chocolate Ganache Cake with Raspberry
   Sauce, 215
Chocolate Raspberry Cupcakes, 225
Fruit Salsa with Cinnamon Tortilla Chips, 9
Raspberry Cheese Danish, 249
Raspberry Pecan Squares, 244
Ricotta Pie with Chocolate and Raspberry, 220

Rice

Curried Chicken Rice Salad, 145
Deep-Fried Rice Balls, 103
N'Orleans Shrimp with Beans & Rice, 150
Pecan Rice Pilaf, 81
Portobello Risotto with Mascarpone, 96
Sunday Paella, 129
Swiss Sweet Onion Casserole, 72
Tender Salsa Beef, 174

Salads

Bacon Kale Salad with Honey-Horseradish
   Vinaigrette, 68
Black-Eyed Pea Spinach Salad, 69
California Chicken Salad, 172
Chicken & Tortellini Spinach Salad, 185
Confetti Jicama Salad, 67
Cornucopia Salad, 105
Cranberry Ambrosia Salad, 57
Cranberry Broccoli Slaw, 61
Crunchy Apple Salad, 74
Crunchy Cool Coleslaw, 90
Fiesta Corn Chip Salad, 60
Fiesta Corn Salad, 53
Greek Salad with Green Grapes, 62
Mediterranean Pasta Salad, 87
Pasta & Sun-Dried Tomato Salad, 89
Quinoa and Black Bean Salad, 59
Reuben Pasta Salad, 64
Roasted Vegetable Pasta Salad, 82
Sesame Spaghetti Salad with Peanuts, 70
Shrimp Mac & Cheese Salad, 158

Salads (continued)

Spicy Cucumber Salad, 73
Spinach Penne Salad, 139
Three Potato Salad, 100
Tossed Salad with Cilantro Vinaigrette, 65
White Bean Tuna Salad, 163

Sandwiches

Cheddar & Bacon Burgers, 144
Cranberry BBQ Pulled Pork, 112
Curried Chicken Sloppy Joes, 170
Italian Grilled Cheese Sandwiches, 124
Mediterranean Turkey Panini, 147
Pesto Grilled Cheese Sandwiches, 119
Turkey Florentine Sandwiches, 165

Sauces

Baked Cranberry Peach Sauce, 95
Black Forest Fudge Sauce, 209
Chive Horseradish Sauce, 98
Pasta with Eggplant Sauce, 184

Sausage

Andouille-Stuffed Pork Loin, 146
Bacon-Sausage Quiche Tarts, 14
Bayou Okra Sausage Stew, 116
Breakfast Biscuit Cups, 102
Canadian Meatballs, 38
Italian Sausage Soup, 93
Italian Wedding Soup, 76
Marinated Antipasto Medley, 40
Pepperoni Lasagna Roll-ups, 111
Sausage & Bean Soup, 83
Sausage Stuffing Muffins, 55
Spicy Chicken Sausage Lettuce Wraps, 181
Sunday Paella, 129

Seafood

Blackened Catfish with Mango Avocado Salsa, 179
Cajun Shrimp, 109
Chesapeake Crab Dip, 27
Crab Soup with Sherry, 51
Creamy Clam Linguini, 149
Grilled Salmon Kyoto, 115
Halibut Chowder, 54
Herbed Salmon Fillets, 175
Mediterranean Cod, 171
N'Orleans Shrimp with Beans & Rice, 150
Pineapple Shrimp Spread, 44
Shrimp Mac & Cheese Salad, 158
Shrimp Salad Cocktails, 19
Shrimp Salsa, 36
Shrimp Spring Rolls, 28
Shrimp-Stuffed Poblano Peppers, 114
Smoked Salmon Quiche, 183
Sunday Paella, 129
White Bean Tuna Salad, 163

Slow Cooker Recipes

Cheese-Trio Artichoke & Spinach Dip, 35
Cranberry BBQ Pulled Pork, 112
Southwest Vegetarian Lentil Soup, 75
Special Sauerbraten, 126
Tender Salsa Beef, 174

Soups & Chili

Beef & Barley Soup, 85

Chipotle-Black Bean Chili, 180
Crab Soup with Sherry, 51
Creamy Turnip Soup, 66
Easy Gazpacho, 78
French Onion Soup, 63
Halibut Chowder, 54
Harvest Pumpkin Soup, 106
Herbed Tomato Bisque, 88
Hot and Sour Soup, 52
Italian Sausage Soup, 93
Italian Wedding Soup, 76
Pumpkin Turkey Chili, 123
Sausage & Bean Soup, 83
Southwest Vegetarian Lentil Soup, 75
Spicy Couscous & Tomato Soup, 92
Sue's Cream of Baked Potato Soup, 101
Tangy Beef Chili, 84
Turkey-Sweet Potato Soup, 108
White Chicken Chili, 113

Spinach

Artichoke & Spinach Enchiladas, 133
Artichoke-Spinach Pinwheels, 32
Black-Eyed Pea Spinach Salad, 69
Cheese-Trio Artichoke & Spinach Dip, 35
Chicken & Tortellini Spinach Salad, 185
Grilled Vegetables & Goat Cheese Napoleons, 162
Ricotta Gnocchi with Spinach & Gorgonzola, 137
Spanakopita Pinwheels, 6
Spinach Penne Salad, 139

Strawberries

Fruit Salsa with Cinnamon Tortilla Chips, 9
I'm Stuffed French Toast, 140
Strawberry Shortcake Cookies, 214

Sweet Potatoes

Favorite Mashed Sweet Potatoes, 91
Grilled Sweet Potato Wedges, 56
Three Potato Salad, 100
Turkey-Sweet Potato Soup, 108

Tomatoes

Artichoke and Sun-Dried Tomato Bruschetta, 25
Easy Gazpacho, 78
Herbed Tomato Bisque, 88
Mediterranean Turkey Panini, 147
Pasta & Sun-Dried Tomato Salad, 89
Pasta Arrabbiata (Angry Pasta), 127
Phyllo-Wrapped Brie with Sun-Dried Tomatoes, 26
Quinoa and Black Bean Salad, 59
Shrimp Salad Cocktails, 19
Slow-Roasted Tomatoes, 58
Spicy Couscous & Tomato Soup, 92

Turkey

Family-Favorite Turkey Egg Rolls, 12
Italian Sausage Soup, 93
Mediterranean Turkey Panini, 147
Pumpkin Turkey Chili, 123
Turkey Cordon Bleu with Alfredo Sauce, 130
Turkey Florentine Sandwiches, 165
Turkey Potpie Cups, 135
Turkey-Sweet Potato Soup, 108
Weeknight Pasta Supper, 168

Vegetables (also see specific kinds)

Bacon Kale Salad with Honey-Horseradish Vinaigrette, 68
Baked Greek Ratatouille, 94
Balsamic Braised Pot Roast, 138
Bayou Okra Sausage Stew, 116
Beef & Barley Soup, 85
Confetti Jicama Salad, 67
Creamy Turnip Soup, 66
Easy Gazpacho, 78
Fiesta Corn Salad, 53
Grilled Vegetables & Goat Cheese Napoleons, 162
Grilled Zucchini with Onions, 79
Halibut Chowder, 54
Harvest Pumpkin Soup, 106
Mediterranean Pasta Salad, 87
Mushroom-Artichoke Brunch Bake, 161
Pasta with Eggplant Sauce, 184
Pork Medallions with Squash & Greens, 173
Quinoa and Black Bean Salad, 59
Ricotta Gnocchi with Spinach & Gorgonzola, 137
Roasted Green Vegetable Medley, 86
Roasted Vegetable Pasta Salad, 82
Shrimp Salsa, 36
Shrimp Spring Rolls, 28
Sicilian Brussels Sprouts, 107
Sizzling Chicken Lo Mein, 164
Southwest Vegetarian Lentil Soup, 75
Spicy Chicken Sausage Lettuce Wraps, 181
Spicy Couscous & Tomato Soup, 92
Spicy Cucumber Salad, 73
Sunday Paella, 129
Taco Salad Tacos, 169
Teacher's Caviar, 47
Tossed Salad with Cilantro Vinaigrette, 65
Turkey Potpie Cups, 135
Tuscan Portobello Stew, 167
Vegetable Beef Stew, 177
Weeknight Pasta Supper, 168

Vegetarian

Artichoke & Spinach Enchiladas, 133
Broccoli Quiche, 121
Caramel-Pecan French Toast Bake, 122
Cheesy Mac & Cheese, 143
Grilled Vegetables & Goat Cheese Napoleons, 162
Italian Grilled Cheese Sandwiches, 124
Mushroom-Artichoke Brunch Bake, 161
Pasta with Eggplant Sauce, 184
Pesto Grilled Cheese Sandwiches, 119
Ricotta Gnocchi with Spinach & Gorgonzola, 137
Southwest Vegetarian Lentil Soup, 75
Spicy Couscous & Tomato Soup, 92
Spinach Penne Salad, 139
Tuscan Portobello Stew, 167

White Chocolate (also see Chocolate)

Cranberry Bars with Cream Cheese Frosting, 206
Lemon Cornmeal Cookies, 242
White Chocolate-Coconut Layer Cake, 216
White Chocolate Cranberry Biscotti, 227

alphabetical index

A

Almond Cake with Raspberry Sauce, 202
Almond-Chocolate Crescents, 221
Andouille-Stuffed Pork Loin, 146
Any Holiday Sprinkle Cookies, 238
Apple-Spice Angel Food Cake, 187
Apricot-Filled Sandwich Cookies, 233
Argentine Lasagna, 154
Artichoke & Spinach Enchiladas, 133
Artichoke and Sun-Dried Tomato
    Bruschetta, 25
Artichoke-Spinach Pinwheels, 32

B

Backwoods Bonfire Bark, 42
Bacon and Fontina Stuffed Mushrooms, 18
Bacon Kale Salad with Honey-Horseradish
    Vinaigrette, 68
Bacon-Sausage Quiche Tarts, 14
Baked Cranberry Peach Sauce, 95
Baked Greek Ratatouille, 94
Baked Reuben Dip, 24
Balsamic Braised Pot Roast, 138
Banana Mocha-Chip Muffins, 245
Barbecued Chicken-Stuffed Potatoes, 166
Bayou Okra Sausage Stew, 116
BBQ Chicken Pizza Roll-Up, 8
Beef & Barley Soup, 85
Beef Stew with Sesame Seed Biscuits, 118
Black-Eyed Pea Spinach Salad, 69
Black Forest Fudge Sauce, 209
Blackened Catfish with Mango Avocado
    Salsa, 179
Blushing Fruit Tarts with Amaretto Truffle
    Sauce, 188
Brandy Pear Pie, 190
Breakfast Biscuit Cups, 102
Broccoli Quiche, 121
Brownie Waffle Sundaes, 191

C

Cajun Shrimp, 109
California Chicken Salad, 172
Canadian Meatballs, 38
Caramel Nut-Chocolate Popcorn
    Cones, 241
Caramel-Pecan French Toast Bake, 122
Caramel-Toffee Apple Dip, 41
Caramelized Onion Dip, 7
Carrot & Raisin Spice Cupcakes, 229
Carrot Cake Cupcakes, 217

Champagne Fruit Punch, 31
Cheddar & Bacon Burgers, 144
Cheddar Bacon Chicken, 159
Cheese-Trio Artichoke & Spinach Dip, 35
Cheesy Mac & Cheese, 143
Cherry Oat Bars, 240
Chesapeake Crab Dip, 27
Chicken & Tortellini Spinach Salad, 185
Chicken Marsala Lasagna, 157
Chicken Portobello Stroganoff, 151
Chicken Tortellini in Cream Sauce, 148
Chipotle-Black Bean Chili, 180
Chive Horseradish Sauce, 98
Chocolate-Coffee Bean Ice Cream
    Cake, 212
Chocolate Eggnog, 33
Chocolate-Filled Cream Puffs, 211
Chocolate Ganache Cake with Raspberry
    Sauce, 215
Chocolate Ganache Peanut Butter
    Cupcakes, 196
Chocolate-Hazelnut Cream Pie, 219
Chocolate Malt Ball Cookies, 235
Chocolate Raspberry Cupcakes, 225
Coffee Roast Beef, 141
Confetti Jicama Salad, 67
Cornucopia Salad, 105
Crab Soup with Sherry, 51
Cranberry Ambrosia Salad, 57
Cranberry Bars with Cream Cheese
    Frosting, 206
Cranberry BBQ Pulled Pork, 112
Cranberry Broccoli Slaw, 61
Creamy Basil-Feta Spread, 5
Creamy Clam Linguini, 149
Creamy Turnip Soup, 66
Crunchy Apple Salad, 74
Crunchy Cool Coleslaw, 90
Curried Chicken Rice Salad, 145
Curried Chicken Sloppy Joes, 170

D

Deep-Fried Rice Balls, 103
Devil's Food Cake, 200
Dill and Chive Bread, 77
Double Cherry Pie, 198

E

Easy Colcannon, 97
Easy Gazpacho, 78
Eggs Benedict Brunch Braid, 117

F

Family-Favorite Peanut Butter Cake, 213
Family-Favorite Turkey Egg Rolls, 12
Favorite Mashed Sweet Potatoes, 91
Feta Cheese Balls, 34
Fiesta Corn Chip Salad, 60
Fiesta Corn Salad, 53
Flank Steak with Cilantro & Blue Cheese
    Butter, 153
French Onion Soup, 63
French Toast Cupcakes, 210
Fruit Salsa with Cinnamon Tortilla Chips, 9
Full-of-Goodness Oatmeal Cookies, 218

G

Gingerbread Hazelnut Biscotti, 237
Gingered Cran-Orange Salsa over Cream
    Cheese, 37
Gluten-Free Chocolate Cupcakes, 193
Gluten-Free Rhubarb Bars, 208
Grandma's Divinity, 236
Grapefruit Layer Cake, 192
Greek Salad with Green Grapes, 62
Grilled Salmon Kyoto, 115
Grilled Sweet Potato Wedges, 56
Grilled Tandoori Chicken Kabobs, 182
Grilled Vegetables & Goat Cheese
    Napoleons, 162
Grilled Zucchini with Onions, 79

H

Halibut Chowder, 54
Ham and Cheddar Scones, 71
Harvest Pumpkin Soup, 106
Hazelnut Espresso Fingers in
    Chocolate, 246
Herbed Lemon Chicken, 142
Herbed Salmon Fillets, 175
Herbed Tomato Bisque, 88
Honey & Oat Yeast Bread, 231
Honey-Glazed Pork Tenderloins, 176
Honey-Roasted Chicken, 160
Hot and Sour Soup, 52
Hot Apple Pie Sipper, 46
Hot Bacon Cheddar Spread, 11
Huevos Diablos, 45

I

I'm Stuffed French Toast, 140
Islander Nachos, 23
Italian Grilled Cheese Sandwiches, 124

Italian Sausage Soup, 93
Italian Wedding Soup, 76

J

Jalapeno Hummus, 10
Jazzed-Up French Bread, 80

L

Layered Curried Cheese Spread, 21
Lemon Cornmeal Cookies, 242
Lemon Curd Chiffon Pie, 207
Lime-Cilantro Marinade for Chicken, 186
Lime Muffins with Coconut Streusel, 204

M

Mango Salsa, 20
Maple-Glazed Corned Beef, 110
Marinated Antipasto Medley, 40
Marshmallow Monkey Business, 234
Mediterranean Artichoke and Red Pepper
  Roll-Ups, 48
Mediterranean Cod, 171
Mediterranean Pasta Salad, 87
Mediterranean Turkey Panini, 147
Mocha Chocolate Chip Cheesecake, 197
Mozzarella Appetizer Tartlets, 17
Mushroom-Artichoke Brunch Bake, 161

N

N'Orleans Shrimp with Beans & Rice, 150
Nutter Butter Truffles, 243

O

Old-Fashioned Butterscotch Cake with
  Penuche Frosting, 239
Orange & Blackberry Panther Tart, 189
Orange Sandwich Cookies, 199

P

Party Sugar Cookies, 247
Pasta & Sun-Dried Tomato Salad, 89
Pasta Arrabbiata (Angry Pasta), 127
Pasta with Eggplant Sauce, 184
Peaches & Cream Jelly Roll, 201
Peanut Butter-Chocolate Cheesecake, 203
Peanut Butter Oatmeal-Chip Cookies, 224
Pear-Blue Cheese Tartlets, 22
Pecan Rice Pilaf, 81
Pepperoni Lasagna Roll-ups, 111
Pesto Grilled Cheese Sandwiches, 119
Phyllo-Wrapped Brie with Sun-Dried
  Tomatoes, 26

Pina Colada Cake, 195
Pineapple-Mango Chicken, 155
Pineapple Shrimp Spread, 44
Pork Canapes, 16
Pork Chops with Honey-Mustard
  Sauce, 120
Pork Medallions with Squash & Greens, 173
Pork Tenderloin with Dried Cherries, 134
Portobello Risotto with Mascarpone, 96
Pumpkin Mousse Dip, 13
Pumpkin Pecan Custard, 205
Pumpkin Turkey Chili, 123

Q

Quick Cajun Chicken Penne, 156
Quinoa and Black Bean Salad, 59

R

Raspberry Cheese Danish, 249
Raspberry Pecan Squares, 244
Red Pepper & Feta Dip, 29
Reuben Pasta Salad, 64
Ricotta Gnocchi with Spinach &
  Gorgonzola, 137
Ricotta Pie with Chocolate and
  Raspberry, 220
Roast Beef Potpie, 136
Roasted Green Vegetable Medley, 86
Roasted Vegetable Pasta Salad, 82

S

Sausage & Bean Soup, 83
Sausage Stuffing Muffins, 55
Savory Oven-Fried Chicken, 178
Schoolhouse Peanut Brittle, 232
Sesame Spaghetti Salad with Peanuts, 70
Shallot-Blue Cheese Dip, 49
Shrimp Mac & Cheese Salad, 158
Shrimp Salad Cocktails, 19
Shrimp Salsa, 36
Shrimp Spring Rolls, 28
Shrimp-Stuffed Poblano Peppers, 114
Sicilian Brussels Sprouts, 107
Sizzle & Smoke Flat Iron Steaks, 131
Sizzling Chicken Lo Mein, 164
Skillet-Roasted Lemon Chicken with
  Potatoes, 128
Slow-Roasted Tomatoes, 58
Smoked Salmon Quiche, 183
Smoky Chipotle Orange Dip, 30
Southwest Vegetarian Lentil Soup, 75
Spanakopita Pinwheels, 6
Sparkling Fruit Punch, 43

Sparkling Party Punch, 50
Special Sauerbraten, 126
Spiced Chocolate Molten Cakes, 194
Spicy Cheese Crackers, 39
Spicy Chicken Sausage Lettuce Wraps, 181
Spicy Coconut Chicken Strips, 125
Spicy Couscous & Tomato Soup, 92
Spicy Cucumber Salad, 73
Spinach Penne Salad, 139
Strawberry Shortcake Cookies, 214
Sue's Cream of Baked Potato Soup, 101
Sugar Plum Sweet Rolls, 230
Sunday Paella, 129
Sweet & Salty Candy, 226
Sweet & Sassy Baby Back Ribs, 152
Sweet Chipotle Pretzels, 223
Sweet Corn and Potato Gratin, 104
Swiss Sweet Onion Casserole, 72

T

Taco Salad Tacos, 169
Tangy Beef Chili, 84
Tarragon Mashed Potato Casserole, 99
Teacher's Caviar, 47
Tender Salsa Beef, 174
Thai Chicken Pizza, 132
Three Potato Salad, 100
Toffee Cheesecake Tiramisu, 222
Tossed Salad with Cilantro Vinaigrette, 65
Trick-or-Treat Pizza, 228
Turkey Cordon Bleu with Alfredo
  Sauce, 130
Turkey Florentine Sandwiches, 165
Turkey Potpie Cups, 135
Turkey-Sweet Potato Soup, 108
Turtle Chips, 15
Tuscan Portobello Stew, 167

V

Vegetable Beef Stew, 177

W

Weeknight Pasta Supper, 168
White Bean Tuna Salad, 163
White Chicken Chili, 113
White Chocolate-Coconut Layer Cake, 216
White Chocolate Cranberry Biscotti, 227

Y

Yummy Cookie Bars, 248